AF566933

chihuly:
glass in architecture

屈胡利：建築中的玻璃

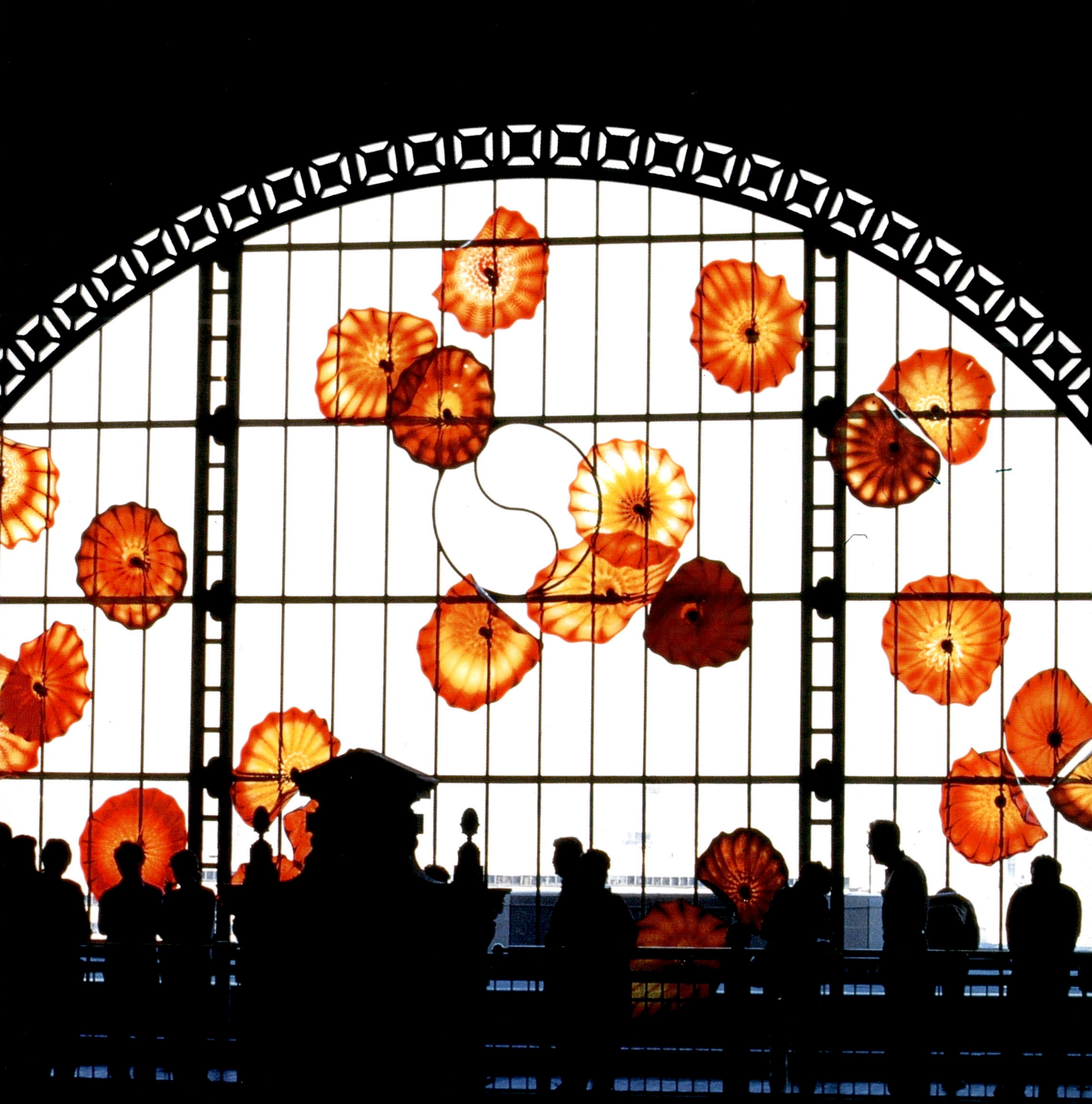

Preface
序文

高雄市立美術館自今年六月開館以來，除致力於國內藝術發展與史料的編整及陳展外，在國際藝術交流方面，也一直戮力不懈。我們引介了歐美着名的藝術家及畫派，並包括了油畫、版畫、雕塑、陶瓷等不同的藝術表現形式，同時也獲得參觀者熱烈的迴響。而此次本館更邀請了美國玻璃造形藝術家德爾・屈胡利至高雄展出其玻璃造形物，讓民衆體驗另一種藝術媒材——玻璃所展現的藝術型態與視覺美感。

屈胡利於一九四一年誕生在華盛頓州的塔科馬。他於華盛頓大學主修室內設計。畢業後，又相繼取得威斯康辛大學理學碩士及羅德島設計學校美術碩士學位。他從一九六一年開始研習玻璃，之後曾赴玻璃工藝重鎮威尼斯習得玻璃吹製技術。屈胡利不拘泥於傳統的玻璃製作形式，他與他的工作夥伴不斷地嚐試與創新，而成功地將材料、色彩、光線及空間作巧妙的結合，將其玻璃作品絢爛瑰麗的視覺效果及奇特造形的空間感完整地傳達給觀賞者。此外，屈胡利也將玻璃裝置運用於建築裝潢中，而增加建築景觀的美感。因此，屈胡利已使玻璃從手工藝的層面躍昇至藝術造景的境界。

屈胡利著迷於玻璃創作，他一再實驗、創新並向玻璃媒材的極限挑戰。自一九七四年起，他陸續創作了「圓桶」、「籃」、「海之形」、「馬其亞」、「波斯」、「威尼斯」、「三島浮球」、「花道」、「吊燈」等不同系列的作品，並在每一系列中作更多的色彩與形體的變化，而創作出變幻無窮、繽紛、綺麗的玻璃作品。屈胡利常至各地旅行，並從旅程中獲得創作的靈感，如「波斯」、「三島浮球」、「花道」等系列即融合了屈胡利對東西方美學的體會，並呈現出異國浪漫的風情與神祕的氣息。

屈胡利的玻璃裝置作品也可與建築空間作完美的搭配，而展現出一獨特而新奇的景觀。他曾將「波斯」系列裝置於窗戶、天花板、棚架等，而「花道」、「吊燈」等亦可裝飾於花園、庭院等地。因此屈胡利的作品，不但廣受博物館收藏，也可見於各大公共建築。近年來屈胡利更爲其故鄉塔科馬的聯合車站作一連串的建築裝置計劃。而本展覽的特色即在展現屈胡利之玻璃作品所具有的建築裝置特質，除了將展出的作品與展覽空間作一完善搭配外，更在專輯中集結了屈胡利歷年來的玻璃裝置作品，讓大家一窺屈胡利之玻璃作品與建築結合的魅力。

黃才郎

高雄市立美術館籌備處　主任

中華民國八十三年十月

Since its opening in June 1994, Kaohsiung Museum of Fine Arts not only devotes entirely to domestic art development and the compilation and display of historical data, but also strives continuously for international art exchange. We have introduced famous Eu-ropean/American artists and artistic schools as well as different forms of arts, including oil painting, woodcut, sculpture, porcelain and ceramics. Our exhibitions are highly appreciated by visitors. Now, we are pleased to invite the glass artist, Dale Chihuly, to exhibit his glass creations in Kaohsiung, so our citizens can experience the artistic style and visual beauty provided by a different artistic media -- glass.

Chihuly was born in Tacoma, Washington in 1941. He graduated from the University of Washington, majoring in interior design. Then, he earned a master's degree of science from the University of Wisconsin and a master's degree of fine arts from Rhode Island School of Design. He began to learn glass blowing in 1961. Later, he went to Venice, an important city for glass art, to learn the skills of glass blowing. Chihuly was not contended with conventional glass production. After continuous tries and innovations, he and his assistants finally succeeded in combining materials, colors, lights and space in a wonderful way, presenting to viewers with brilliant and fabulous visual effects and outstandingly styled sense of space. Chihuly also applied glass installation to architectural decoration in order to increase the beauty of architectural designs. In other words, Chihuly has enhanced glass from handicraft to artistic landscaping.

Chihuly is fascinated with glass making. He makes experiments and innovations over and over again and challenges the limits of glass materials. Since 1974, he has created different series of glass works, including Cylinders, Baskets, Seaforms, Macchias, Persians, Venetians, Niijma Floats, Ikebanas, and Chandeliers. In adddition, he has made various changes in colors and shapes and consequently more different resplendent and gorgeous glass works. Chihuly often travels around the world and derives inspiration from his trips. For example, the series of "Persians", "Niijima Floats", and "Ikebana" series blend Chihuly's understanding to oriental and western esthetics and express the feelings and mysteries of exoticism and romanticism.

Chihuly's works in glass installation also match perfectly with architectural space design and present a unigue and new atmosphere. He has applied the "Persians" series to windows, ceiling, pergola, and "Ikebana" and "Chandelier" series to gardens and yards. Therefore, Chihuly's works are not only collected extensively by museums, but also seen very often in many public buildings. In recent years, Chihuly has made a series of architectural installation plans for the Union Station in his hometown, Tacoma. The features of the exhibition "Chihuly : Glass in Architecture" are to display the architectural characteristics in his glass works. In addition to presenting the perfect combination of the exhibited works and the exhibition space, we have compiled a catalogue to introduce the collection of Chihuly's glass installation works in past years and to provide an opportunity for people to experience the charm of the combination of Chihuly's glass works and architecture.

Tsai-Lang Huang
Director / Kaohsiung Museum of Fine Arts
October 1994

目次

CONTENTS

dale chihuly: spontaneity and space

德爾.屈胡利:自發性與空間

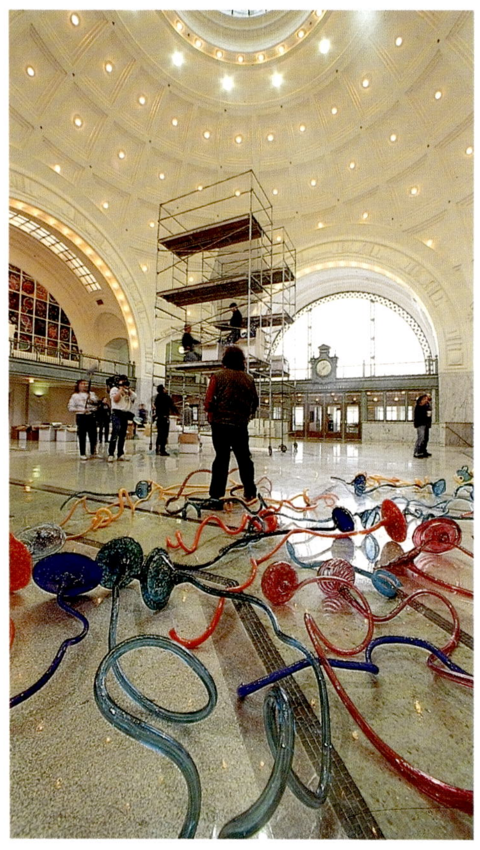

"屈胡利在聯合車站"
展覽中之裝置
塔科馬, 1994
攝影: R. Johnson

installation for
"Chihuly at Union Station"
Tacoma, 1994
photo: R. Johnson

If one person has been responsible for transforming the scope and reputation of glass as an artistic medium, it is Dale Chihuly. Once considered decorative rather than aesthetic, glass has risen to the ranks of high art, ascending from the tables of craft shows to the pedestals of art museums, due largely to the efforts of Chihuly and the extraordinary appeal of his glass sculptures. Chihuly has shown his work in solo and group exhibitions throughout the world and is one of only four Americans to have had a solo exhibition at the Musée des Arts Décoratifs in the Louvre in Paris. In 1992 he received the first National Living Treasure Award given by the United States.

Chihuly was born in 1941 in Tacoma, Washington. He received a B.A. from the University of Washington in 1965, an M.S. from the University of Wisconsin in 1967 and an M.F.A. from the Rhode Island School of Design in 1968. Although he counts his formal education as important, he considers his boyhood penchant for observation and discovery as invaluable. His upbringing thoroughly informs his large, diverse vocabulary of shapes and forms. Walking the shores of Washington State, the young Chihuly observed the flow and undulation of the ever-changing sea and examined the delicate, intricate patterns and shapes of rocks and shells at his feet. At home he watched his mother cut and arrange colorful flowers from the family garden. His father, a butcher, died in 1957, a year after the artist's only sibling, an older brother, had been killed in a Naval Aviation training flight.

What Chihuly has assimilated from his travels has been crucial to his personal and artistic development. In 1968 a Fulbright Fellowship allowed him to study the art of glassmaking in Venice. In a city known for its glasswork as well as for its canals and stunning light, Chihuly learned the art of glassblowing and that of teamwork—a crucial and integral part of his production. At the Venini factory, he was the first American glassblower to work on the island of Murano, which had been a carefully guarded and isolated epicenter of glassblowing since the 13th century.

Chihuly's own studio, now located in the Boathouse, a converted racing scull factory on scenic Lake Union in Seattle, is a busy workshop of crew members, each of whom plays an essential role, from gaffer to installation designer to registrar. Chihuly rarely blows glass himself, as a near-fatal car accident in 1976 left him sightless in one eye. Rather, he is the maestro who orchestrates with flair, finesse and unlimited energy. Although Chihuly is the conductor, he is quick to credit his players. Moreover, he cites people who influenced his artistic development as if to perpetuate the master/apprentice paradigm, thought to be a lost model in modern times, but a central premise of Chihuly's work since his Venice days. The painter and sculptor Italo Scanga and sculptor and designer James Carpenter are two significant influences, and Chihuly's travels around the globe have resulted in many friendships and collaborative ventures.

Chihuly's artistic development has gone through numerous stages. While an interior design student at the University of Washington, he experimented with glass as an aesthetic element. Not yet a glassblower, he wove a tapestry with glass inclusions and became fascinated by the visual implications of meshed shapes and planes of translucent color. In 1966 he studied with the famous glass artist Harvey Littleton, who himself had sparked a glass renaissance. By the end of the year, Chihuly had started exploring new forms. He blew glass around steel, and incorporated neon and glass in Plexiglas containers, reminiscent of the works in colored translucent materials by California "light and space" artists such as Larry Bell and Dewain Valentine. Later, at the Rhode Island School of Design, Chihuly worked with James Carpenter to create indoor and outdoor environments of plastic, neon and ice.

During the past two years, Chihuly has created neon-and-ice sculptures similar in sensibility and concept to his early explorations of color, reflection and materiality. He has produced these pieces for sites as diverse as the new Seattle Art Museum; the Tacoma Dome; the Contemporary Arts Center, Cincinnati and the Honolulu Academy of Arts. In these environmental works, polychromatic neon tubes are frozen into large blocks of ice, averaging about three-hundred-pounds each. As the ice melts, a visual transformation occurs that mirrors the metamorphosis of ice to water, uniting the aesthetic to the physical. This duality of "science" and art is not in conflict, but rather a carefully cultivated interaction that comes from a mastery of the materials and a knowledge of their inherent properties.

Chihuly is totally aware of the complexities of glass as a physical substance and draws upon its seemingly contradictory properties: ephemeral and eternal, clear and opaque, decorative and functional, fluid and brittle, material and immaterial, solid and liquid. Glassblowing itself, an intense and difficult technique involving hot and hazardous conditions, permits a small margin for the all-important element—chance. On this border of controlled accident, Chihuly not only operates but excels.

In 1971 Chihuly, with Northwest art patrons Anne Gould Hauberg and John Hauberg, founded the Pilchuck Glass School on a tree farm 50 miles north of Seattle. At first a rustic counterculture camp for artists and 16 students from the Union of Independent Colleges of Art, which helped fund the initial year, the school has since burgeoned into a major art hub, enrolling over 250 students during its summer sessions. Throughout its growth, Pilchuck has remained true to Chihuly's mission to produce ideas as much as objects and to encourage experimentation as much as technical advances. Consequently, the school has been a successful artists' think-tank, a center of creative interaction and development, with an impressive staff and student roster. Pilchuck has caused a veritable boom in glass that has put the Northwest on the map, while Seattle itself now has over 35 hot shops.

The 1970s and 1980s were productive decades for Chihuly, during which he concentrated on the glass object, creating a vocabulary of diverse forms and shapes. He began working in series, developing the *Cylinders* (1974), *Baskets* (1977), *Sea Forms* (1980), *Macchia* (1981), *Persians* (1986) and *Venetians* (1988).

The *Basket* series was inspired by Northwest Coast Indian baskets that Chihuly saw while visiting the Washington State Historical Society with his good friends, Italo Scanga and James Carpenter. Captivated by the graceful sagging forms, he decided to replicate them in glass. The rumpled, distressed and asymmetrical appearance of the glass baskets was unlike anything previously associated with objects crafted of glass.

The *Sea Forms* are delicate and fanciful works that recall marine life: seaweed, shells, sea urchin skeletons. They came about in true Chihuly fashion — by accident. As the *Baskets* were being blown into the ribbed molds to allow for the glass to be thinner and thus have a pliable, malleable appearance, it was remarked that the striations looked like those of sea shells and the glass looked like water. Also, the color had shifted from earthy tones to more pale pinks, greys and white—a very aquatic palette. Later it seemed only natural to name the series after the organisms they resembled, the sea creatures so important in the artist's childhood.

The *Macchia*, multicolored, speckled, wavy-edged forms, came into being after Chihuly woke up one morning intent on using the array of 300 colors available in the hot shop. [The most important "art historical" influences on Chihuly relative to color have been the writings of Clement Greenberg and the color-field paintings of Morris Louis and Kenneth Noland as well as the watercolors of Homer, Prendergast, Demuth and Marin.] On a personal level, Chihuly simply loves color and colors—during a 60-hour train trip from Vancouver to Montreal in 1964, he mixed as many colors from his Winsor-Newton watercolors as possible to make the time pass quickly. The *Macchias* are distinguished by their bright colors (created by "jimmies" of colored glass, large chunks of glass and "dustings" of powdered glass), spotted appearance (*macchia* means spotted in Italian) and by the bold color contrasts of the lip wrap, interior and exterior surfaces. The *Macchia* represented a turning point—they were often large and were not merely objects but integral parts of successful installations.

> It turns out that size is extremely important to the *Macchias* and with them I felt for the first time that a piece of glass held its own in a room.
> (Dale Chihuly, Chihuly: Color, Glass and Form, 1986, p.21.)

The *Persians,* variously shaped and intricately patterned forms, were the result of a series of technical experiments. When Chihuly noticed that one of his glassblowers, Martin Blank, valued experimentation, he paired him with Robbie Miller, a particularly fine technical craftsman.

> I would make large pencil drawings for Martin and Robbie with a couple of dozen small forms and then I would put an *X* under the ones I wanted them to go for. Over the next year, we made more than 1,000 miniature experimental forms.
> (Dale Chihuly, Chihuly: Form from Fire, 1993, p. 45.)

The resultant series is marked by busy, striped surfaces, supple and elastic forms and an overall aura evocative of the ancient Middle East. This series suggests as much as it depicts, it conjures up as much as it represents romance and exoticism. *Persians* are often installed on windows or spread on glass ceilings, creating pergolas or passageways under which viewers walk. They form seductive environments that attract viewers from a distance. For his one-man exhibition at the Seattle Art Museum, Chihuly installed *Persians* along the 50-foot long window and named it the "Venturi Window" for the building's architect.

The *Venetians* came into existence when renowned glassmaker Lino Tagliapietra collaborated with Chihuly on a series derived from Art Deco glass. *Venetian*s are classic Chihuly, combining art historical references, contemporary experimentation and a sense of the outrageous. The vessel forms are "ornamented" with organic and biomorphic shapes and motifs, so that each *Venetian* becomes its own flamboyant organism. Coils, corkscrews, curls, spirals, snakes, wings, horns, putti and other protrusions enhance the vessels, endowing them with mobility and life.

More recent additions to Chihuly's vocabulary of objects are the *Niijima Floats (*1991), glass spheres reminiscent of the blue-green Japanese fishing floats that dotted the shorelines of Chihuly's youth, and the *Ikebana* (1990), long, graceful stems that recall Japanese floral arrangements, inspired by a trip to Buddhist temples in Japan. The *Floats* must be the largest glass spheres known—often measuring over a yard in diameter and weighing approximately 80 pounds each. Alone, each sphere is its own planet, sometimes appearing hollow, sometimes appearing solid. In groupings, the *Floats* seem to form their own magnetic field. The shadows cast by each sphere add to the sense of mystery, suggesting an uncanny absence and presence. It must be more than a coincidence that a "float" is not only an object but a gravitational term, meaning "to be suspended in space or move through space as if supported by a liquid."

The *Ikebana* were fashioned from forms that were originally meant to embellish the *Venetians*, an example of decoration becoming the actual object, surface becoming substance. The *Ikebana* run the gamut from elongated, tangled, viney tendrils to bulbous gourd- or pear-like sculptures. They have been installed on the ground, in courtyards, on the walls. In Chihuly's studio/home, the Boathouse, the *Ikebana* were transformed into an "arbor of blooming glass," a presentation that was duplicated for the Seattle Art Museum's exhibition, "Dale Chihuly: Installations 1964-1992."

Related directly to the *Ikebana* are the *Chandeliers*. Both series use the forms and motifs of flora—stems, tendrils, leaves, blossoms, buds. The *Chandeliers* cross many boundaries, employing clusters of bulbous shapes reminiscent of the *Sea Forms* or the biomorphic bulbs of Chihuly's early "Pilchuck Pond Installation" (1971); conical forms somewhat similar to the *Venetians* but more ribbed, as hornets' nests; dripping, elongated icicles/stalactites that are suspended with putti, again reminiscent of the *Venetians* ornamentation. The *Chandeliers*, inverted pyramids or large clusters, connect ceiling to floor in colorful blasts of pink, cadmium red, lemon yellow, orange or blueberry. As the *Ikebana* vary according to placement—ground, wall or ceiling—the *Chandeliers* prove the importance of placement and of gravity. They are suspended from ceilings or overhead supports. Frequently they are installed over reflective pools of water or glass. They can light their environs serving as illuminated sculpture.

The drawings and faxes are energetic and expressive—immediate and spontaneous notations and plans. Chihuly is perpetually developing new ideas and projects, despite (or maybe *because of*) a constantly booked schedule. For him, continuous activity is as necessary and vital as the continuous flow of blood through his body. The drawings and faxes are proposals to be shared, discussed and, finally, taken on by his staff. Frequent travel does not hinder but is part-and-parcel of his modus operandi. Not only is the artist in constant dialogue with his studio and staff via phone and fax, but the act of travel—of dislocation, movement, exploration and excitement—is key to his creative process.

Faxes provide instantaneous communication and an opportunity to combine word and image in an often comic-strip-like form. Plans and projects are described not only in graphic and literal terms but also in terms of anticipated response. Many of the faxes delineate works that are surrounded by appreciative audiences, who react to the (future) projects with enthusiasm. For example, a fax describing a "Chihuly Chandelier in the Canal of Venice" (2/21/94) is a sketchy drawing of a chandelier suspended between two buildings while remarks in bubbles float over those peering out of their windows: "fantastico," "incredible," "bellisimo," "buono," "superbo" and "wow." Other faxes anticipate a varied response; a fax depicting the Tacoma Dome project (5/8/94) shows clusters of people (small scratchy blobs) reacting to the work: "I'm cold," "awesome," "let's go," "wow," "stupid," "kool" and "groovy."

Chihuly's drawings are above all colorful and energetic renderings. He often works on the floor, on his deck, splashing paint about with mops and brooms in a physical and theatrical manner. His entire body is used in making these creations, which becomes apparent in the lively swirling lines; in the blobs of paint that burst out of their outlines (and off the page); through the splats, drips and blotches. He paints so thickly and quickly that many drawings retain a just-made moistness, a soft, squishy, tactile quality that makes them seem alive, as if they are part of an ongoing process. And they are.

A recent installation in Dallas is formed of color drawings on Plexiglas mounted on an atrium-high window. Chihuly drew with transparent chemicals, "see-thru" colors as it were, that reflect on the opposite wall while they float in their own space. Large swirls of color are dematerialized from their support, and due to the transparency of both the Plexiglas and window, color is form and color is light. The installation is a brilliant distillation of previous projects and, in its simple elegance, addresses all of the concerns so central to Chihuly's work: color, form, dematerialization, transience and permanence. This work gives strength to the claim that Chihuly is primarily an installation artist, that when he conceives of an artwork, he is thinking not merely about how objects will be placed but how he can deliver a cogent and successful architectural, aesthetic and experiential statement. Scale never scares but excites. Limitations of any sort are challenges. As the artist himself says, "I'm as interested in the way my art works in a space as in the art itself." (Carol Soucek King,"Public Works: Dale Chihuly's Glass Sculptures Showcased at the New Seattle Art Museum," Designers West, November 1992, p. 43.)

Chihuly recently designed the sets for the Seattle Opera's production of Debussy's *Pelléas et Mélisande*. This story of passion and jealousy set in a surreal landscape intrigued Chihuly, who was inspired and encouraged by the fact that fellow artist David Hockney had designed sets for the opera stage. Creating 12 sets, including 35-foot trees made from mylar, Chihuly evoked the moods and nuances of Debussy's symbolist opera of dream and reality. Matching material with mood, substance with suggestion, the sets are not realistic depictions but rather reflective shimmering structures that allow room for the imagination.

Chihuly's art is indeed all encompassing in its goals and scope, going far beyond the successful creation of objects and even beyond installation as it anticipates audience reaction. Everything is informed by his interest in the phenomenological significance of color, light, space and atmosphere, which are intrinsic to the viewer's experience—whether it be of a *Venetian* or of *Pelléas et Mélisande*.

It seems only natural, therefore, that Chihuly is attracted by interdisciplinary projects. Perhaps the most ambitious project to date is the Tacoma Union Station in Washington. Once the western terminus for the transcontinental railroad and now a courthouse, this Beaux Arts masterpiece (1911) was placed on the National Register of Historic Places in March of 1974, the first Tacoma landmark to be designated as such. Designed by Reed and Stem, who built Grand Central Station in New York, the grandiose structure is now undergoing a $10 million restoration.

> It is a tough space...it's like decorating the inside of a cathedral. You have to be very sensitive to what this place is.
> (Dale Chihuly quoted in Douglas McLennan, "Ever-changing imagination marks Chihuly's work," The News Tribune, March 27, 1994, pp. A1, A14.)

Chihuly considered several installations for Union Station, including window walls of flowers and stems, a "Monarch Window" of large *Persians*, a "Macchia Window", a disk/frieze "Lakawana Ikebana," a half-circle mural of *Basket* drawings and a 24-foot high, 2,750-piece blueberry *Chandelier*. The project is an ongoing five-year "laboratory" during which ideas—and their material manifestations—are accepted, rejected or altered according to how they work within the space. Chihuly knows the power of architecture and knows how each line, each color, each object plays a role in the overall success of the whole. He must be in agreement with Winston Churchill who once said: "We shape our buildings; thereafter, they shape us."

The Union Station project extends into 1999, and is administered by the Tacoma Art Museum. Tours at Union Station are available and attendance has been phenomenal, a major boost for the morale and economic health of the community. While this project is a significant step in the revitalization of downtown Tacoma, it has particular meaning and resonance for Chihuly, for Tacoma is his hometown.

All of this is consistent with Chihuly's desire to reach all sectors of the community, to touch "non- art" audiences as well as those already familiar with his work. For this artist, who constantly challenges limitations, who loves to work in the public arena, who loves to ask anybody and everybody what they think, Tacoma Union Station is a wonderful way to come home again.

by Sarah Bremser
Independent Curator

德爾·屈胡利：自發性與空間

莎拉布瑞塞　撰

若有人曾經負責將玻璃的領域和聲譽轉變成一種藝術媒材，那則非德爾·屈胡利莫屬。由於屈胡利的努力，以及他的玻璃雕塑品獨特的吸引力，一向只被認爲具有裝飾價值而非美學價值的玻璃，已從手工藝品櫥窗躍上博物館的展示枱，步入高級藝術的殿堂。屈胡利曾在全球各聯展與個展中展示他的作品。至目前爲止在巴黎羅浮宮裝飾藝術博物館舉辦過個展的美國人只有四名，而屈胡利就是其中之一。1992 年，美國特別頒發當代國寶獎給他。

1941 年，屈胡利誕生於華盛頓州的塔科馬。1965 年，他以文學士學位畢業於華盛頓大學。1967 年，他取得威斯康辛大學理學碩士學位，並於 1968 年再度獲得羅德島設計學校美術碩士學位。雖然他重視自己的正式教育，卻更珍惜童年時代養成的觀察、探索的興趣。他的成長過程完全反應在他那浩瀚多變的作品形態與造形上。年幼的屈胡利常漫步於華盛頓海岸，觀察永無休止的潮汐與海浪、瞬息萬變的海面，並仔細研究脚邊大小岩石細緻、複雜的花紋和形狀。在家時，他也常看母親從花園剪下各色花朵插在室內擺飾。他的父親在 1957 年逝世——剛好是屈胡利唯一的哥哥在海軍航空訓練飛行中意外罹難的一年之後。

屈胡利從旅行中獲得的經歷對他個人及藝術上的發展皆具有重大的影響。1968 年他獲得富爾布來特獎助金赴威尼斯研習玻璃製作藝術。威尼斯除了運河、絢爛的夜景之外，也以玻璃藝品聞名。在這裏，屈胡利學到了吹製玻璃的藝術，更學到了團體合作，這一點對於他日後的作品具有重大的影響。在威尼斯工廠裏，他是第一個在慕拉諾島上的美籍玻璃吹製者，此地自十三世紀起即被嚴密的看守，與外界隔離。

屈胡利目前的個人工作室位於西雅圖觀光湖區的船屋，係由一間划漿賽舟工廠改建的。工作室的成員相當忙碌，從師傅、裝置設計師、到登記員，每一位成員扮演的角色都十分重要。屈胡利很少親自吹玻璃，因爲 1976 年一場嚴重的車禍已使他單眼失明。然而，如同一個交響樂團的指揮家，他仍領導團員演奏出優雅、奔放、又充滿活力的曲子。儘管他位居指揮家的地位，卻從不吝於歸功於樂手。此外，他也常常褒揚那些影響他藝術發展的人，雖然這種師徒典範在今日社會已蕩然無存，但卻是屈胡利從威尼斯時期以來作品的中心前提。影響屈胡利最深刻的兩位藝術家是：畫家兼雕塑家義塔洛·史坎加，以及雕塑家兼設計家詹姆士·卡本特。屈胡利的全球旅行更爲他贏得許多友誼和合作事業。

屈胡利走過許多個藝術發展階段。在美國華盛頓大學唸室內設計時，他以玻璃爲美學素材做實驗。當吹玻璃工人的時期，他用含有玻璃的礦物編成織錦，且立即被那網狀組織在視覺上的糾結和半透明的結晶面深深吸引。1966 年，他師從著名的玻璃藝術家哈維·里多頓，這位名師曾點燃玻璃的文藝復興之火。同年年底，屈胡利開始嚐試新形體。他在鋼鐵外表吹上玻璃，並在塑膠玻璃容器中融合了霓虹與玻璃，以紀念緬懷加州「光與空間」的藝術家（如賴瑞・貝爾、迪文・瓦倫泰等），以彩色半透明材料創作作品。之後，在羅德島設計學校求學時，他與詹姆士・卡本特聯手創作了以塑膠、霓虹、冰爲素材的戶內、戶外環境藝術作品。

近兩年來，屈胡利完成了一些霓虹與冰的雕塑品，在感覺性與概念上類似他早期在顏色、反射、材料上做的嚐試。這些作品是爲各種場所特別設計的，包括新西雅圖藝術館、塔科馬圓頂華廈、辛辛那提當代藝術中心，以及檀香山藝術學院。這些環境作品是將多色霓虹管凍結成平均每個三百磅重的大冰磚製成的。當冰融化時，產生了一種視覺變轉，反映出冰化成水時的變形過程，是物理和美學的綜合體。這種科學與藝術並存的現象並不衝突，反而是對於材料的精通和材料本質的知識費心構思交織出來的。

屈胡利十分了解玻璃在物理上的複雜性，因而把重點放在它呈對比的特性：短暫與永恆，清晰與透明、裝飾與功能性，流動體與易碎體，物質與非物質，固體與液體。玻璃吹製的過程本需要專注而艱深的技術，在高熱而危險的狀況下進行。僅留下十分有限的時空讓創作者把握瞬間即逝的良機。在這個侷促的空間裏，屈胡利不但游刃有餘，甚至超越巔峰。

1971 年，屈胡利和西北藝術守護者——約翰・荷伯夫婦——共同創辦了比恰克玻璃學校。該校位於西雅圖北方五十哩的一座農場上。起初它只不過是反體制藝術家的一處粗糙的集會場所，加上十六名來自獨立藝術學院聯盟的學生，合力度過了第一個年頭。翌年夏天暑期時，該校已蓬勃發展成擁有兩百五十名學生的藝術輻軸點。比恰克玻璃學校在它整個發展過程中，始終不負屈胡利的期望與使命感，激發理想和目標，鼓勵實驗和技術提昇。目前，該校已成爲藝術家的智囊中心，也是創作交流和成長的所在，擁有陣容堅強的師資和潛力無窮的學生。比恰克爲玻璃藝術帶來了眞正的春天，也使西北部著名的藝術再度光大。如今，西雅圖市區已林立了三十五家藝術玻璃工廠。

西元七〇至八〇年代是屈胡利最多產的時期。在這段期間，他專攻玻璃藝品，創造出豐富多樣的形態與造形。同時，他開始進行系列創作，共計有「圓桶」（1974），「籃」（1977），「海之形」（1980），「馬其亞」（1981），「波斯」（1986）及「威尼斯」（1988）。

「籃」系列是屈胡利和好友義塔洛・史坎加、詹姆士・卡本特同遊華盛頓州立歷史社區時激發而得的靈感。屈胡利被那優雅下垂的造型深深吸引，決定要用玻璃來表現這種美感。他創作出各種縐紋狀、凌亂、不對稱的玻璃籃，完全迴異於傳統細緻的玻璃藝品。

「海之形」則較精緻花俏，令人聯想到海底世界：海草、貝殼、海膽骨架，全都在屈胡利的手中呈現出意想不到的效果。就像「籃」系列的作品，是把玻璃吹在模型外層，所以看起來薄軟、有延展性，上面的溝紋猶如貝殼花紋，玻璃的質感仿佛水紋。另外在顏色方面，也從大地色系轉變爲較輕淡的粉紅、灰和白，簡直是海洋世界的調色盤。因此，很順理成章的將這個系列的作品以它們的外形來命名。這些海洋生物在屈胡利童年具有重大的意義和影響力。

「馬其亞」系列色彩豐富、點狀與波紋邊緣的形狀，是屈胡利一天清晨起床時突發奇想，要把工廠裏三百種現有的顏色全部用在一系列的作品裏。在藝術史中，有關色彩方面，克萊蒙・格林勃的著作和莫里斯・路易斯、肯尼士・諾蘭的水彩寫生畫，以及荷墨爾、普蘭德・蓋斯特、狄姆斯、馬林的水彩畫，對屈胡利的影響最大。對他個人而言，在 1964 年他從溫哥華旅行到蒙特婁的六十小時內，就愛上了顏色的搭配組合，用他的文瑟一紐頓水彩調配出各種顏色來打發漫長的旅途。「馬其亞」最出色之處就是它們鮮艷的色彩（「吉米斯」的彩色、大塊的玻璃，以及「粉塵」的玻璃粉），和斑點圖案（「馬其亞」在印弟安語即指「斑點」），還有在包邊、內層、外層大膽的對比色。「馬其亞」代表一個轉捩點——它們多半是大塊的，而且不僅是一個物體，更是一體系列的各個部份組合成的完美裝置。

> 對「馬其亞」而言，體積是相當重要的一環，看著它們，我才初次感受到一件玻璃品在房間裏是一個獨立的個體。
> （摘自 1986 年屈胡利的「屈胡利：顏色、玻璃、形體」第 21 頁。）

「波斯」系列形狀多樣化，形體複雜，是一系列技術實驗的成果。當屈胡利注意到他手下一名吹玻璃工人馬丁・布蘭克很重視實驗，他就把馬丁和另一名手藝精巧的玻璃師傅洛比・米勒搭檔成一組來進行創作。

> 我先替馬丁和洛比用鉛筆畫出數十種形體的大張草稿畫，然後在選定的形體下打「×」，讓他們依樣發揮。接著的整個年度裏，我們總共實驗出一千個縮小比例的形體。
> （摘自 1993 年德爾・屈胡利的「屈胡利：火之形」第 45 頁。」

這些實驗成品的特色包括：熱鬧的條紋外表、柔軟有彈性的形體，以及令人聯想到古代中東的氣息。這一系列作品兼具敍述性與暗示性，表現出浪漫與異國風情。「波斯」系列多半安裝在窗戶上或玻璃天花板上，搭成蔓棚小徑或通道，讓參觀者從下面走過。它們的魅力吸引了無數遠道而來的參觀著。在西雅圖藝術館的個展，屈胡利把「波斯」系列安裝在一扇五十呎長的窗戶上，並將它命名爲「泛突利窗」以紀念該棟建築物的設計師。

「威尼斯」系列是著名的玻璃師傅里諾・達里歐派特拉和屈胡利合作的成果，靈感則來自裝飾藝術玻璃。它們呈現出屈胡利古典的一面，結合了藝術史典故，當代實驗風格，以及一點點荒謬感。這些船形玻璃作品上面「裝飾」著有機性和生態性的形狀與主題，所以每件「威尼斯」作品都作爲一個裝飾華麗的有機體。盤繞的線圈、拔塞鑽、捲曲體、螺旋體、蛇、翅膀、角及其它許多種突出形，無一不豐富了這些玻璃船，且賦與動感和生命。

屈胡利較近期的作品「三島浮球」(1991 年)，也是他擅於變化主題物的成果之一。本系列是屈胡利懷念童年在海邊常看到的日本漁船浮標所創作出的玻璃球系列作品。而他 1990 年的「花道」系列則得自一次參觀日本廟宇的經驗靈感。造型高雅、修長的柄狀作品，令人聯想到日本插花。「三島浮球」是目前全世界最大的玻璃球，每件作品的直徑多半在一碼以上，重量也大於八十磅。每個玻璃球看起來仿佛都是宇宙中獨立的星球；有時候看起來是空心的，有時又好像實心的。全部擺在一起時，這些玻璃球宛如擁有其獨立的磁場。投射在玻璃球上的陰影造成一種神秘感，暗示著不可思議的存在與非存在。「浮球」一詞不僅指一件物品，更是一個重力術語，意味著「懸浮在空間裏，或者在空間裏移動，仿佛有液體托浮一般」。

「花道」系列的造型脫胎自一些原本要用來潤飾「威尼斯」系列的形體。「威尼斯」已成爲化實物爲裝飾、化表面爲實質的成功範例。「花道」淋漓盡致地以玻璃雕塑表現長卷糾纏的蔓藤和球根狀、梨形的葫蘆。它們被安裝在地面、庭院、牆壁上。在屈胡利的住家兼工作室「船屋」，「花道」轉變成一座「玻璃涼庭」，也是他在西雅圖藝術館的展覽「德爾・屈胡利 1964—1992 紀念展」中的作品仿製。

跟「花道」有直接關聯的是「吊燈」。兩個系列皆以花卉爲主題，包括枝柄、蔓藤、葉片、花朵、花蕾。「吊燈」系列跨越了多重界限，擷取「海之形」中的球根形狀，或屈胡利早期的「比恰克池塘」(1971 年) 中的生態球根形狀；而角錐狀的形體則類似「威尼斯」，不過骨架較多，猶如蜂巢；滴垂、長條狀的冰柱/鐘乳石懸浮著，則聯想到「威尼斯」的華麗裝飾。「吊燈」系列的倒金字塔或大花果串形作品從天花板垂到地板，充滿明亮耀目的粉紅、鮮紅、檸檬黃、橙或寶藍的色彩。猶如「花道」可以隨著佈署位置而改變，「吊燈」再一次證明了位置和地心引力的重要性。它們直接吊在天花板上，或屋頂的支撐物上。它們最常被安裝在會反射的水池或玻璃池上方。它們可以當作發光的雕刻品照明周遭的環境。

屈胡利畫的草稿和傳眞稿充滿活力，予人深刻的印象，也是他立即、自發性的筆記和計劃。屈胡利永遠不停地發展新構想和新方案，儘管（或許可以說「因爲」）他的行程表一直排得滿滿的。對他而言，持續不停的活動就如血液在身體裏流動一樣，是非常必要的。他的草稿和傳眞是要和工作夥伴共同分享、討論，最後再由他們去執行。經常的旅行並不會妨礙，反而是他日常生活的一部分。他隨時和工作室和工作夥伴以電話和傳眞保持連繫，旅途的活動——移位、遷移、探險、興奮——都是他創作過程的關鍵。

傳眞內容常爲連環漫畫的形式，提供立即的通訊，以及將文字與圖畫結合起來的機會。不僅可用圖畫和文字表達計劃和方案，更能夠以預期的反應來表達。許多傳眞內容勾畫出一些工程被觀衆圍繞著，他們對（未來的）方案反應十分熱絡。例如，有一張傳眞描述「威尼斯運河上屈胡利的吊燈」(2/21/94)，畫著一張草圖，一盞吊燈懸掛在兩棟建築物之間，從窗戶探頭外望的人們發出的驚嘆話語寫在他們頭上的圓圈泡泡裏：「太驚人了！」，「不可思議！」，「美極了！」，「太帥了！」，「出色至極！」其它一些傳眞的內容則表示出各種不同的反應；有一張傳眞稿描述「塔柯瑪圓頂華廈方案」(5/8/94)，畫著一群群圍觀的人（小墨點般的大小）對這個工程的反應：「我好冷！」，「令人敬畏！」，「我們走吧！」「蠢！」，「酷！」，「老套！」

屈胡利的素描是最佳的彩色透視圖，充滿了活力。他常常在地板上工作，在船甲板上工作，抹布沾著顏料灑得到處都是。他的全身都可以用來作畫，所以作品很明顯的呈現許多自然的弧線，甚至畫到紙張外面。他的顏料用得相當濃，畫筆下得又快，以致許多畫都保留著剛畫完的濕潤感，那種柔軟、泥濘、立體的質感讓這些畫顯得生動，如同進行過程中的一部分。

最近屈胡利在達拉斯的一件裝置作品，是由畫在塑膠玻璃上的彩色素描構成的，安裝在一扇中庭高窗上。屈胡利用一種透明彩色顏料作畫，可以反映在牆的另一面。大塊的顏色浮在半空中，顯出超脫了物質的感覺，顏色透過塑膠玻璃呈現出形體和光。這套裝置是無數次事先規劃方案的結晶，單純、高雅，同時也表達了屈胡利關心的重點：顏色、形體、非物質化、短暫無常與永恆。這個工程證明了一種說法：基本上，屈胡利是一位裝置藝術家，當他構思一件藝術作品時，不僅會考慮到物件如何擺放，更考慮到要如何表現出有說服力、成功的建築、美學和實驗的效果。世俗的標準尺度永遠無法衡量屈胡利造成的意外驚喜，任何形式的限制對他而言都是一種挑戰，誠如他自己說過：「我對我的藝術作品在空間中的表達方式很感興趣，就像我對藝術本身的興趣一樣濃厚。」(摘自「西方藝術家 1992 年十一月刊，卡羅・蘇塞克京著「公共工程：德爾・屈胡利在新西雅圖藝術館的玻璃雕塑展」，第 43 頁。）

屈胡利最近爲西雅圖歌劇院上演的德布西作品「貝蕾亞絲與梅力松」設計佈景。這個激情嫉妒的故事以超現實派的風景爲佈景，深深吸引著屈胡利，因爲他的工作夥伴大衛・哈克尼曾爲這個劇舞台設計佈景，引起屈胡利這個靈感。他設計了十二套佈景，包括高達三十五呎的樹木。屈胡利喚起了德布西象徵主義戲劇中夢幻與現實的心境和感情，融合物與情、意與實，他設計的佈景已不僅是現實主義的表現，更在層層反映的結構中爲觀衆留下想像的空間。

屈胡利的藝術的確超越了它的目標和領域，超越了成功創造出的物件，甚至超越了裝置本身，因爲它可以預期觀衆的反應。透過他重視的顏色、光、空間和氣氛——觀衆直覺的經驗——所有事物都在他的作品中呈現出截然不同的風貌，無論是「威尼斯」或「貝蕾亞絲與梅力松」。

因此，很自然的，屈胡利對於綜合多種專門領域的方案特別有興趣。或許，到目前爲止，他最有野心的方案應該是華盛頓的塔科馬聯合車站。曾經是美國內陸鐵路西端終站，如今則是郡政府所在地。這個美術鉅作完成於 1911 年，在 1974 年三月列入美國國家歷史古蹟登記名單上，也是塔科馬郡指定的第一個陸標。它是由曾設計過紐約中央車站的建築師李得和史坦姆設計的。這棟宏偉的建築物目前正以十萬美元的經費進行修復工作。

> 這個地方要修復起來是相當費力的……好像爲教堂的內部做裝潢一樣。你必須隨時提醒自己這是什麼地方。
> （摘自新聞論壇 1994 年三月二十七日，道格拉斯・麥克林南著「永遠改變中的想像力即屈胡利作品的特色」。）

屈胡利爲聯合車站考慮過好幾個裝置，包括花葉構成的窗戶牆，大型「波斯」系列作品中的一扇「帝王窗」，一扇「馬其亞窗」，「花道」系列中的一件作品，「籃」系列素描中的一幅半弧形壁畫，以及一盞 24 呎、2750 件組合的藍莓吊燈。這個方案相當於爲時六年的實驗，各種構想和實施不斷地被接受、拒絕或更改，以求達到最完美的空間配置。屈胡利深知建築的力量，也很了解每個線條、每種顏色、每個物件在整個成功的裝置中扮演的角色。相信他一定十分同意溫斯頓邱吉爾說過的一句話：「我們塑造了我們的建築物，然後，它們塑造我們。」

聯合車站的方案將一直進行到 1999 年，由塔科馬藝術館監督。目前仍可以到塔科馬聯合車站觀光，管制只是暫時的，是爲了社區士氣和經濟狀況帶來更美好的未來。這個方案一方面代表塔科馬市區復興的重要一大步，另一方面對屈胡利的聲譽也具有重大的意義，因爲塔科馬是他的家鄉。

所有這些活動都是爲了配合屈胡利希望深入社區每個角落的心願，他要感動那些「非藝術」的觀衆，就如同感動那些已經很熟悉他作品的觀衆一樣。對這些藝術家而言，他不斷向各種限制挑戰，熱愛在公共競技場工作，喜歡問別人的想法，塔科馬聯合車站修復方案是他回家最好的方式。

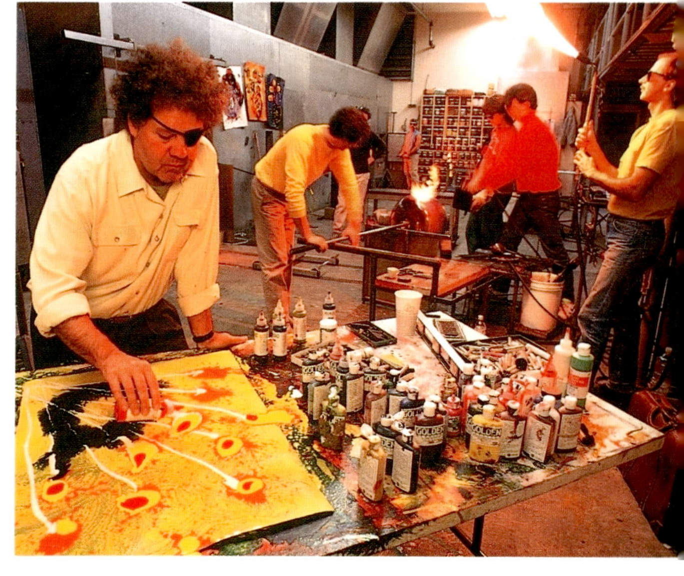

工作室中之素描
西雅圖, 1991
攝影：M. Wexler

drawing in the hot shop
Seattle, 1991
photo: M. Wexler

Plates

圖版

macchias

馬其亞

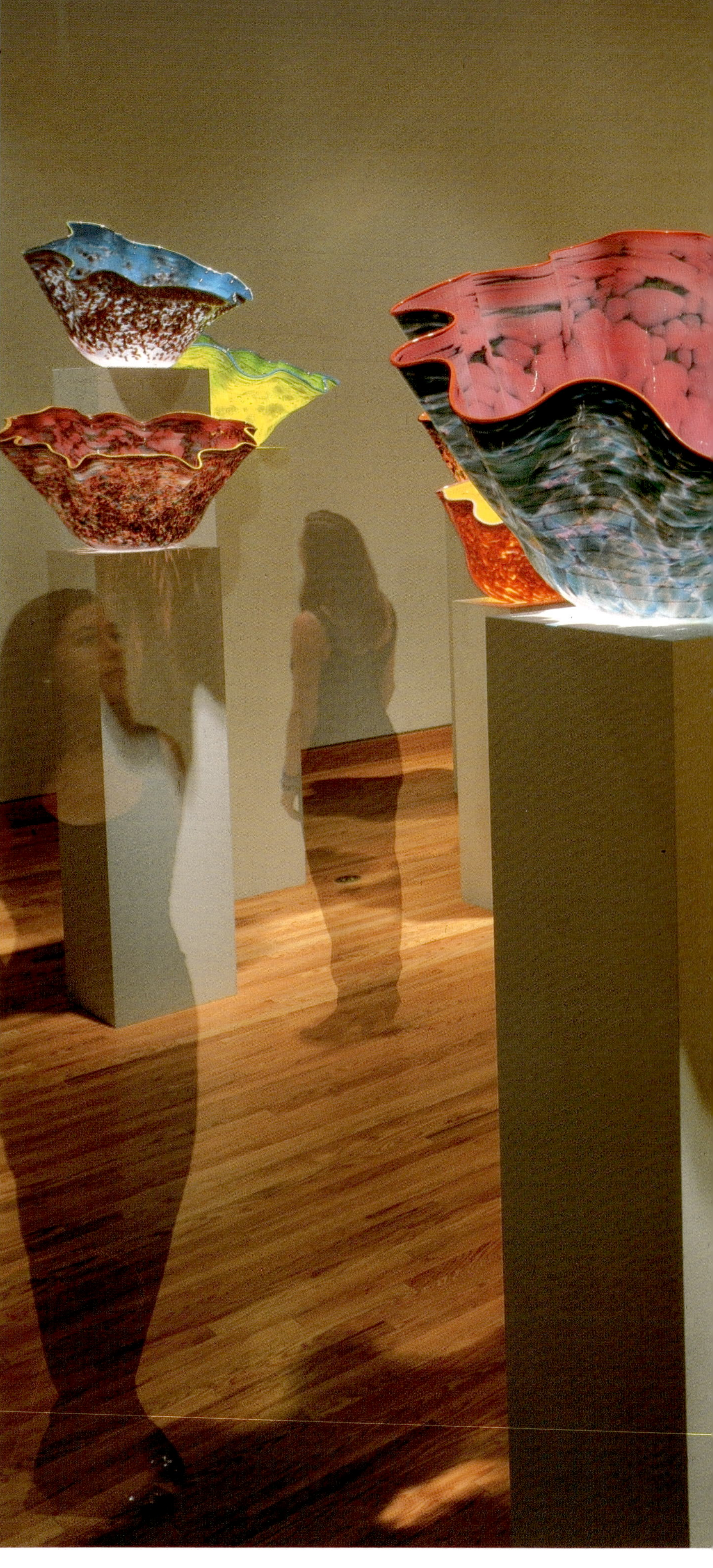

馬其亞森林
45 x 25 x 10呎
"德爾．屈胡利：裝置藝術
1964-1992"
西雅圖藝術館
西雅圖, 1992
攝影：E. Calderon

Macchia Forest
45 x 25 x 10'
"Dale Chihuly: Installations
1964-1992"
Seattle Art Museum
Seattle, 1992
photo: E. Calderon

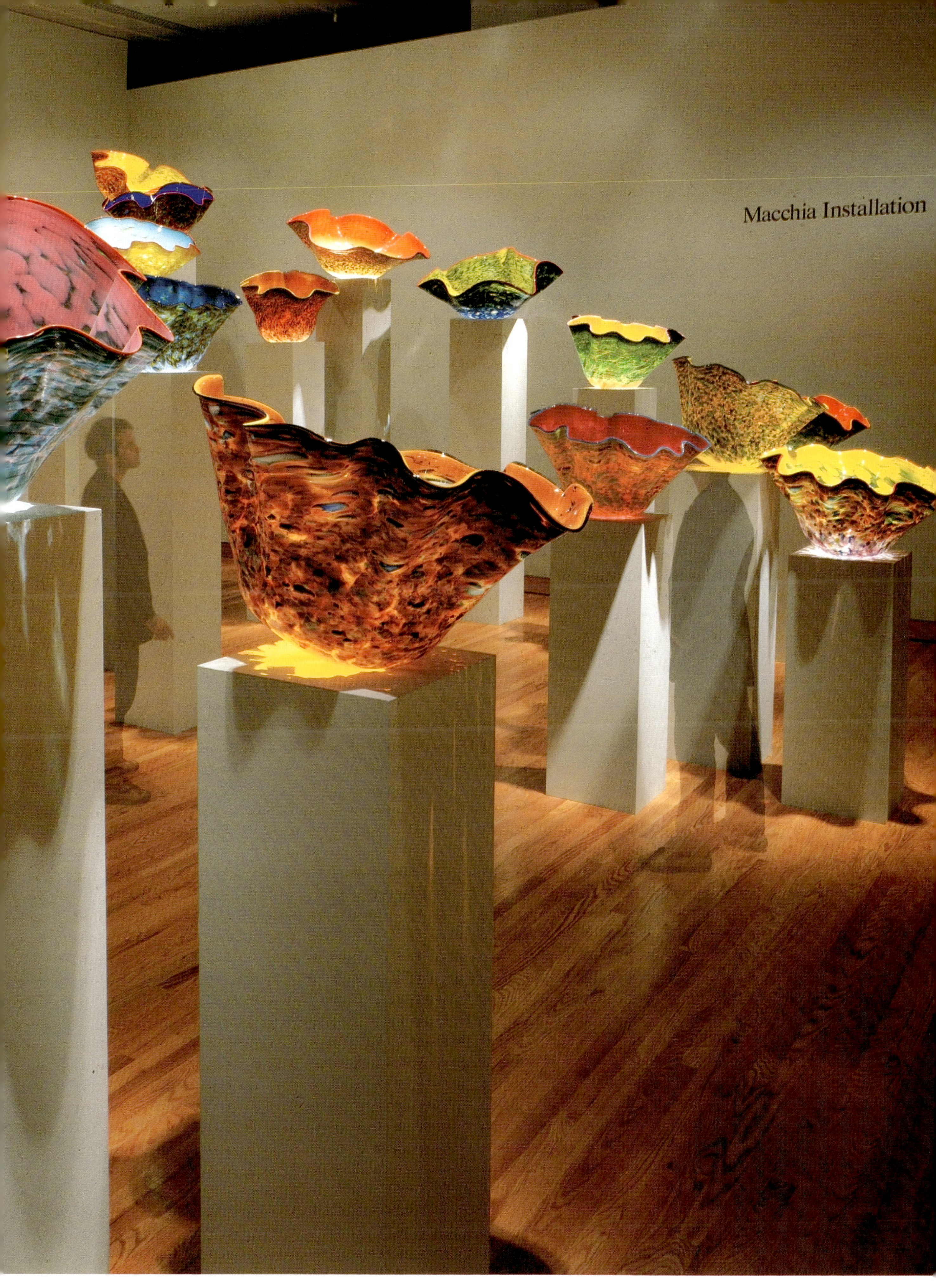
Macchia Installation

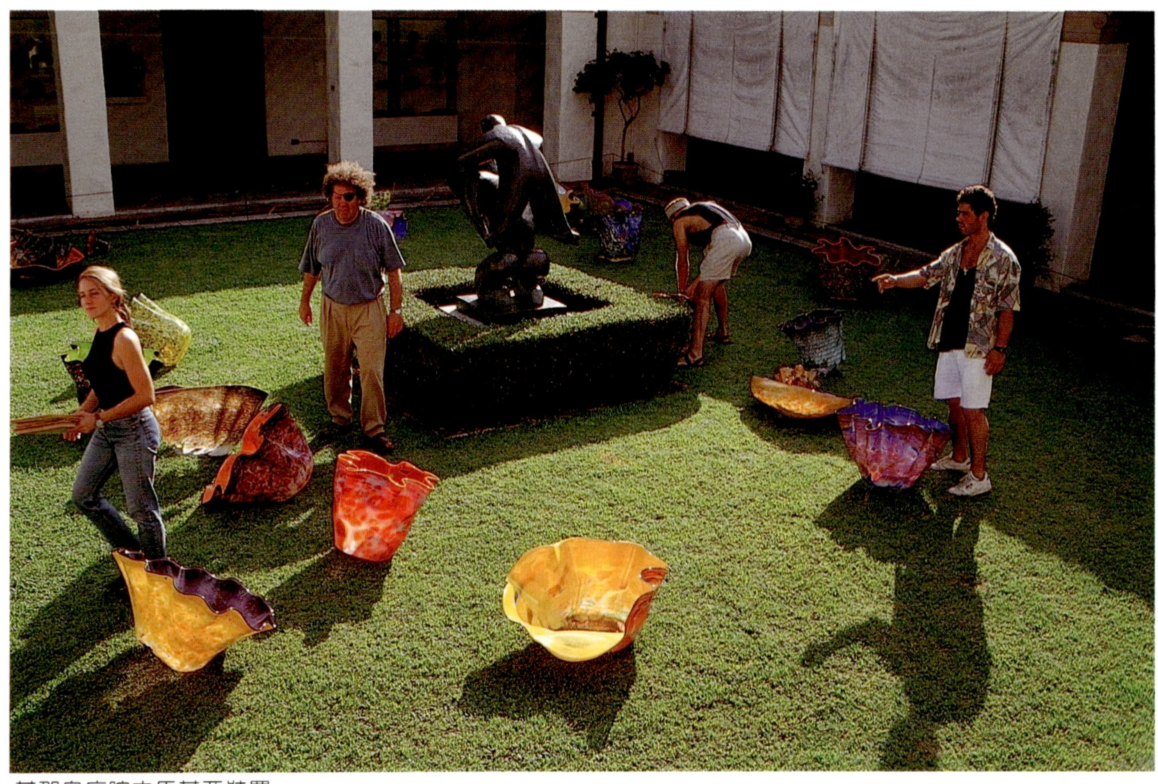

其那烏庭院之馬其亞裝置
"屈胡利庭院展"
檀香山藝術學院
檀香山, 1992
攝影: R. Johnson

Macchia Installation in the Kinau Court
"Chihuly Courtyards"
Honolulu Academy of Arts
Honolulu, 1992
photo: R. Johnson

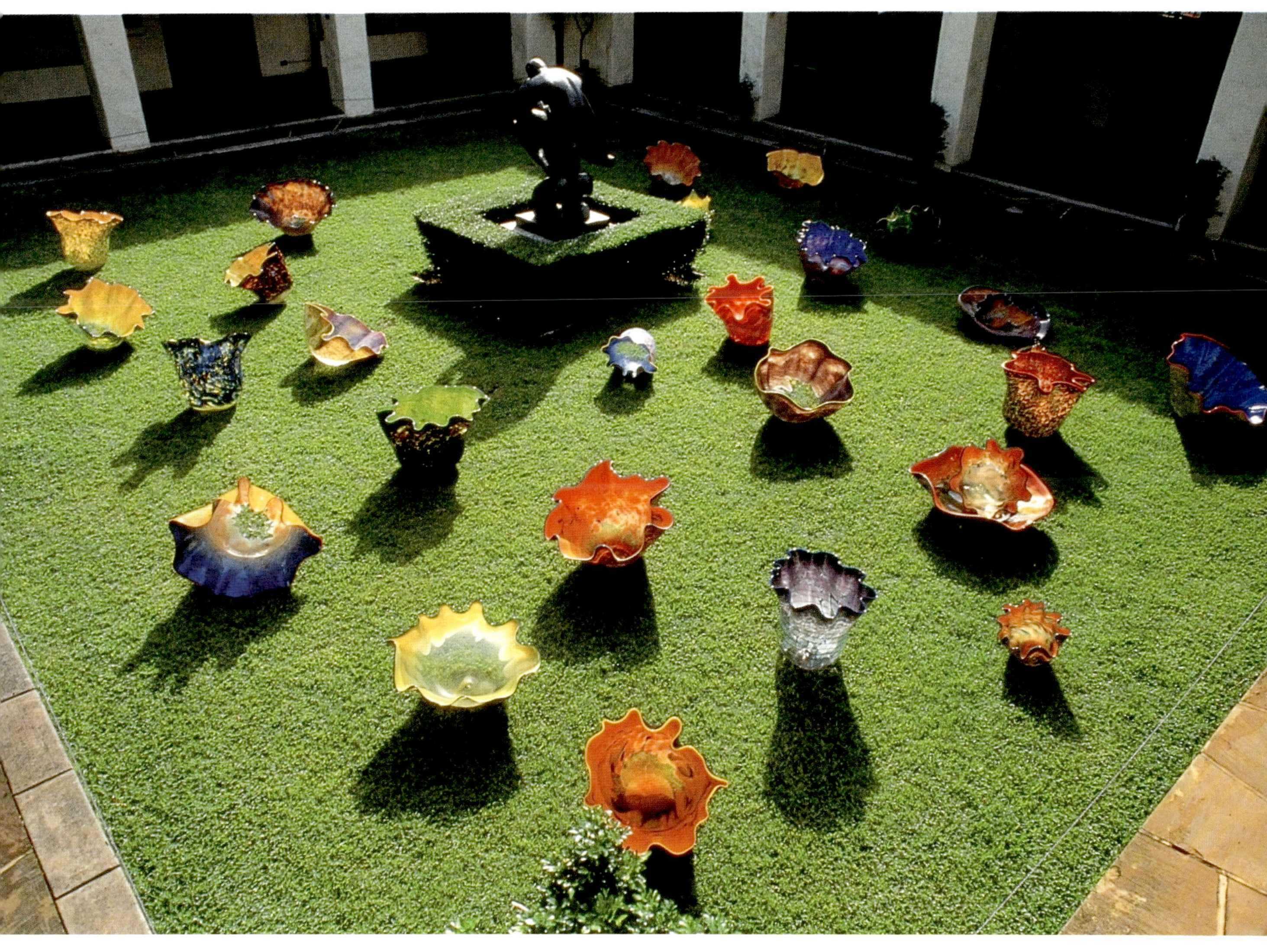

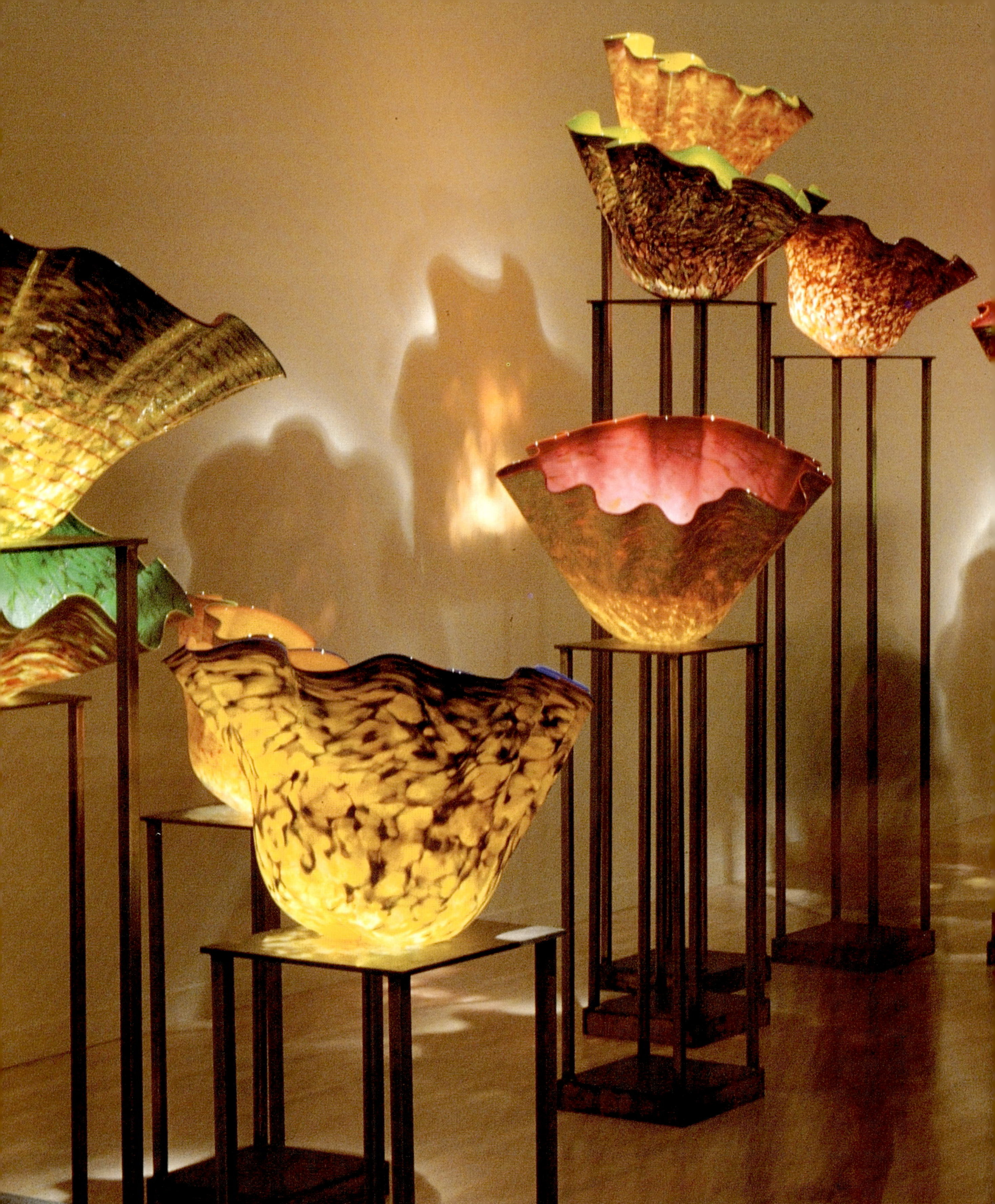

馬其亞森林
"德爾.屈胡利:裝置藝術 1964-1994"
達拉斯藝術館,達拉斯 1994
攝影: S. Hagar

Macchia Forest
"Dale Chihuly: Installations 1964-1994"
Dallas Museum of Art
Dallas, 1994
photo: S. Hagar

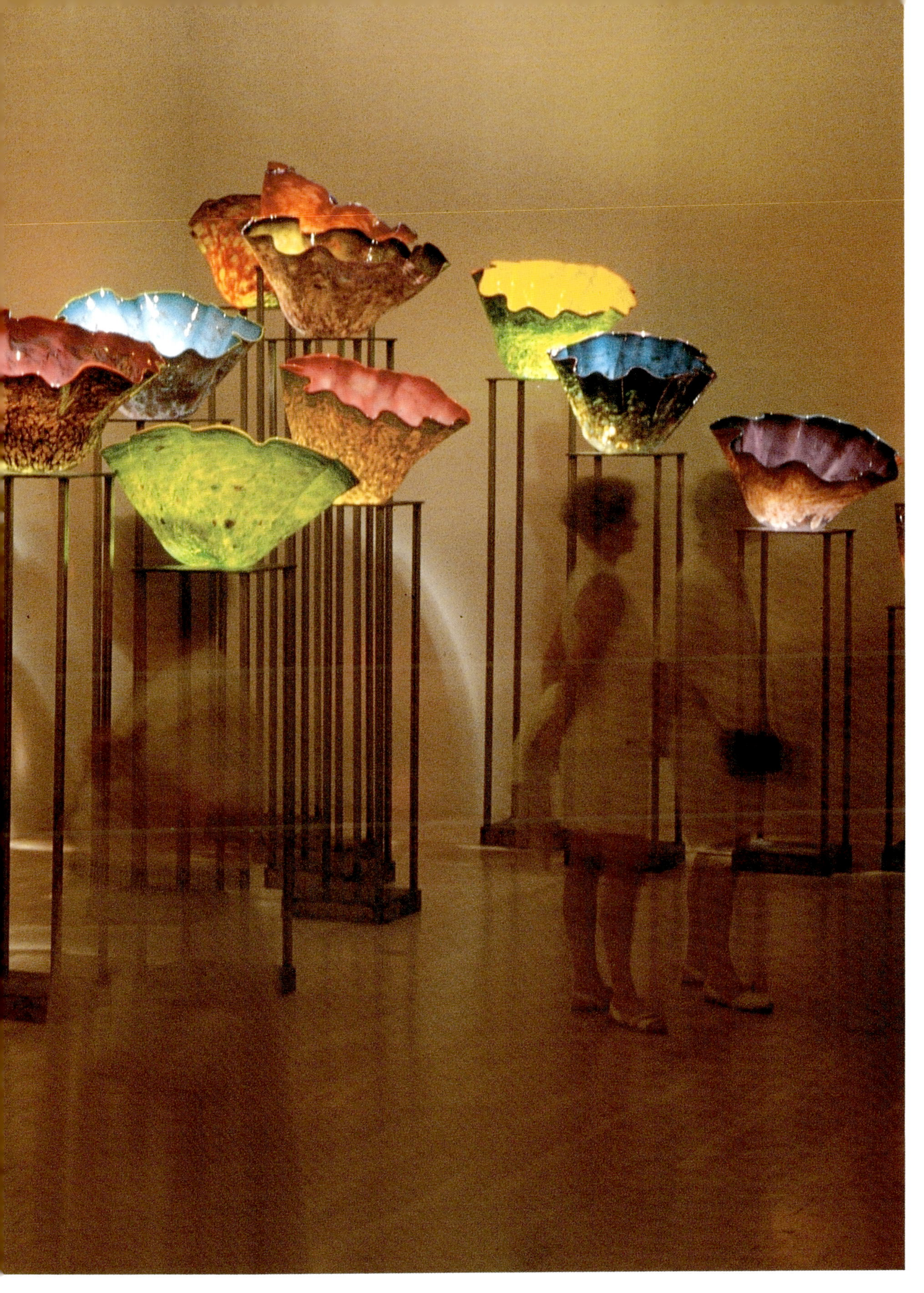

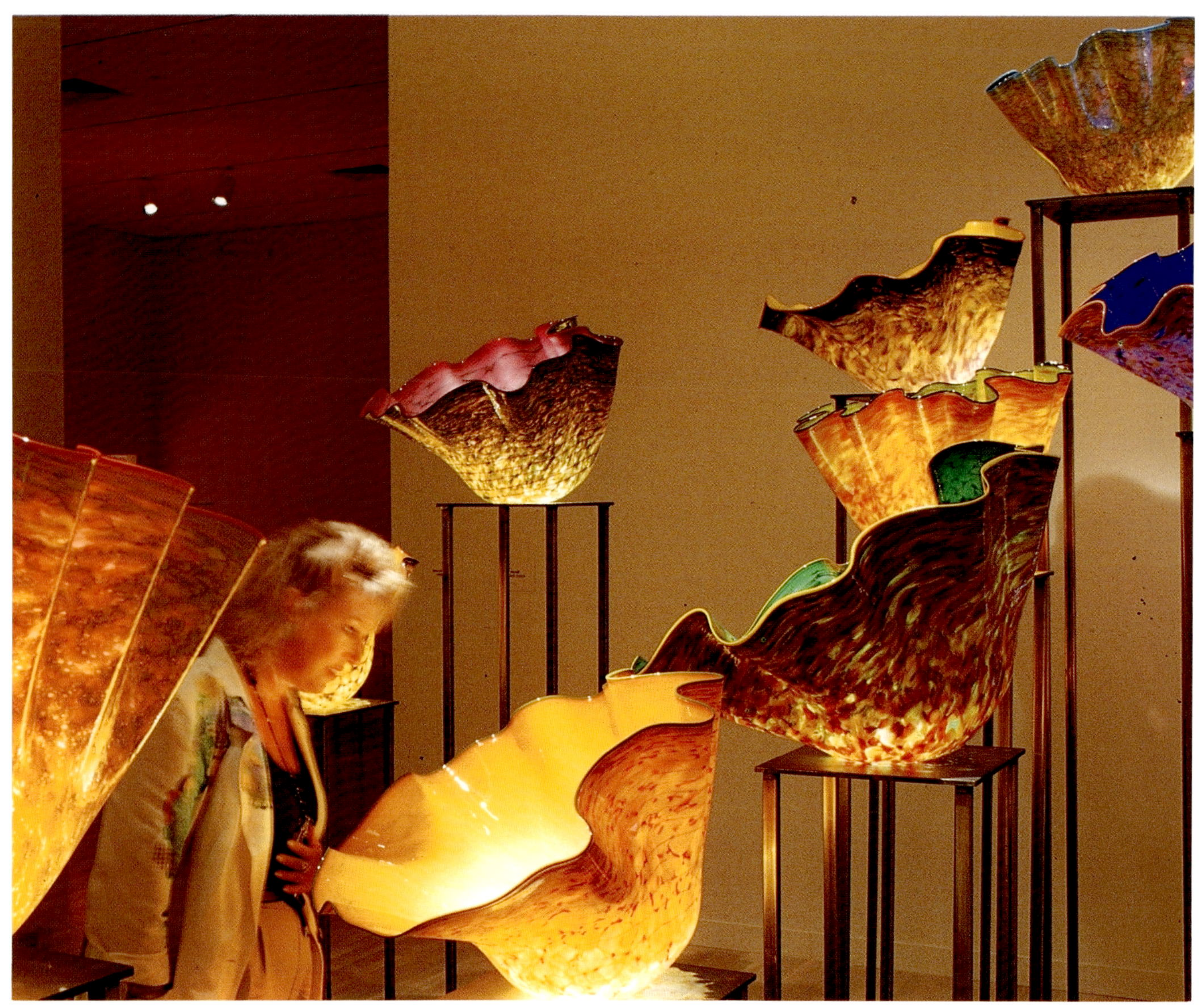

馬其亞森林
"德爾.屈胡利:裝置藝術 1964-1994"
達拉斯藝術館
達拉斯, 1994
攝影 S. Hagar

Macchia Forest
"Dale Chihuly: Installations 1964-1994"
Dallas Museum of Art
Dallas, 1994
photo: S. Hagar

馬其亞森林
"德爾.屈胡利:裝置藝術
1964-1993"
底特律藝術學院
底特律, 1993
攝影: R. Johnson

Macchia Forest
"Dale Chihuly:
Installations 1964-1993"
**The Detroit
Institute of Arts**
Detroit, 1993
photo: R. Johnson

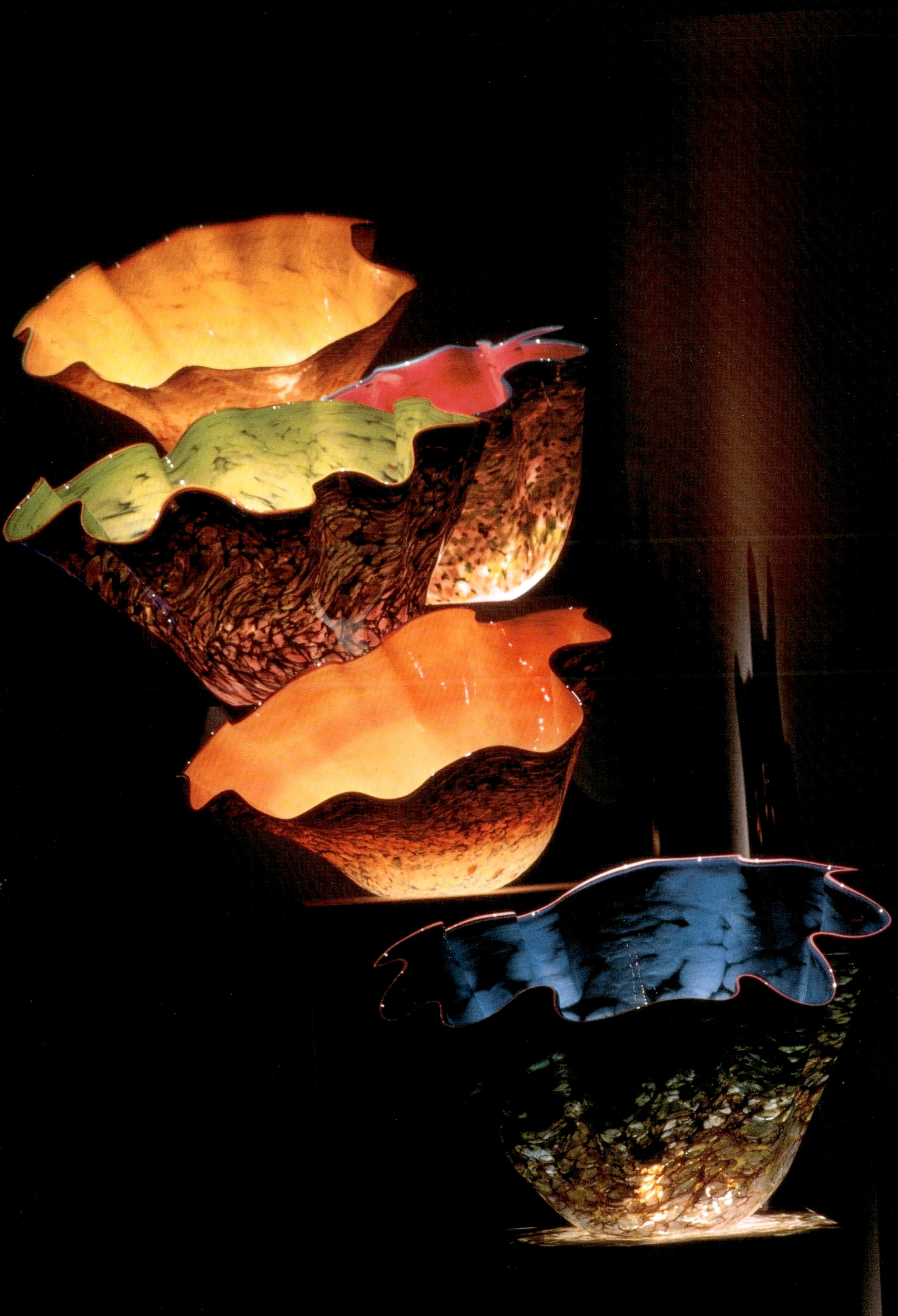

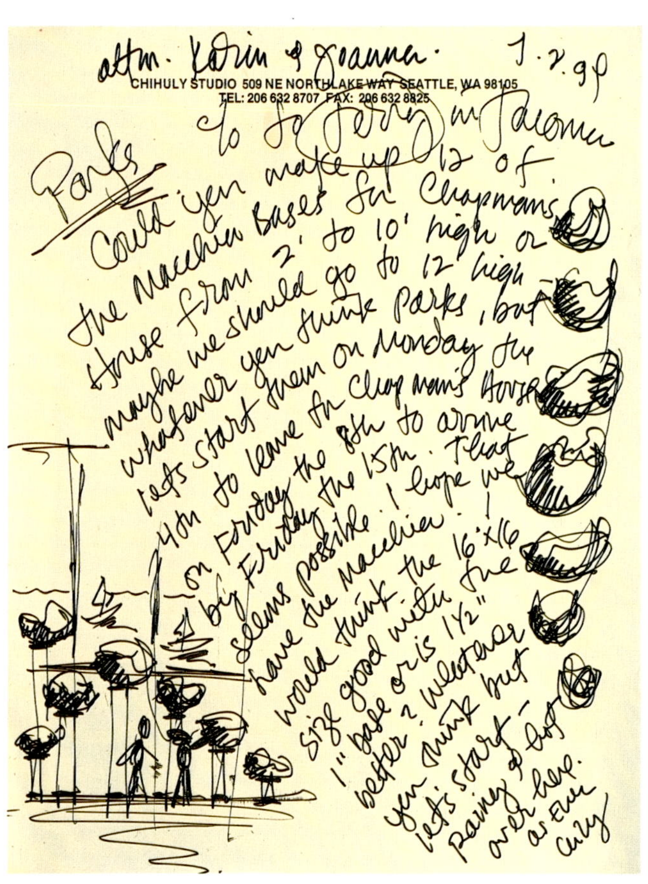

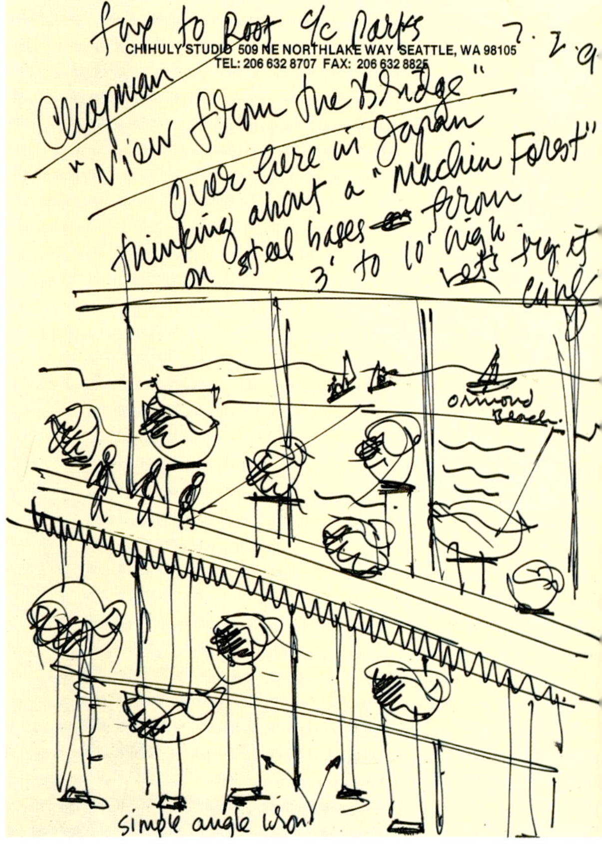

馬其亞森林素描
8.5 x 11吋
1994
攝影：C. Garoutte

Macchia Forest Sketches
8.5 x 11"
1994
photos: C. Garoutte

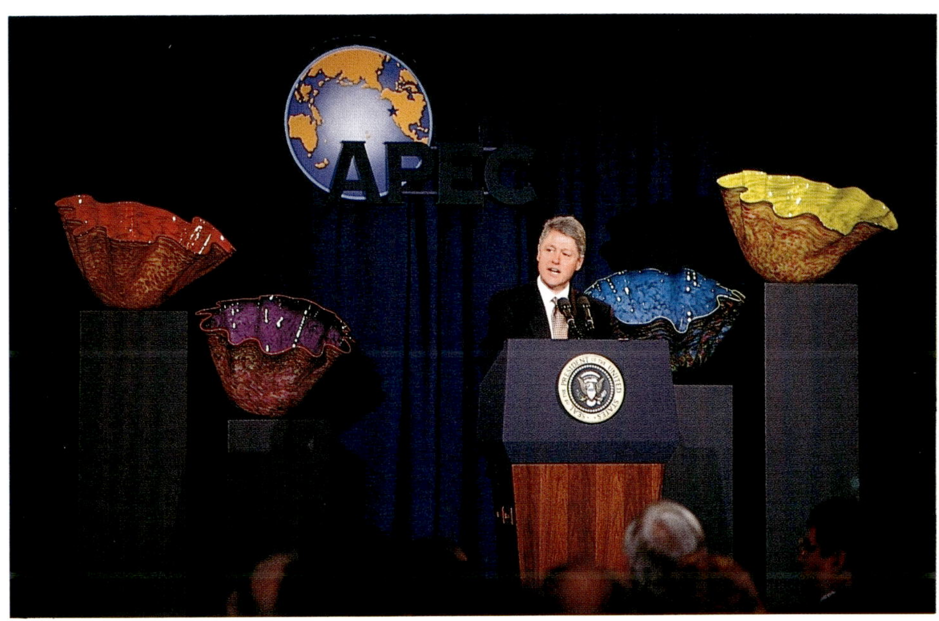

總統馬其亞
亞太經濟會議
西雅圖, 1993
攝影: R. Johnson

Presidential Macchia
APEC Conference
Seattle, 1993
photo: R. Johnson

window installations

窗之裝置

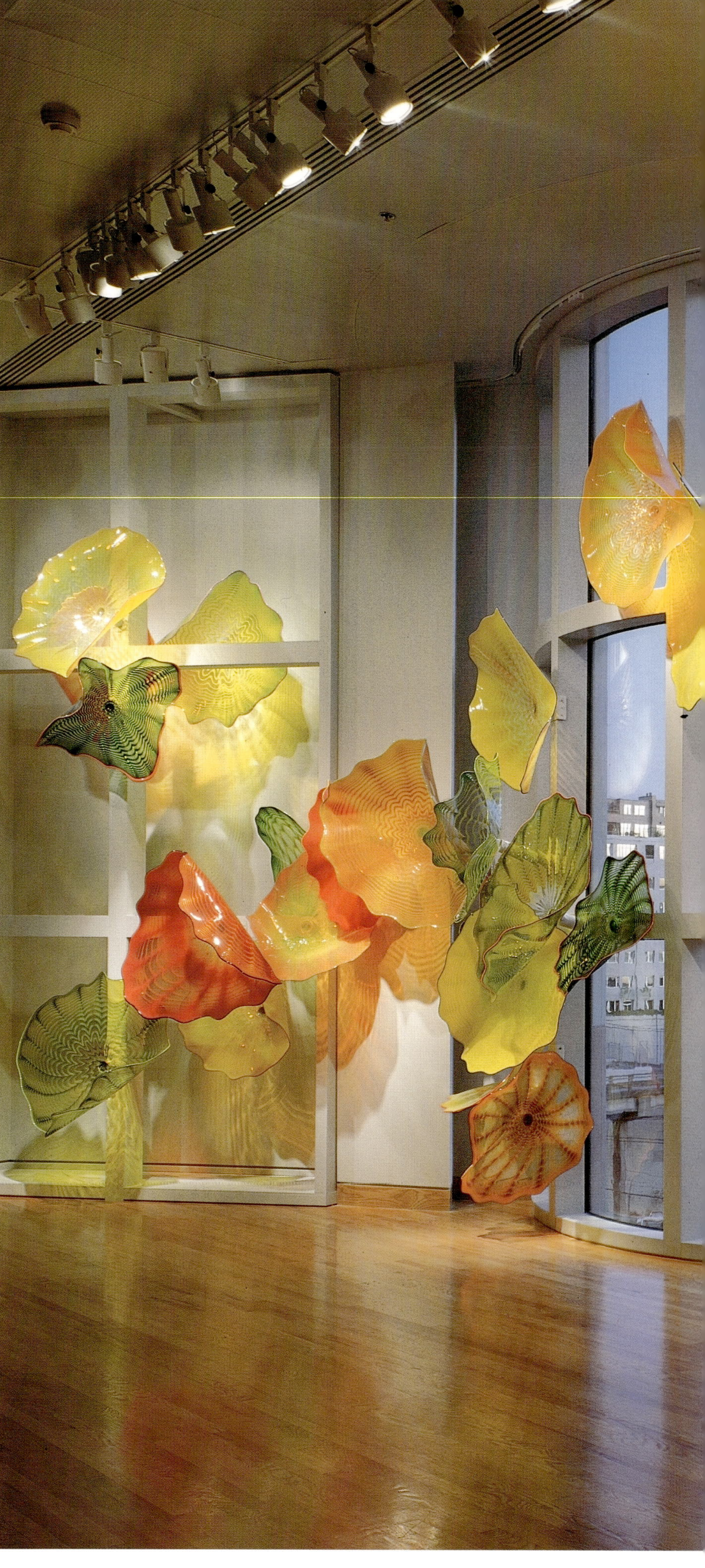

泛突利窗
48 x 16 x 7呎
"德爾.屈胡利： 裝置藝術
1964-1992"
西雅圖藝術館
西雅圖, 1992
攝影: E. Calderon

Venturi Window
48 x 16 x 7'
"Dale Chihuly:
Installations 1964-1992"
Seattle Art Museum
Seattle, 1992
photo: E. Calderon

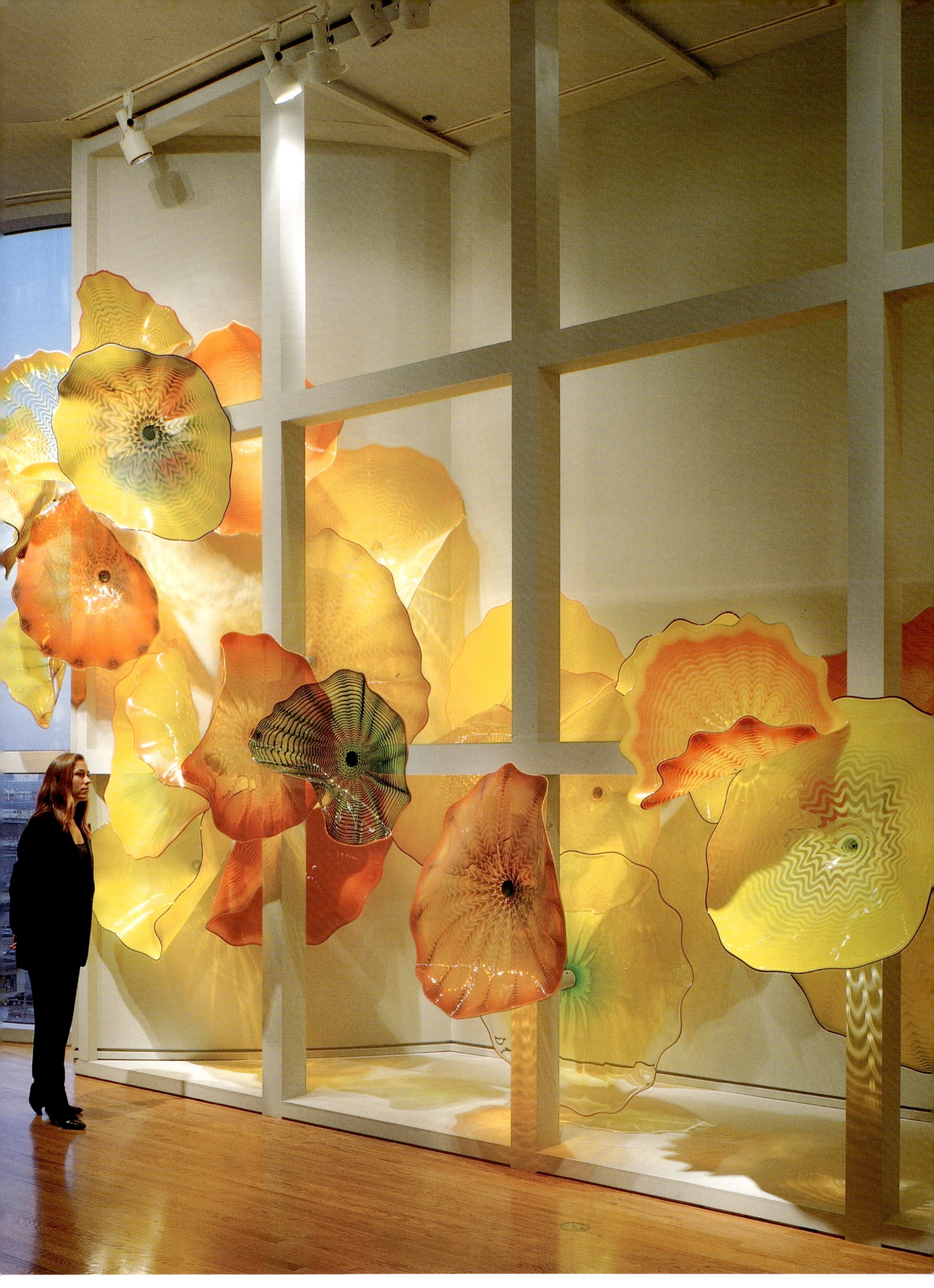

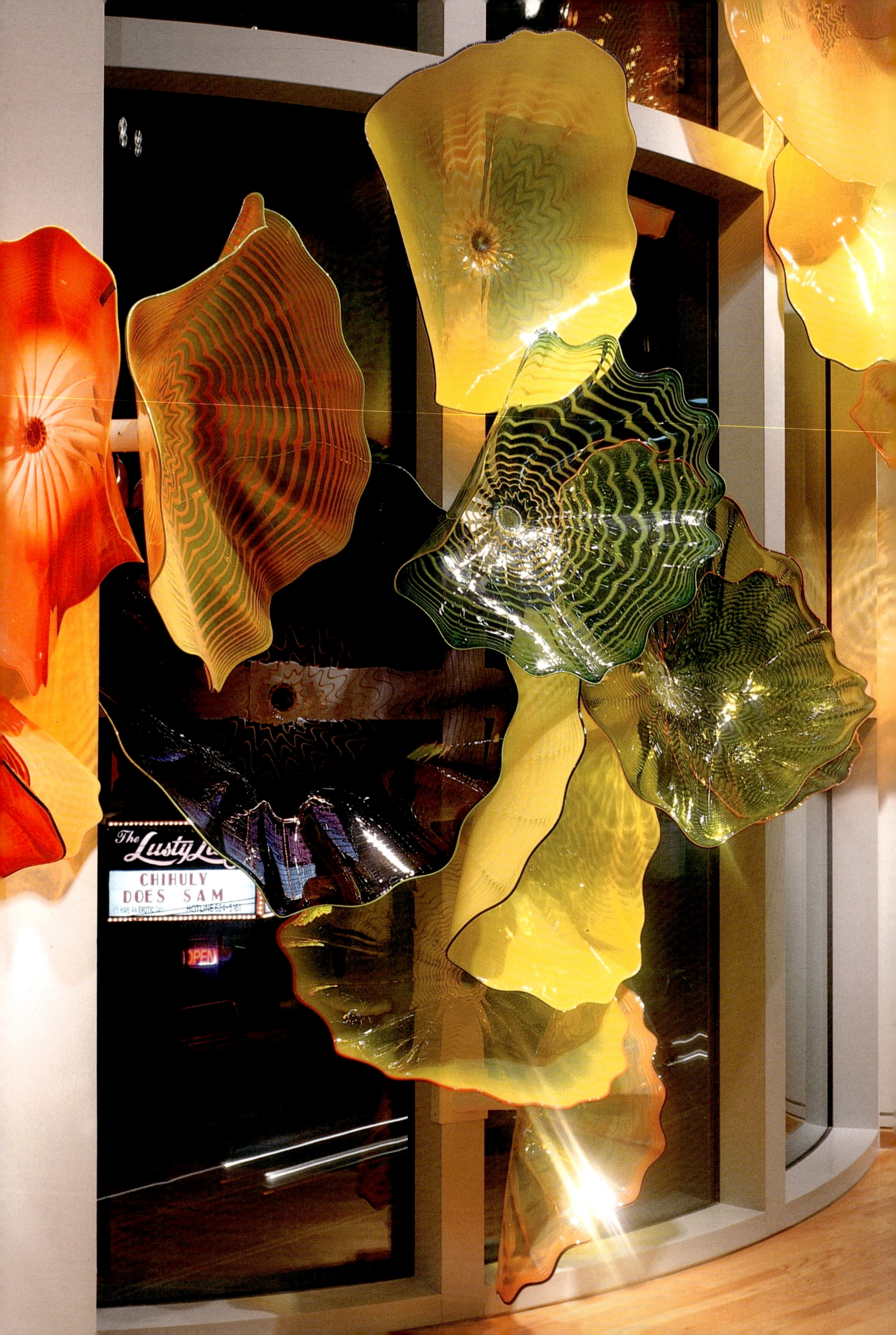
The Lusty
CHIHULY
DOES SAM
HAVE AN EROTIC DAY
HOTLINE 624-5161

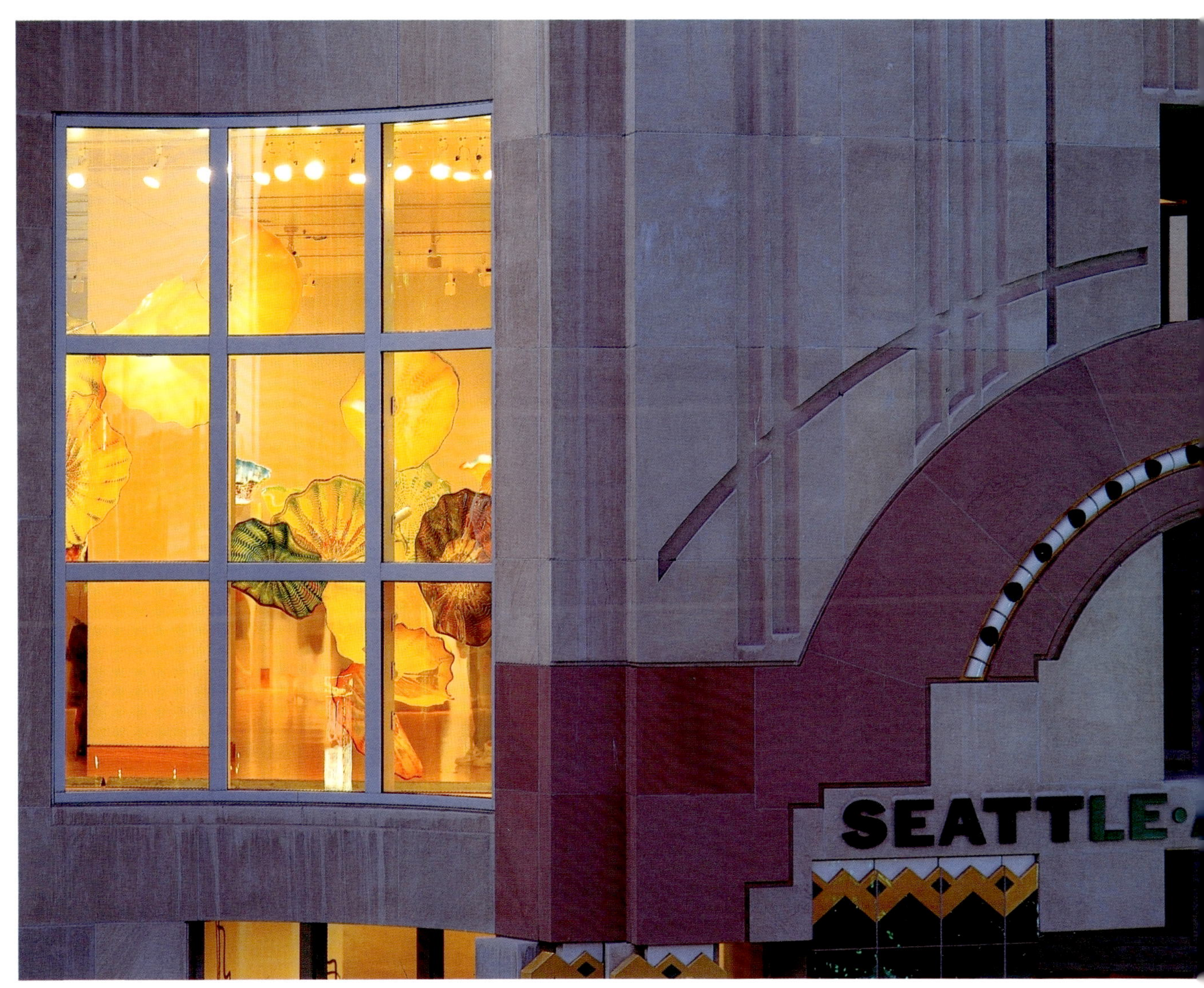

泛突利窗
"德爾.屈胡利： 裝置藝術
1964-1992"
西雅圖藝術館
西雅圖，1992
攝影：C. Garoutte

Venturi Window
"Dale Chihuly: Installations
1964-1992"
Seattle Art Museum
Seattle, 1992
photo: C. Garoutte

泛突利窗
外部景觀

Venturi Window
outside view

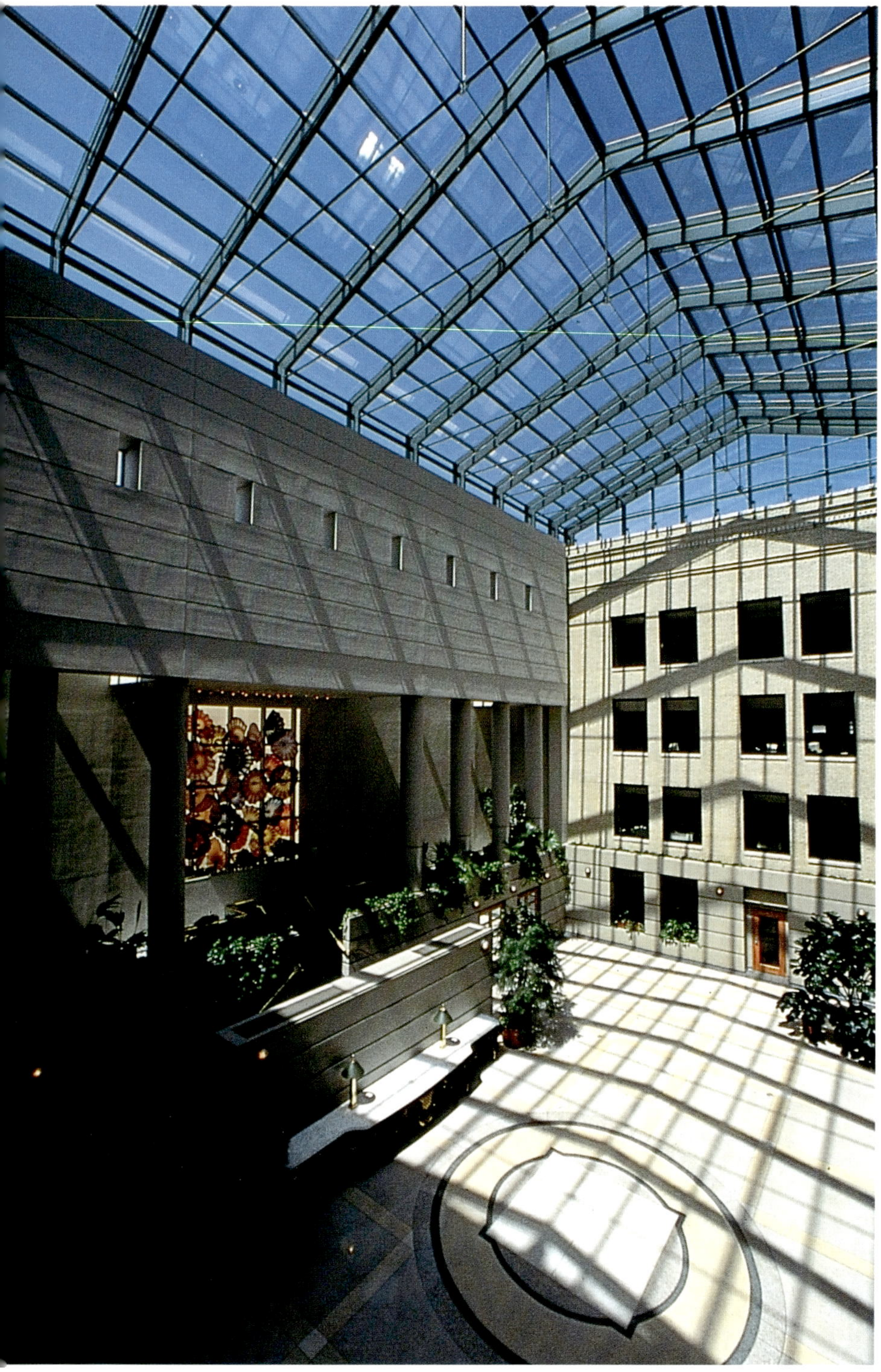

瑪利娜窗
16 x 16呎
小凱撒企業世界總部
底特律, 1993
攝影: R. Johnson

Malina Window
16 x 16'
Little Caesars World Headquarters
Detroit, 1993
photo: R. Johnson

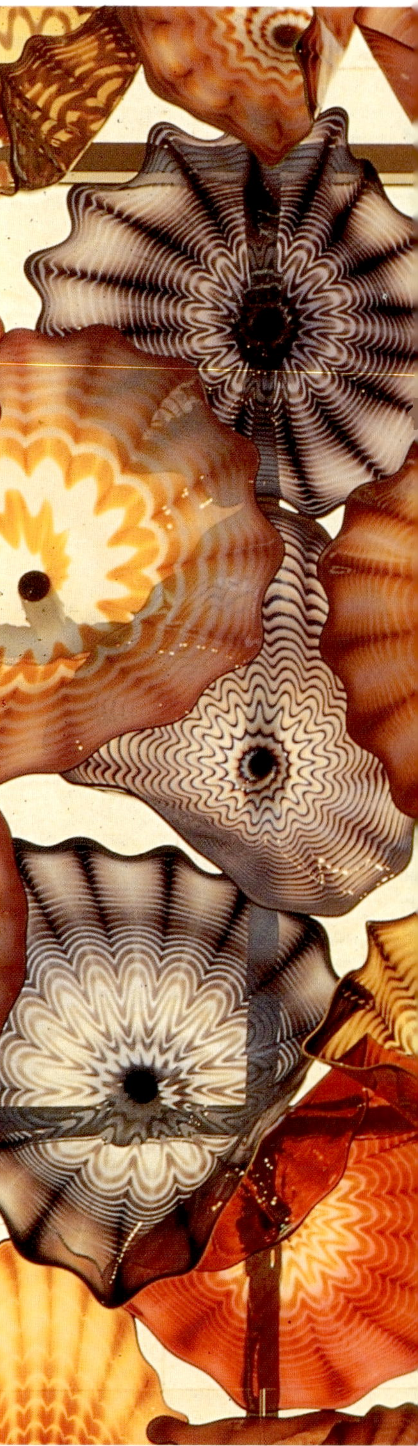

日間景觀 / daylight view

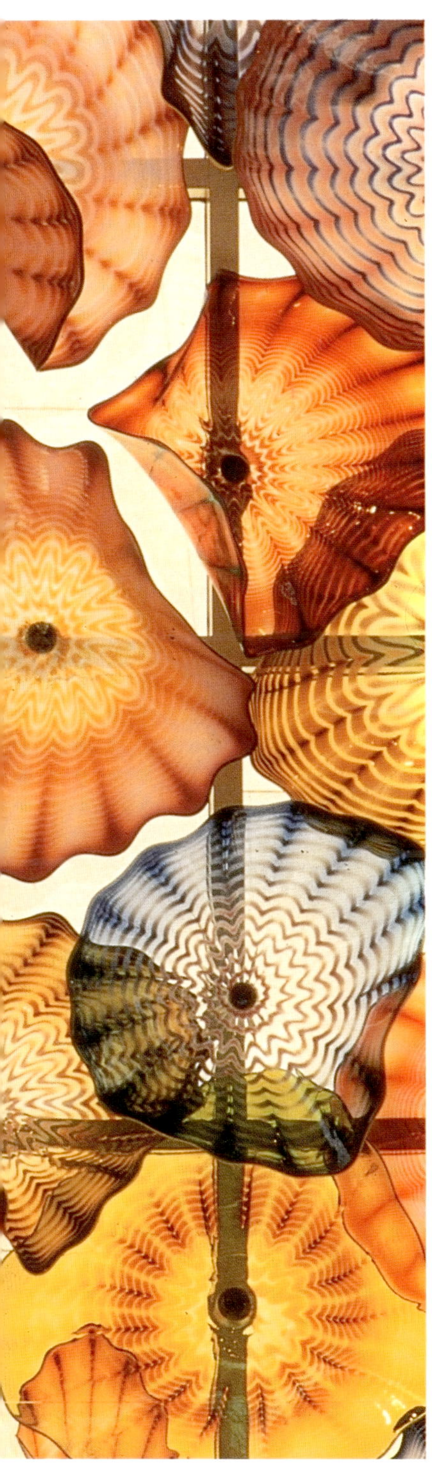

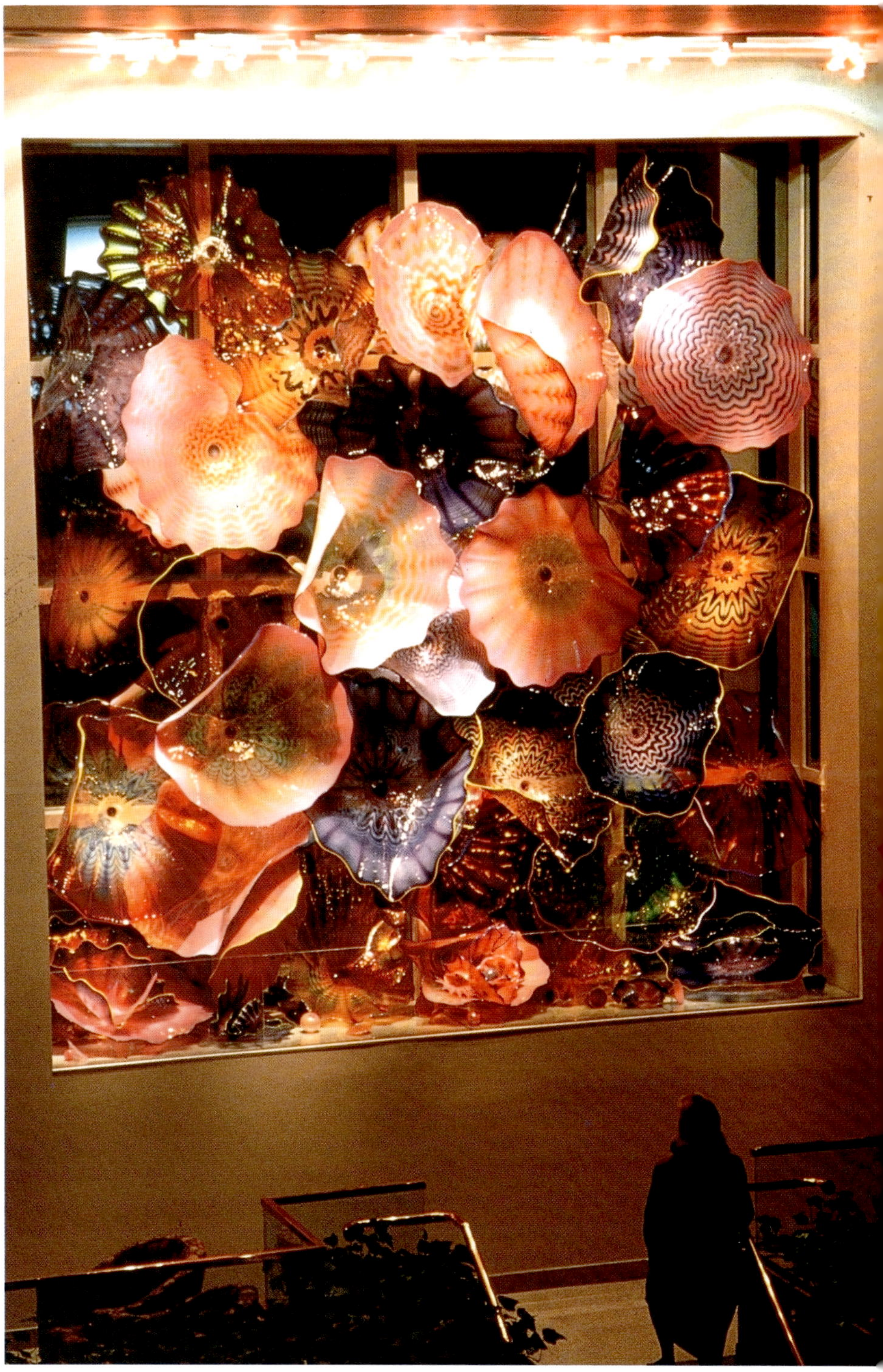

夜間景觀 / night view

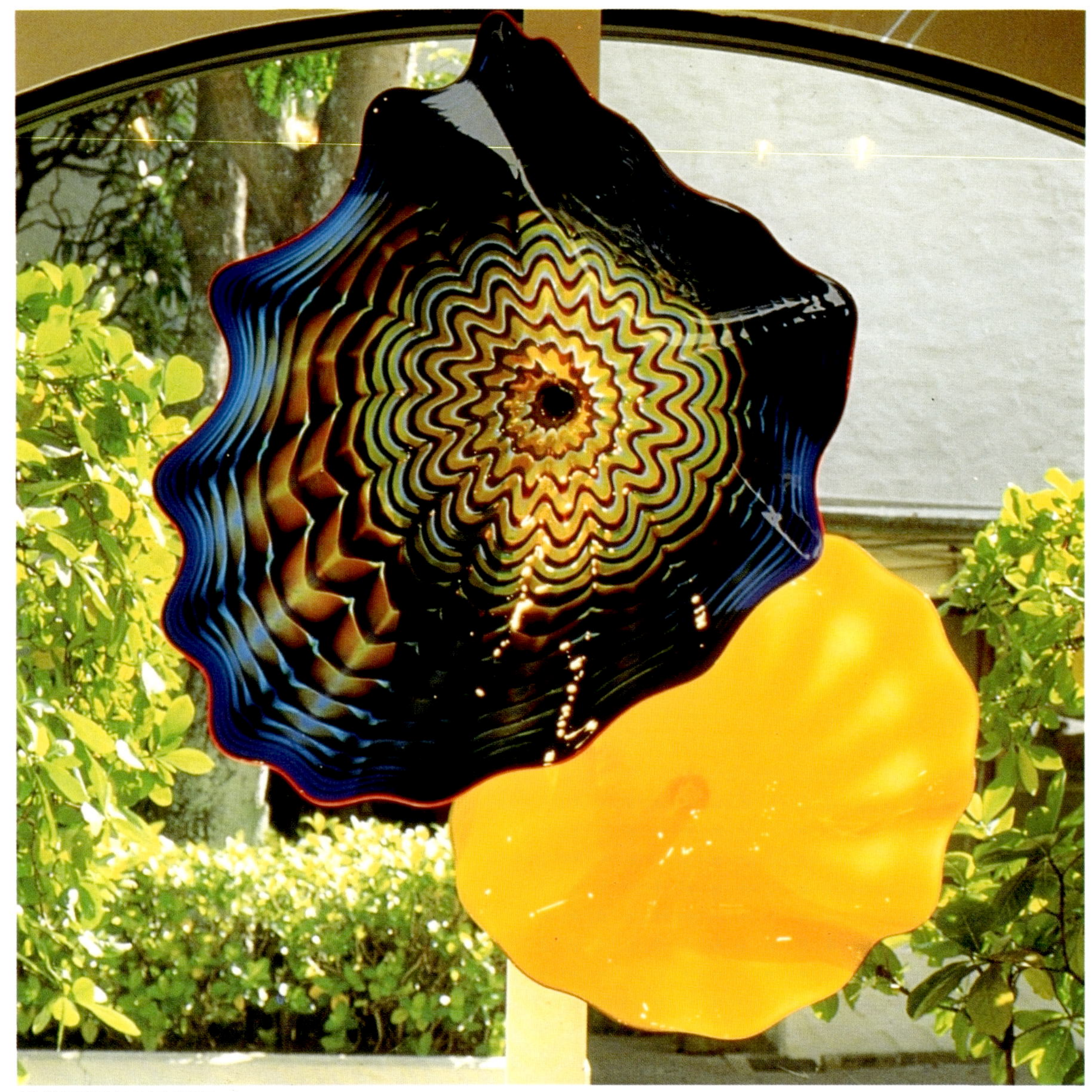

露絲展覽室之波斯窗
"屈胡利庭院展"
檀香山藝術學院
檀香山, 1992
攝影: R. Johnson

Persian Window in the Luce Gallery
"Chihuly Courtyards"
Honolulu Academy of Arts
Honolulu, 1992
photo: R. Johnson

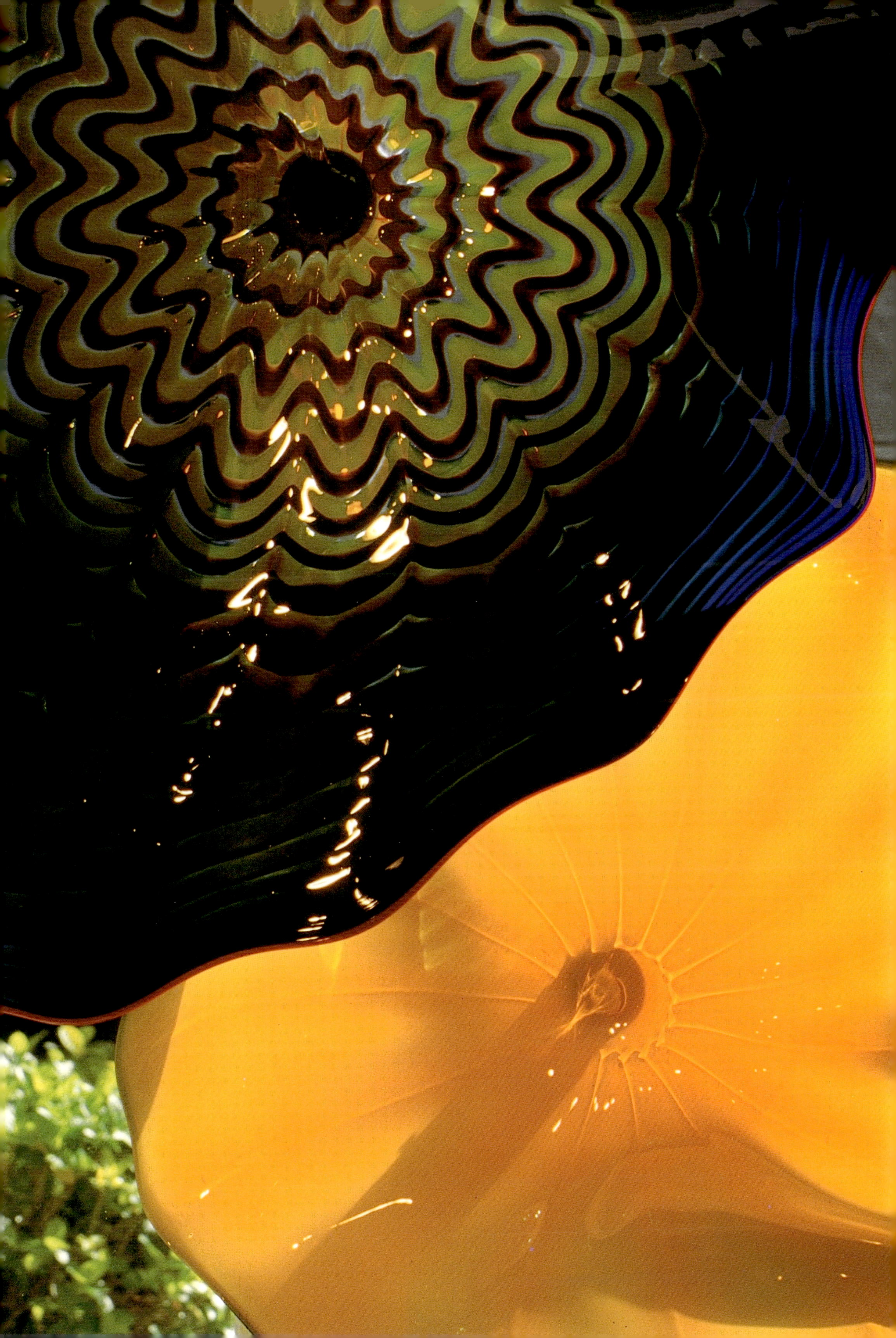

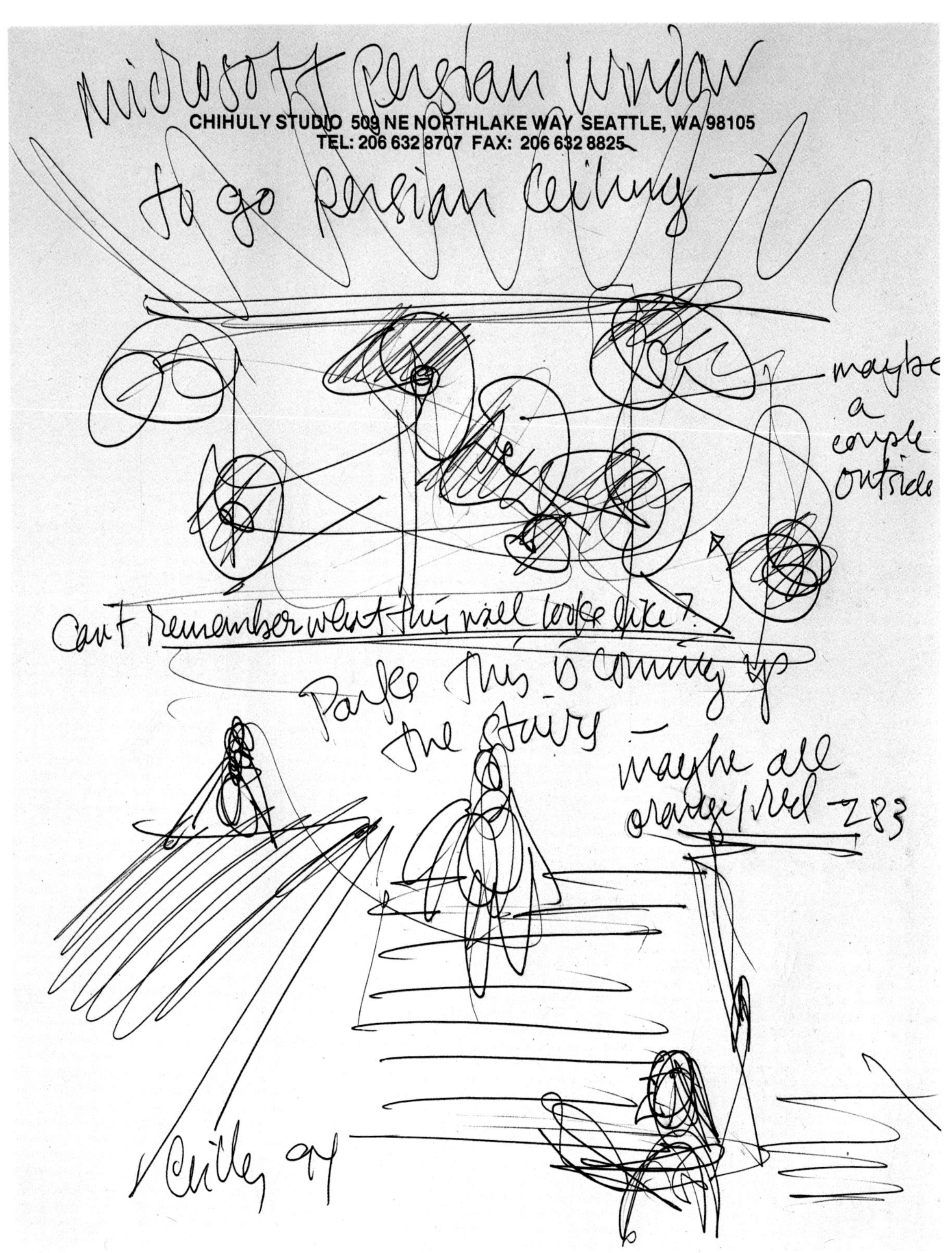

微軟窗素描
8.5 x 11吋
1994
攝影：C. Garoutte

Microsoft Window Sketch
8.5 x 11"
1994
photo: C. Garoutte

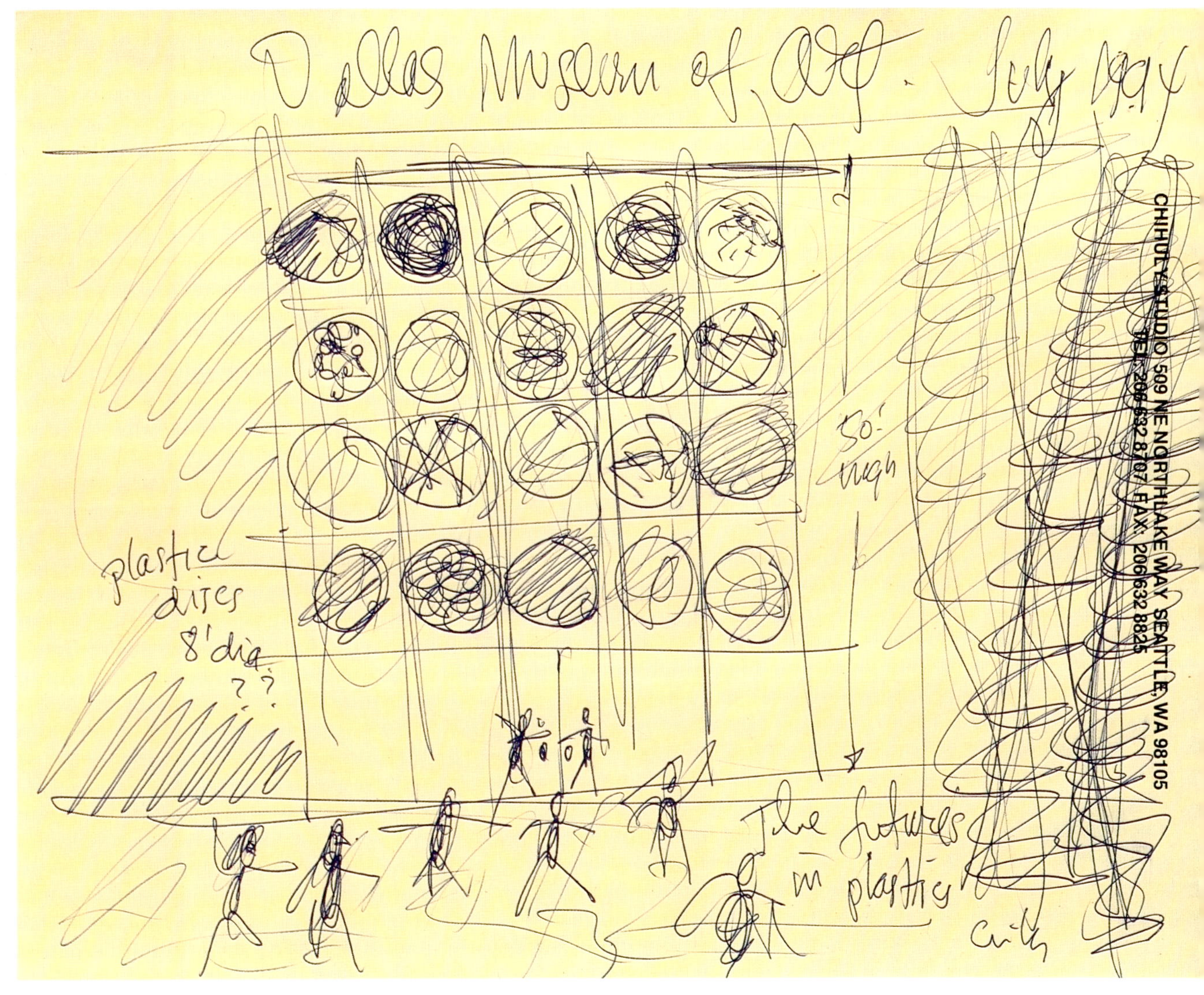

達拉斯窗素描
8.5 x 11吋
1994
攝影：C. Garoutte

Dallas Window Sketch
8.5 x 11"
1994
photo: C. Garoutte

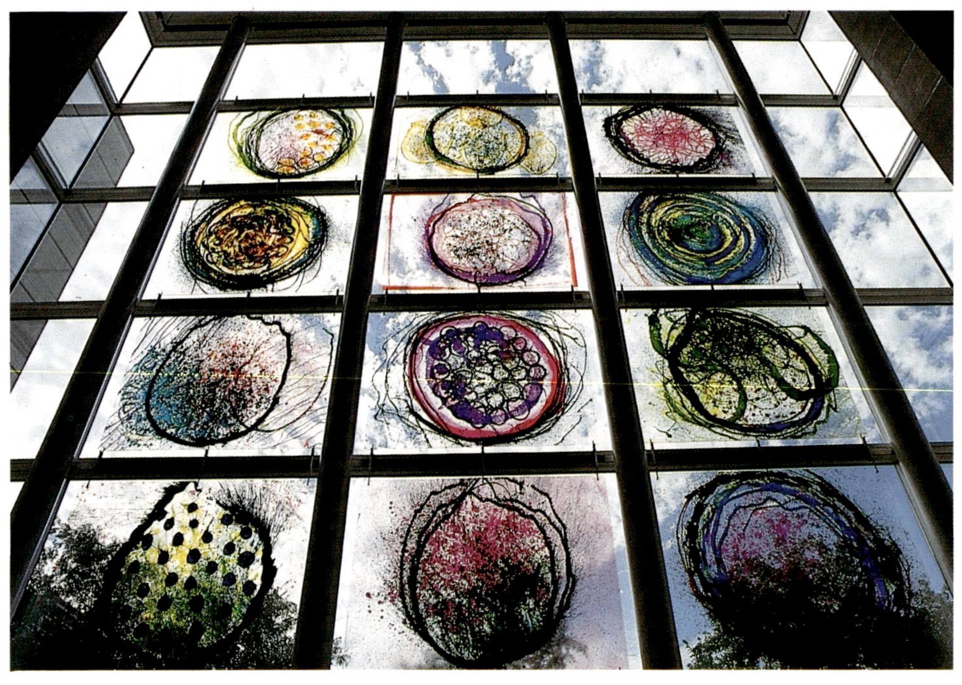

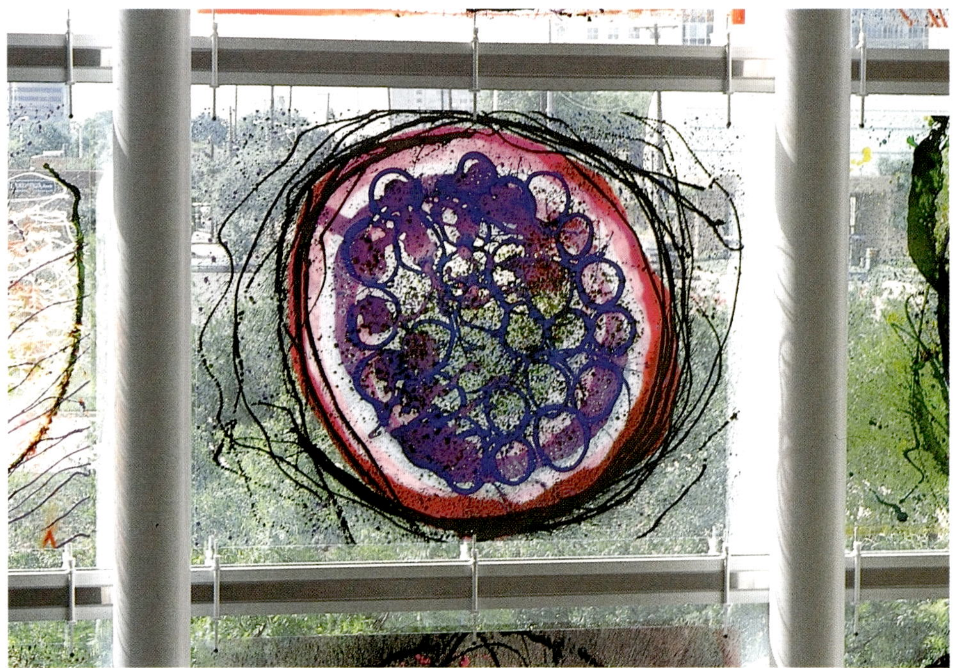

藍素描窗
“德爾.屈胡利:裝置藝術 1964-1994”
達拉斯藝術館
達拉斯, 1994
攝影: S. Hagar

Basket Drawing Window
“Dale Chihuly: Installations 1964-1994”
Dallas Museum of Art
Dallas, 1994
photo: S. Hagar

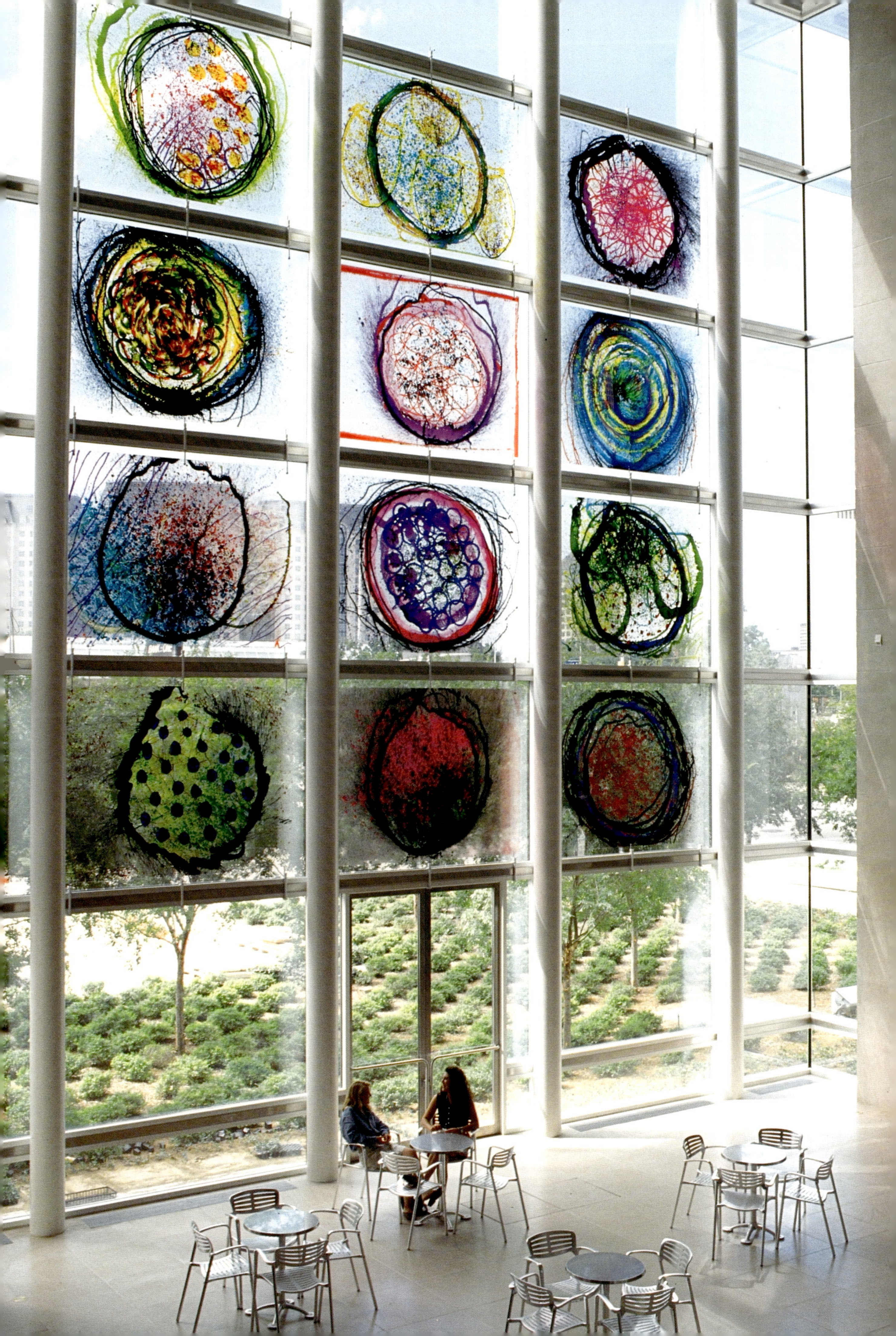

wall installations

牆之裝置

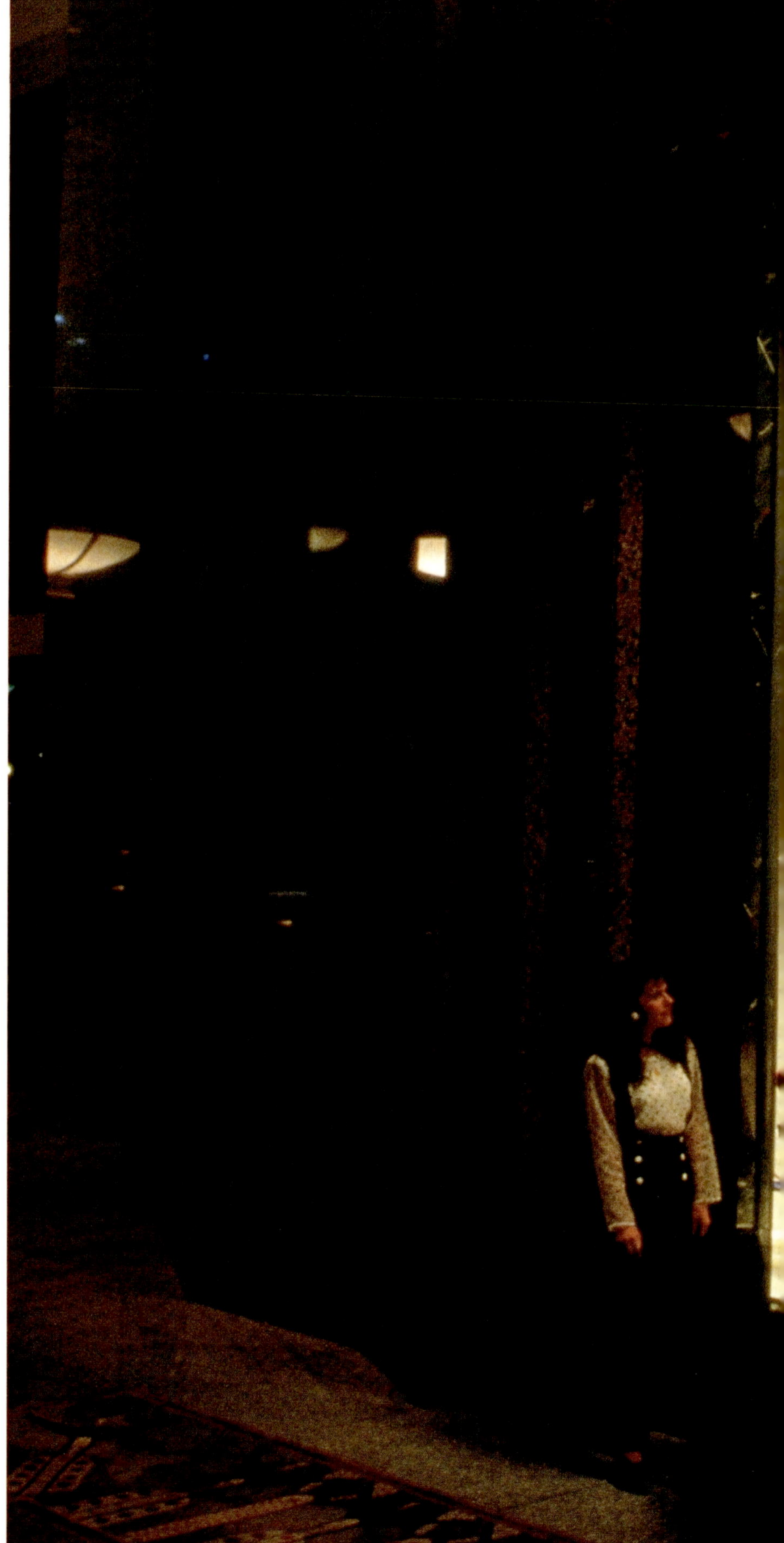

太平洋第一波斯裝置
美國銀行中心
西雅圖, 1992
攝影: C. Garoutte

Pacific First Persian Installation
U.S. Bank Centre
Seattle, 1992
photo: C. Garoutte

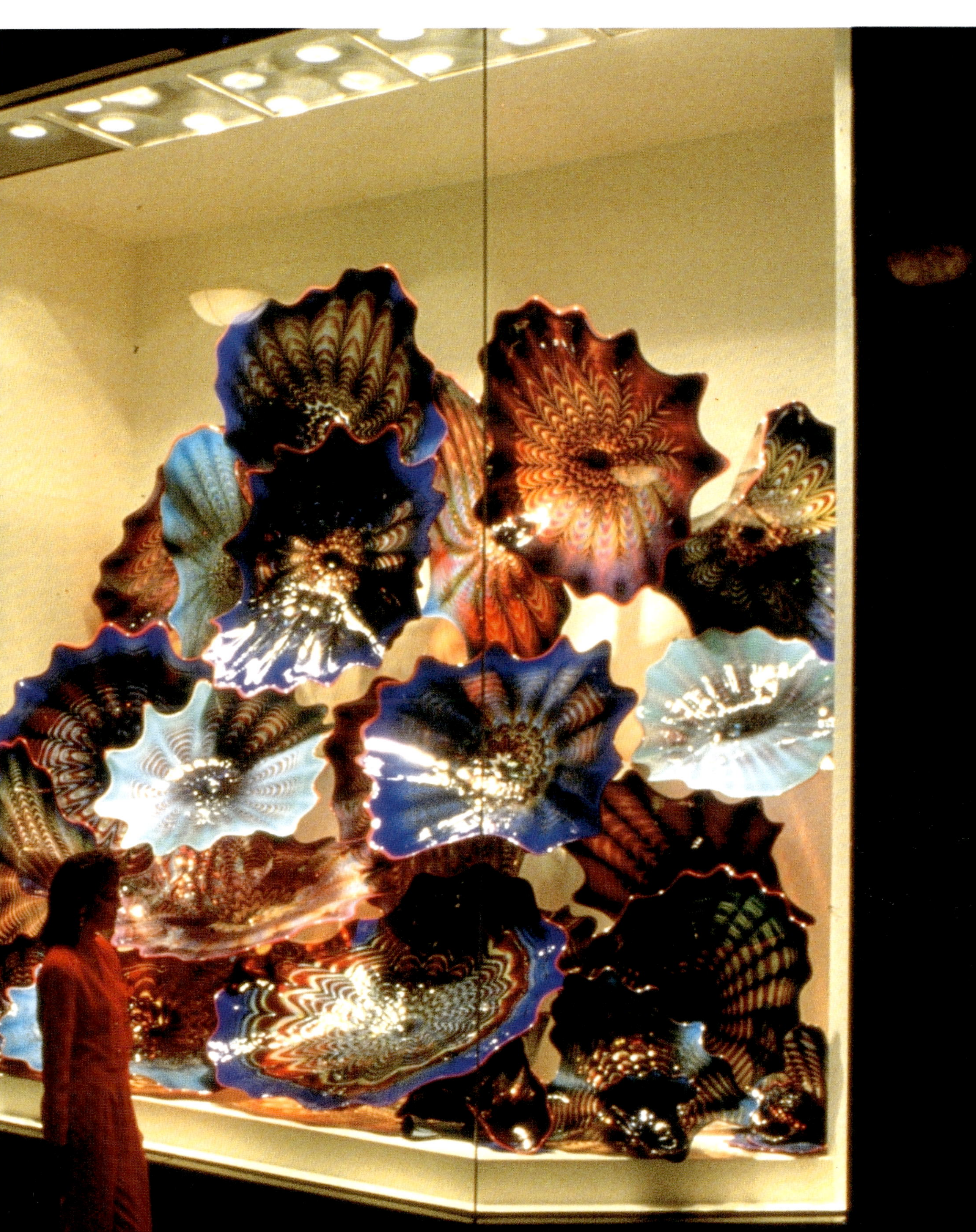

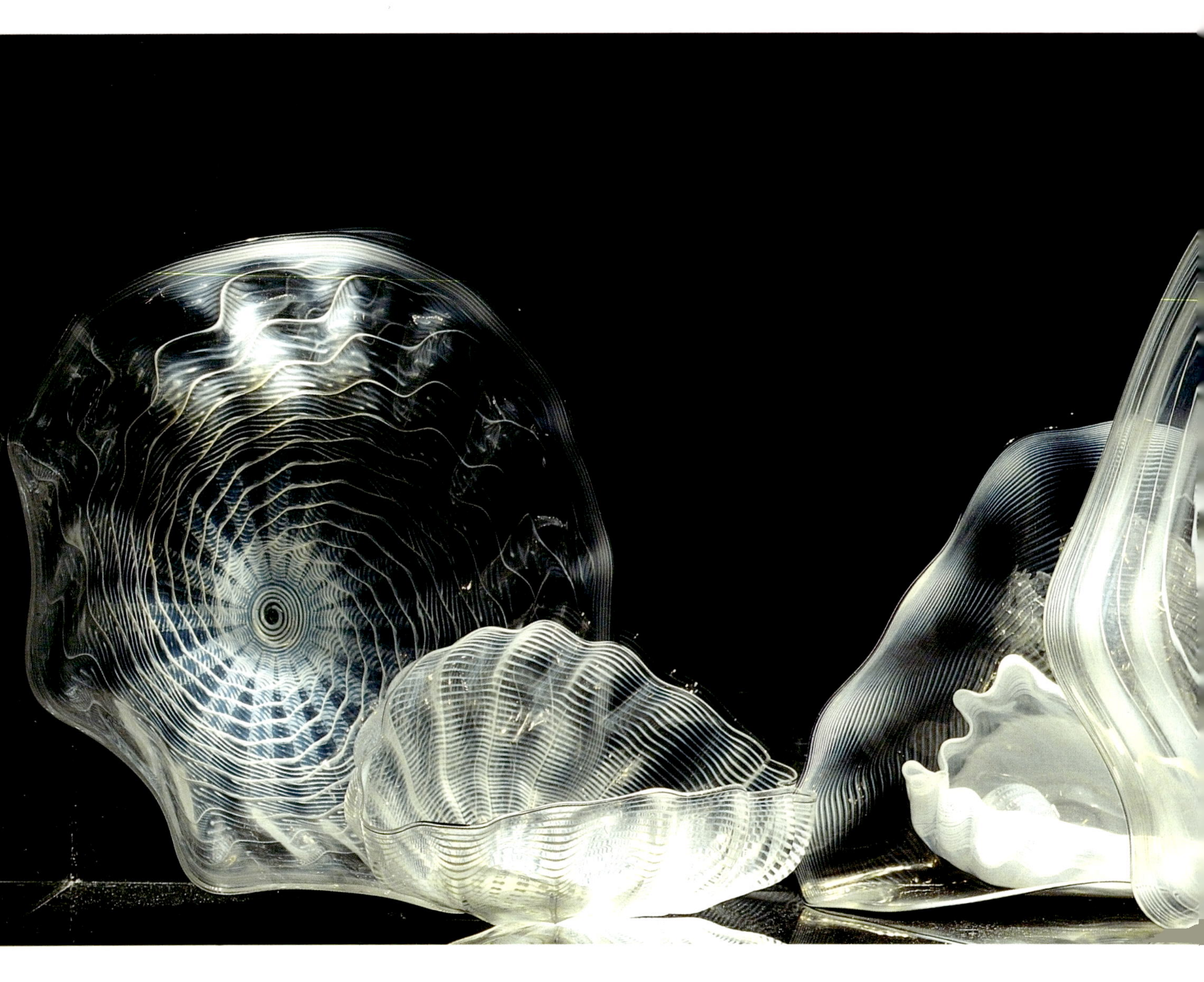

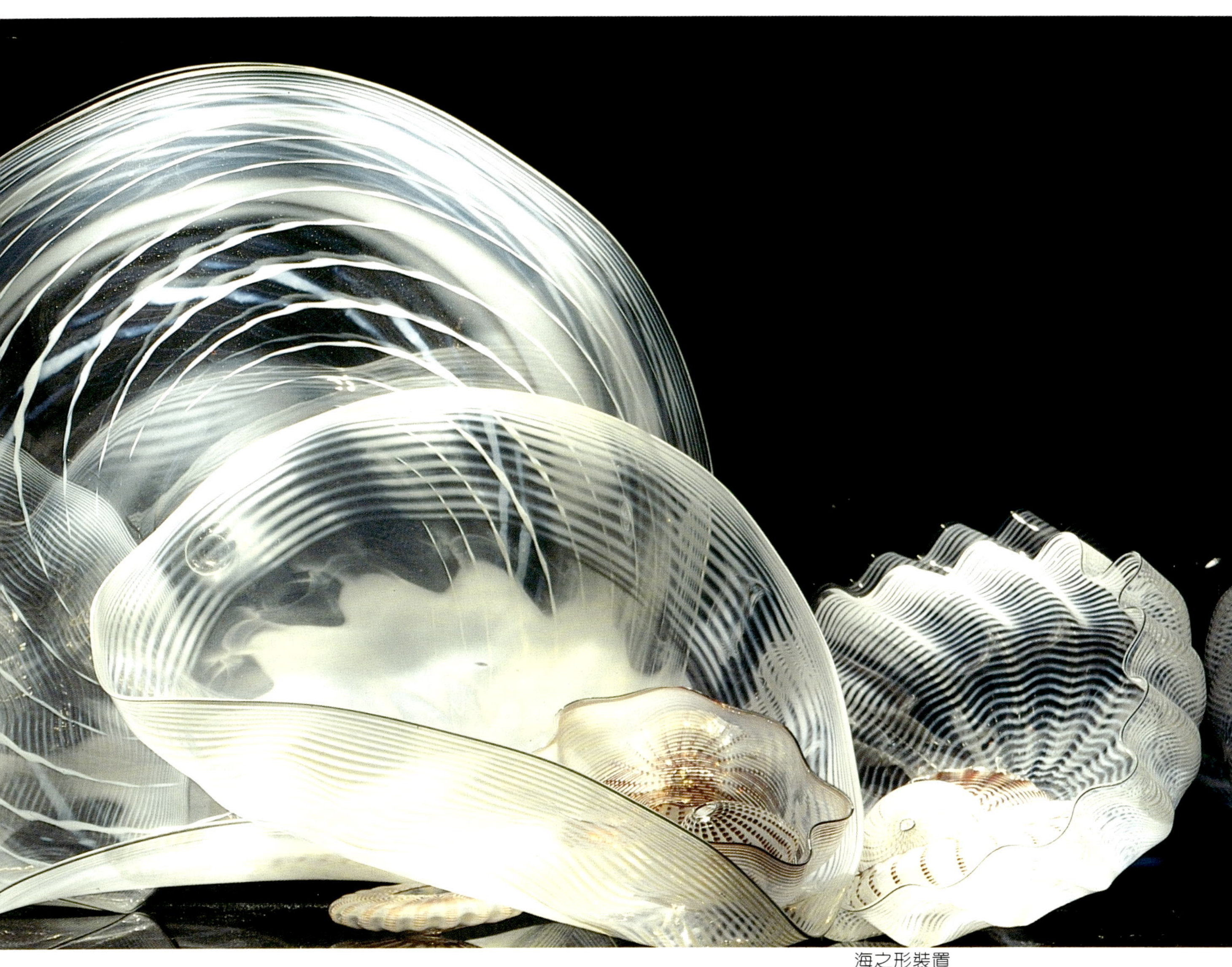

海之形裝置
3 x 5 x 2.5呎
塔科馬金融中心
塔科馬，1984
攝影：D. Busher

Sea Form Installation
3 x 5 x 2.5'
Tacoma Financial Center
Tacoma, 1984
photo: D. Busher

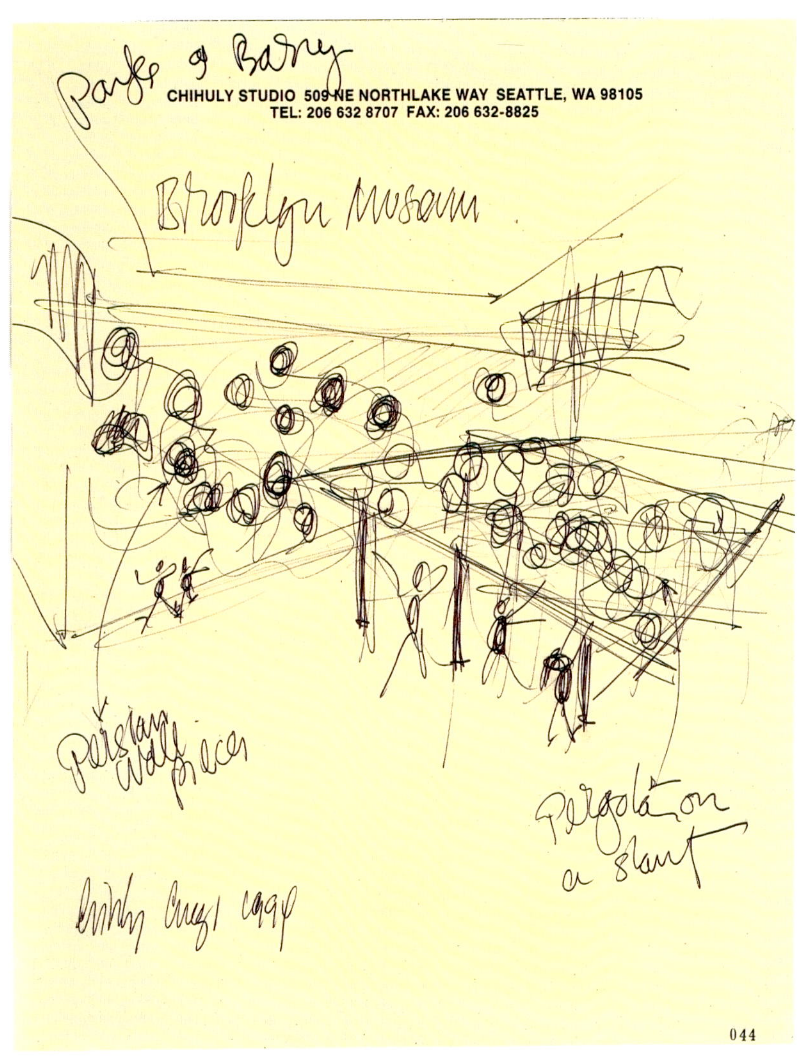

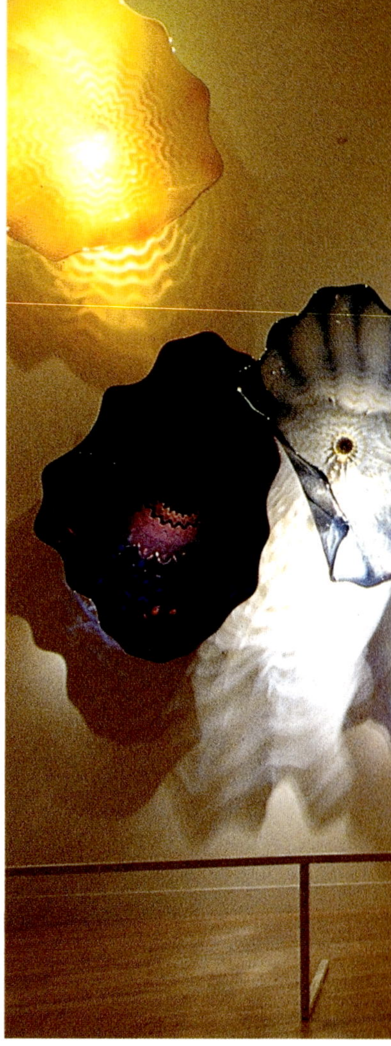

布魯克萊博物館素描
8.5 x 11吋
1994
攝影：C. Garoutte

Brooklyn Museum Sketch
8.5 x 11"
1994
photo: C. Garoutte

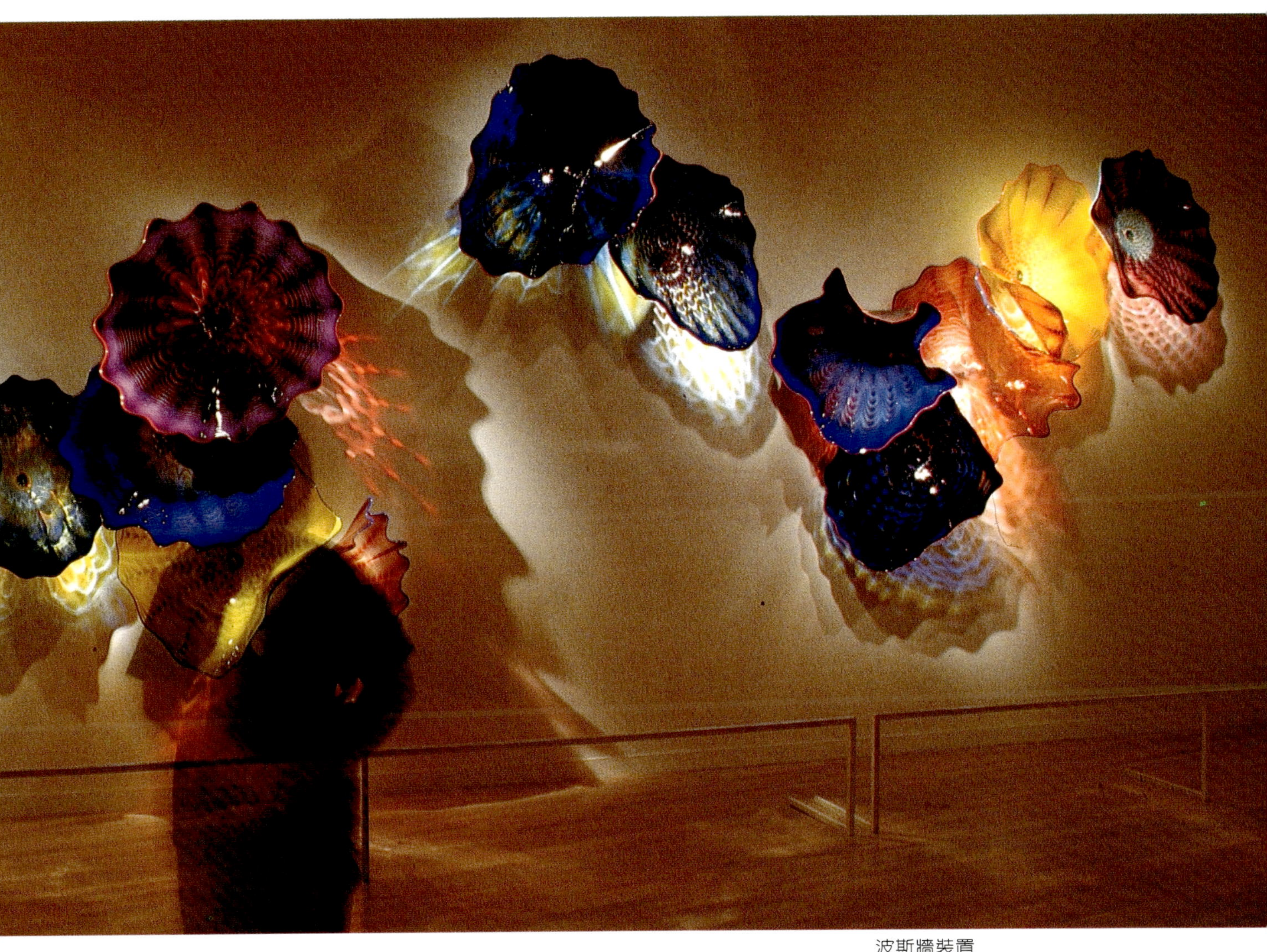

波斯牆裝置
"德爾.屈胡利:裝置藝術
1964-1994"
達拉斯藝術館
達拉斯, 1994
攝影: S. Hagar

Persian Wall Installation
"Dale Chihuly: Installations
1964-1994"
Dallas Museum of Art
Dallas, 1994
photo: S. Hagar

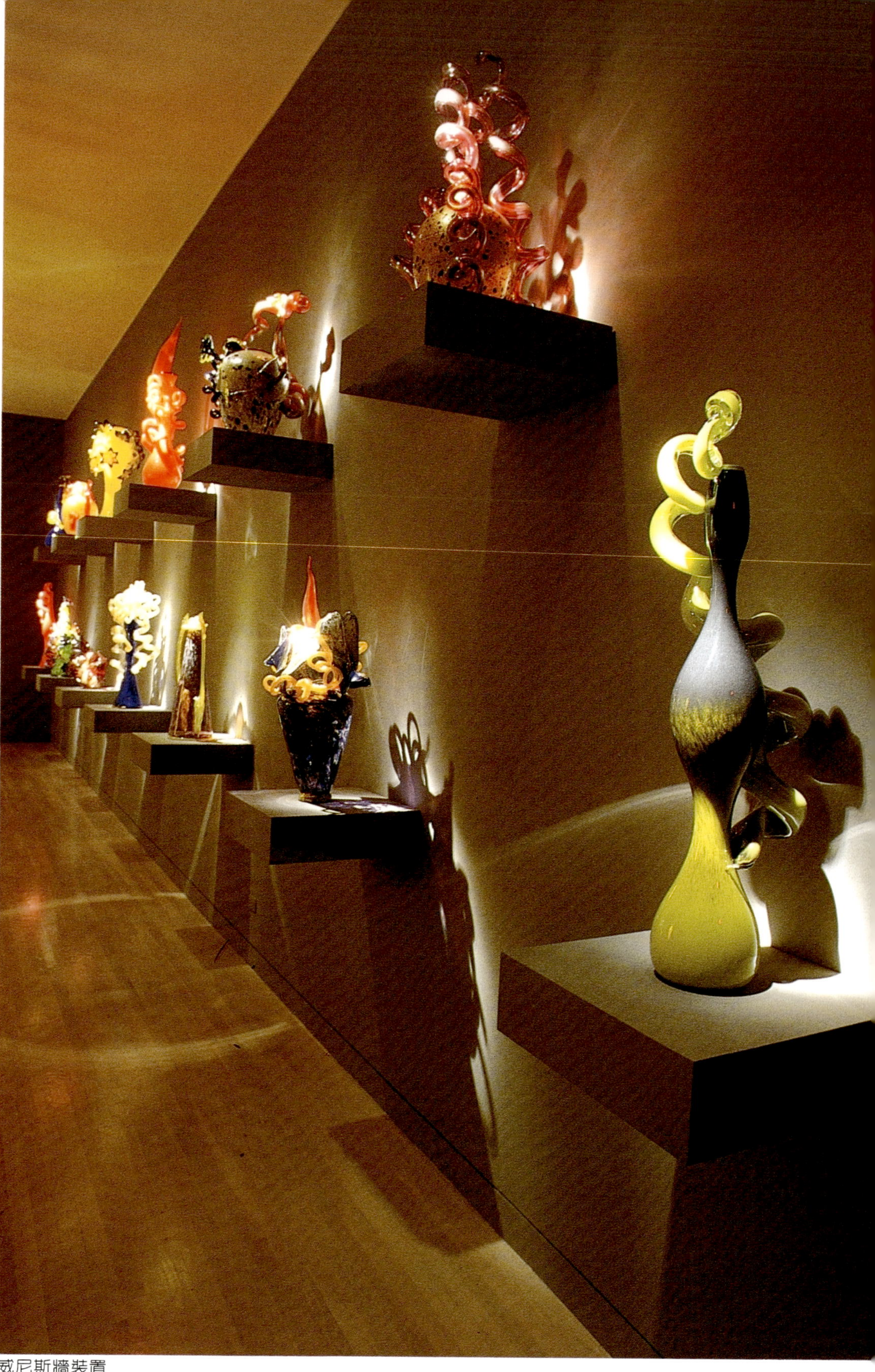

威尼斯牆裝置
"德爾.屈胡利:裝置藝術
1964-1994"
達拉斯,1994
攝影: S. Hagar

Venetian Wall Installation
"Dale Chihuly: Installations
1964-1994"
Dallas Museum of Art
Dallas, 1994
photo: S. Hagar

有飾帶的紅黃色威尼斯
37 x 14 x 14吋
1991
攝影：C. Garoutte

Red Over Yellow Venetian with One Coil
37 x 14 x 14"
1991
photo: C. Garoutte

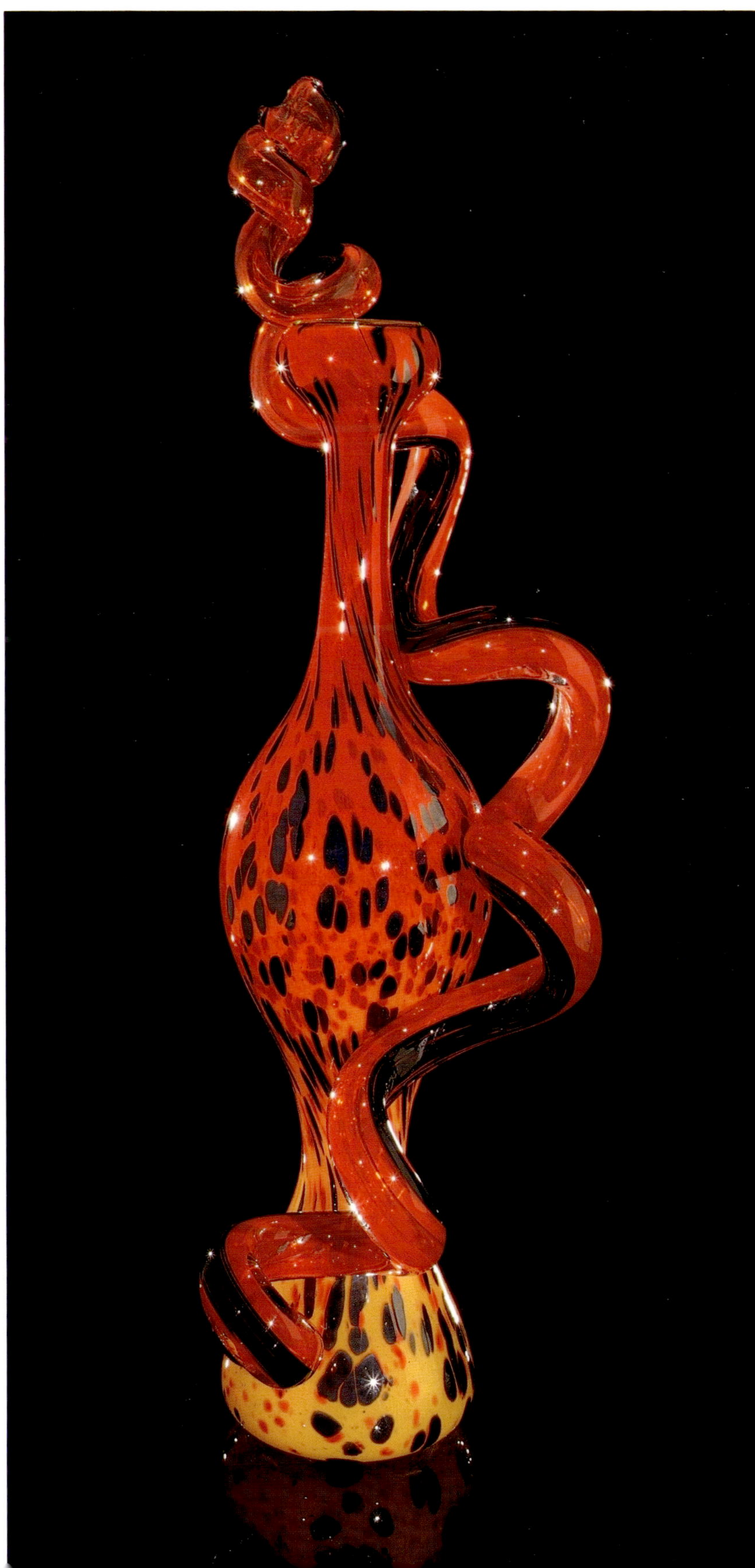

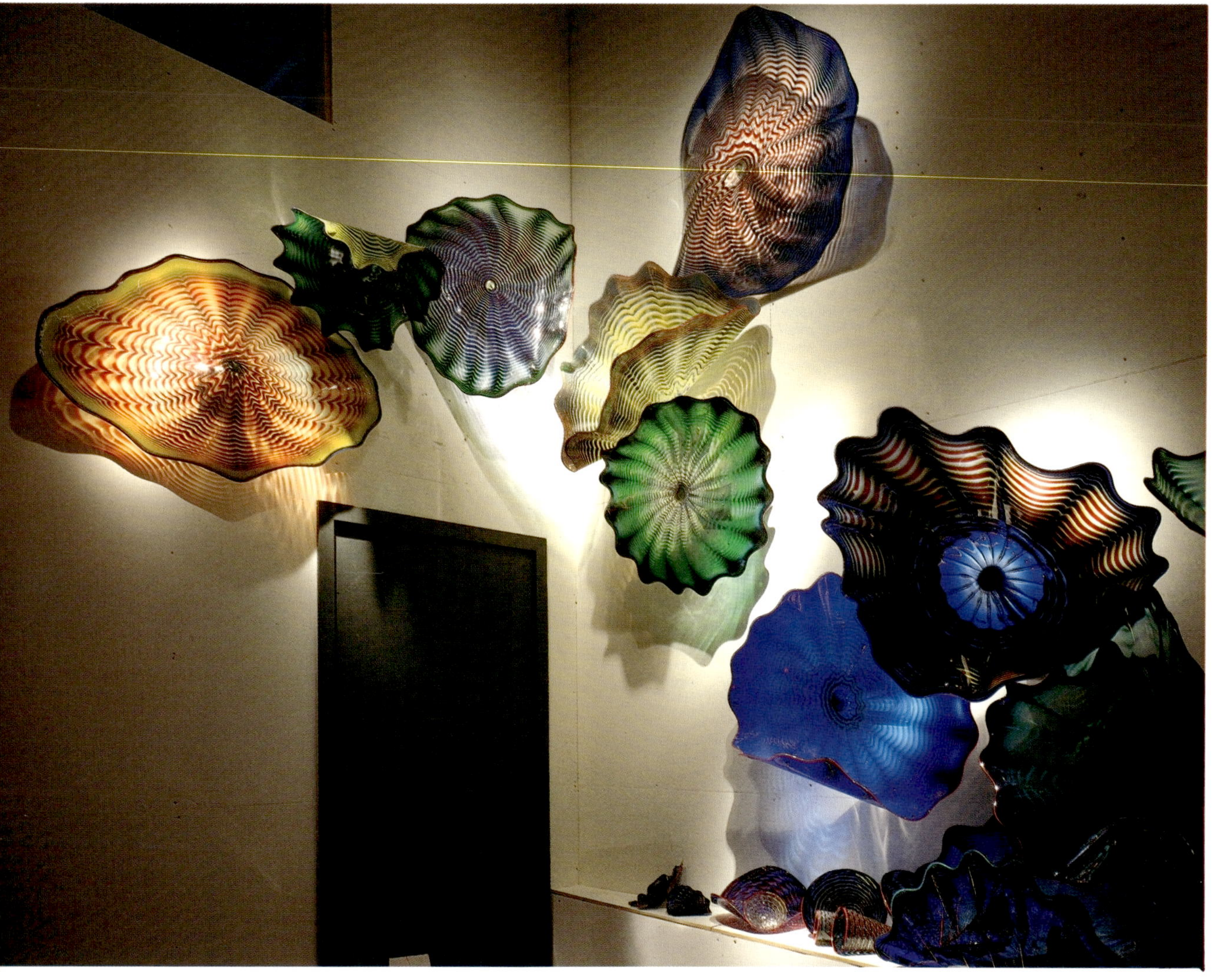

蘇珊與諾曼柯漢裝置
私人住宅
費城, 1989
攝影: R. Schreiber

Suzanne and Norman Cohn Installation
Private residence
Philadelphia, 1989
photo: R. Schreiber

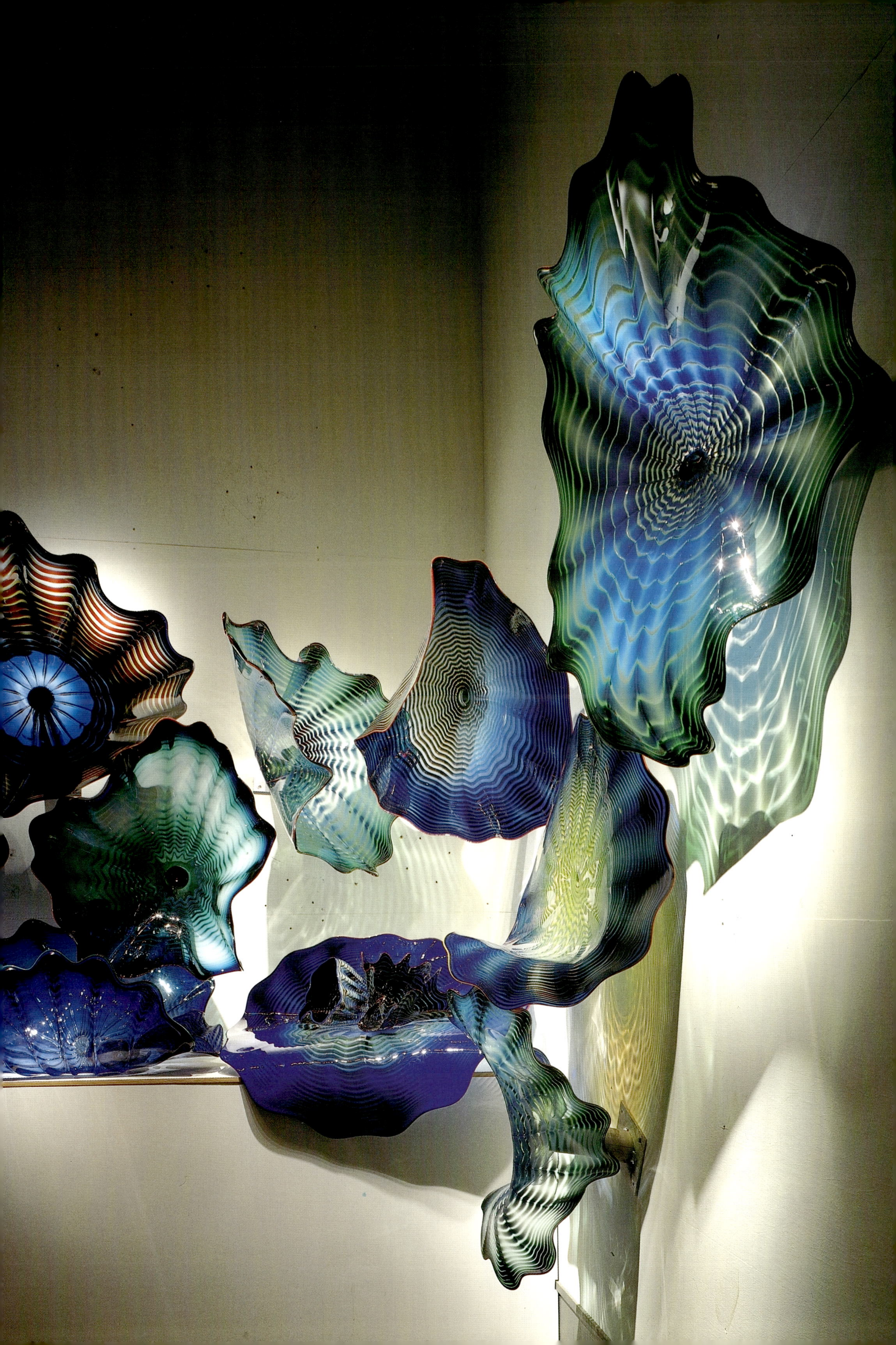

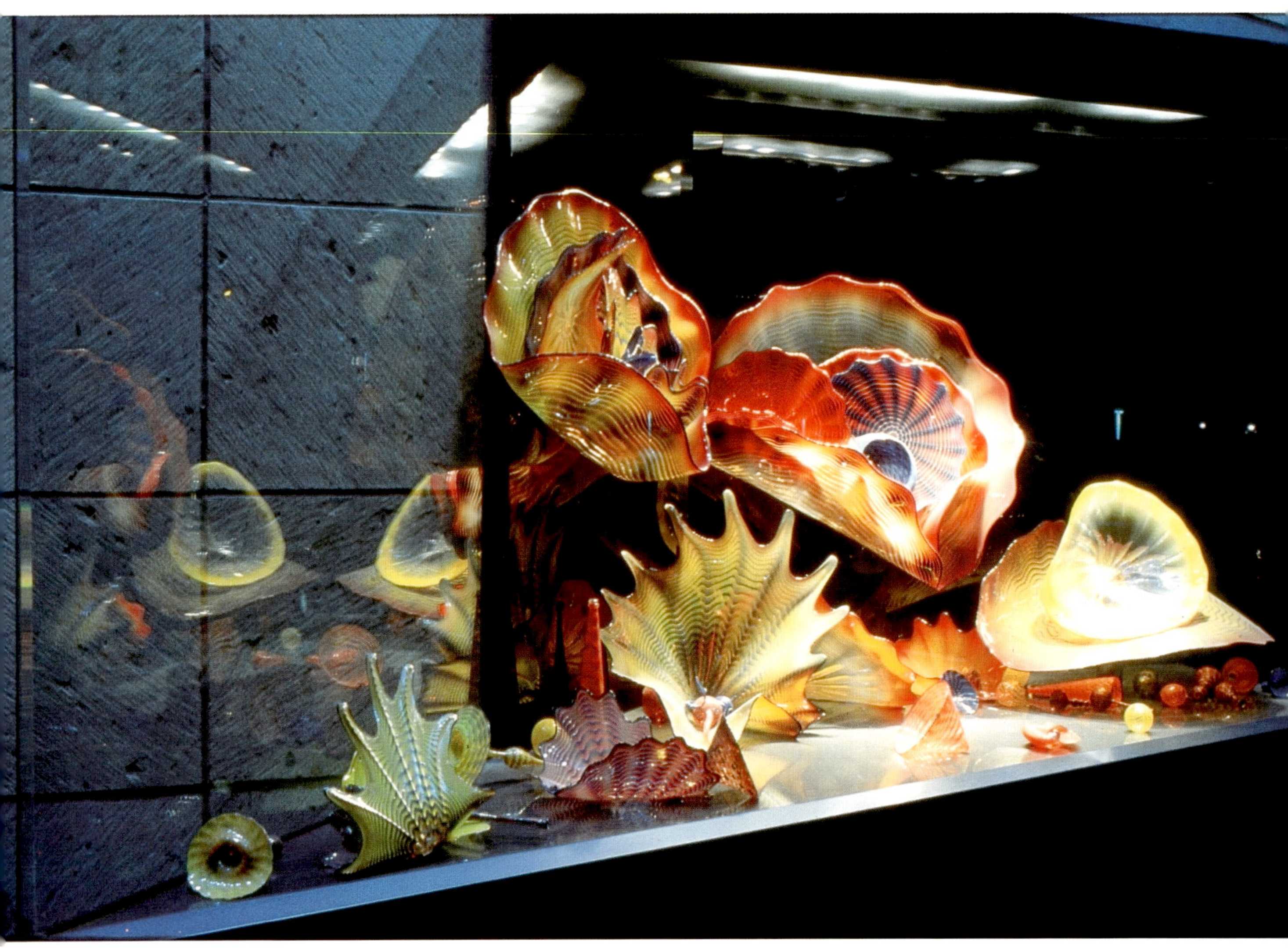

首相公園之波斯裝置
72 x 14 x 144吋
拉荷雅，1988
攝影：E. Calderon，R. Schreiber

Chancellor Park Persian Installation
72 x 14 x 144"
La Jolla, 1988
photos: E. Calderon, R. Schreiber

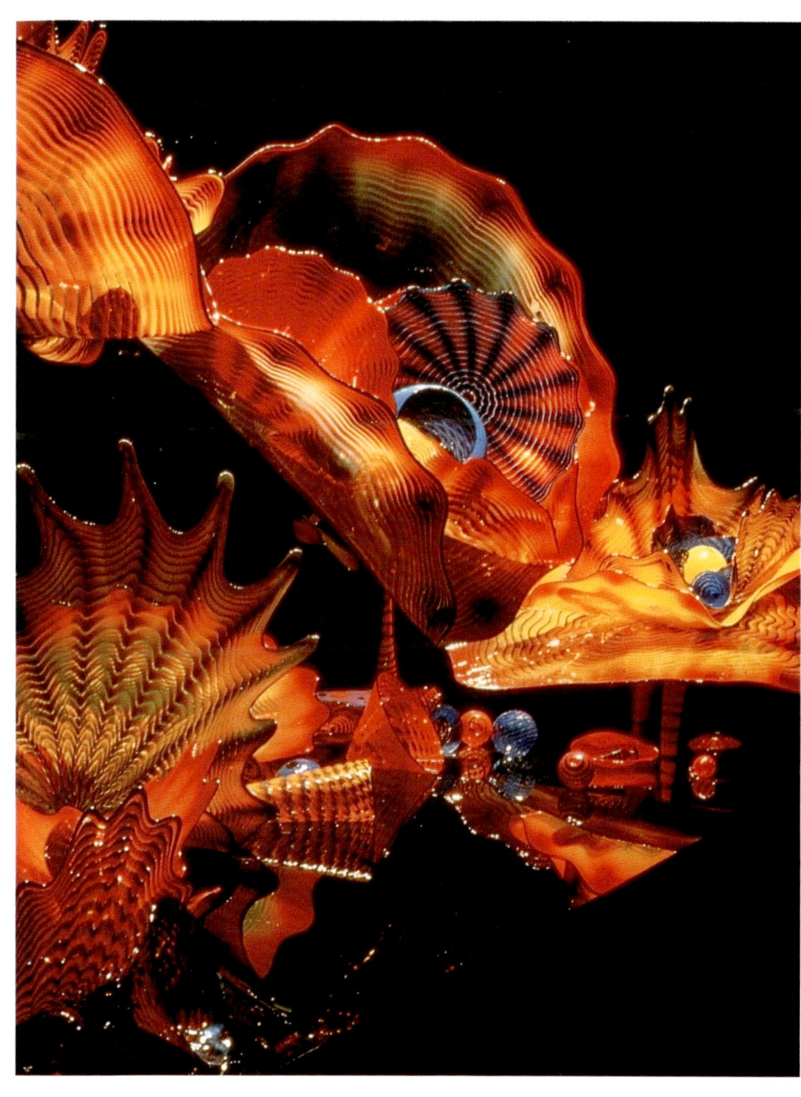

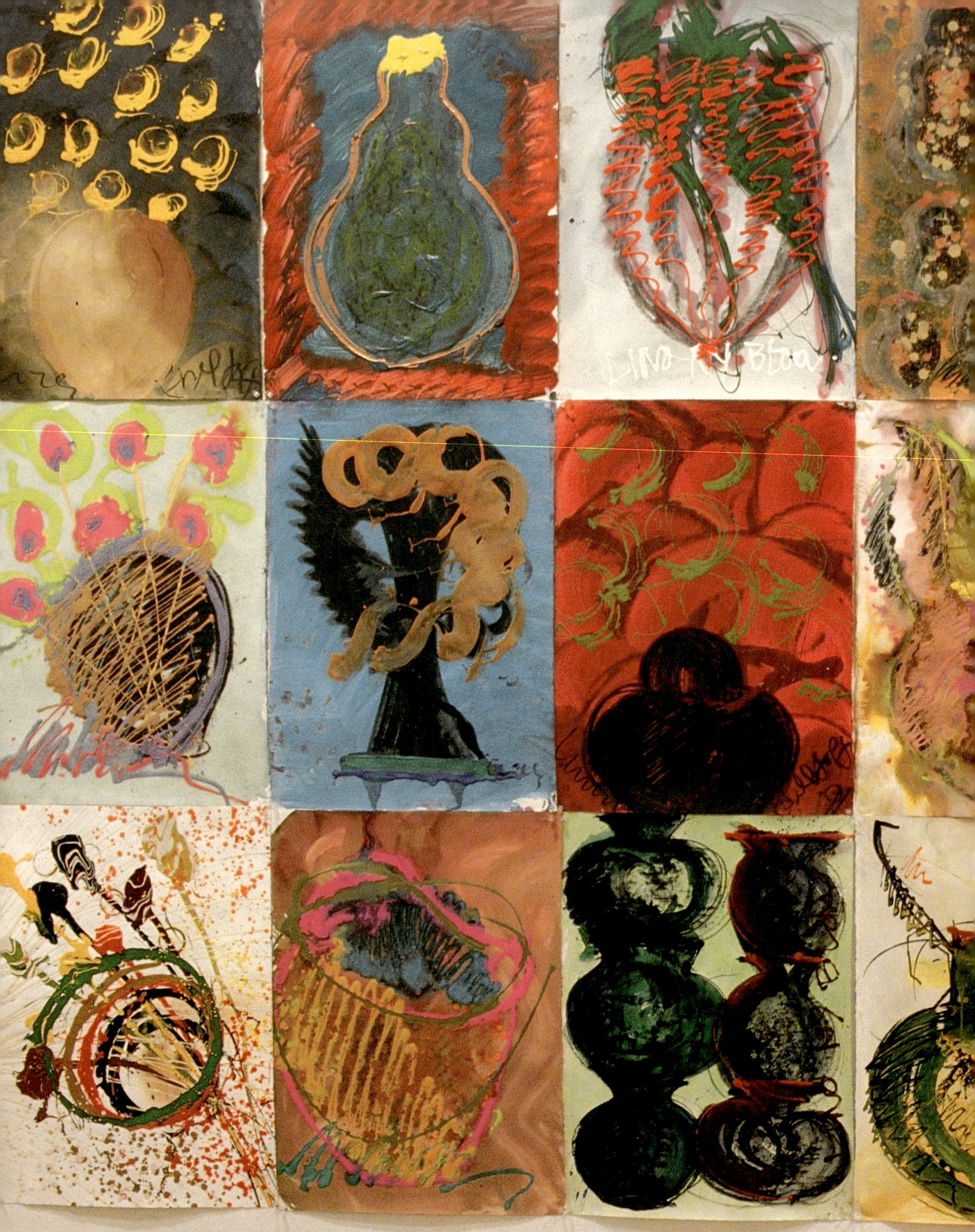

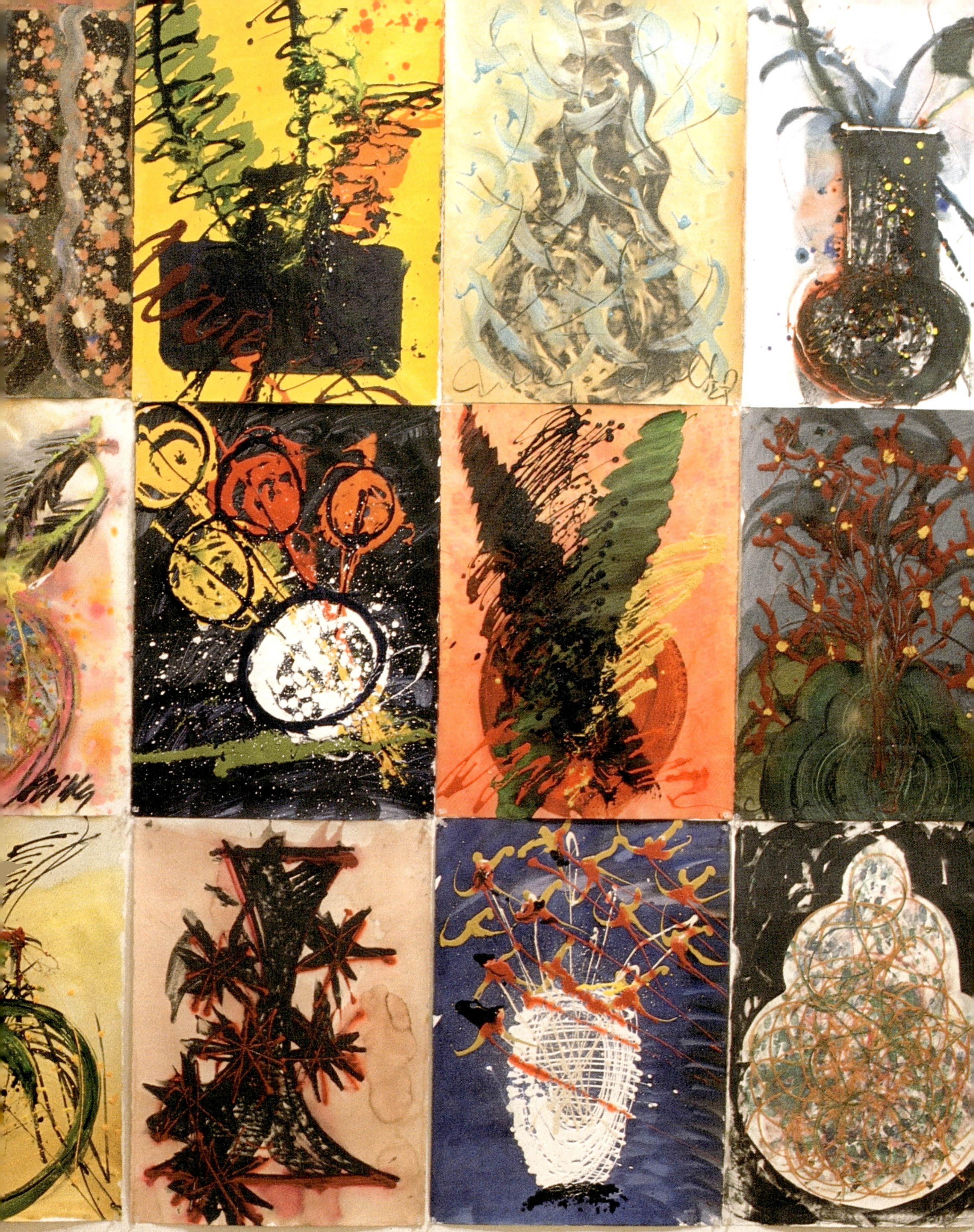

pergola

棚架

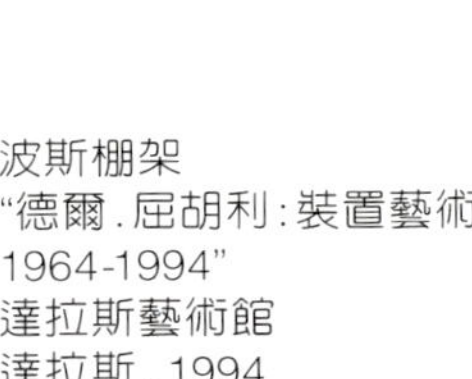

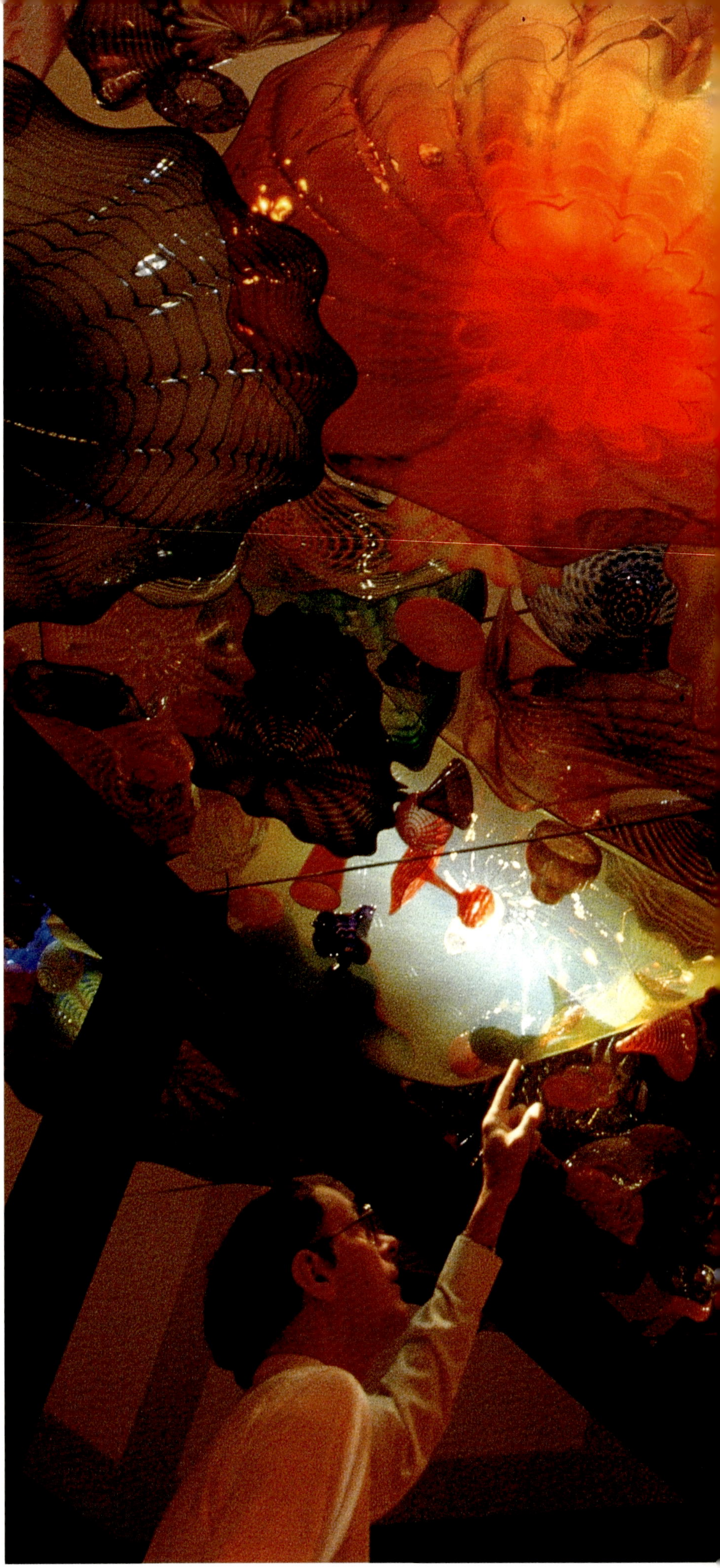

波斯棚架
“德爾．屈胡利：裝置藝術
1964-1994”
達拉斯藝術館
達拉斯，1994
攝影：S. Hagar

Persian Pergola
“Dale Chihuly: Installations
1964-1994”
Dallas Museum of Art
Dallas, 1994
photo: S. Hagar

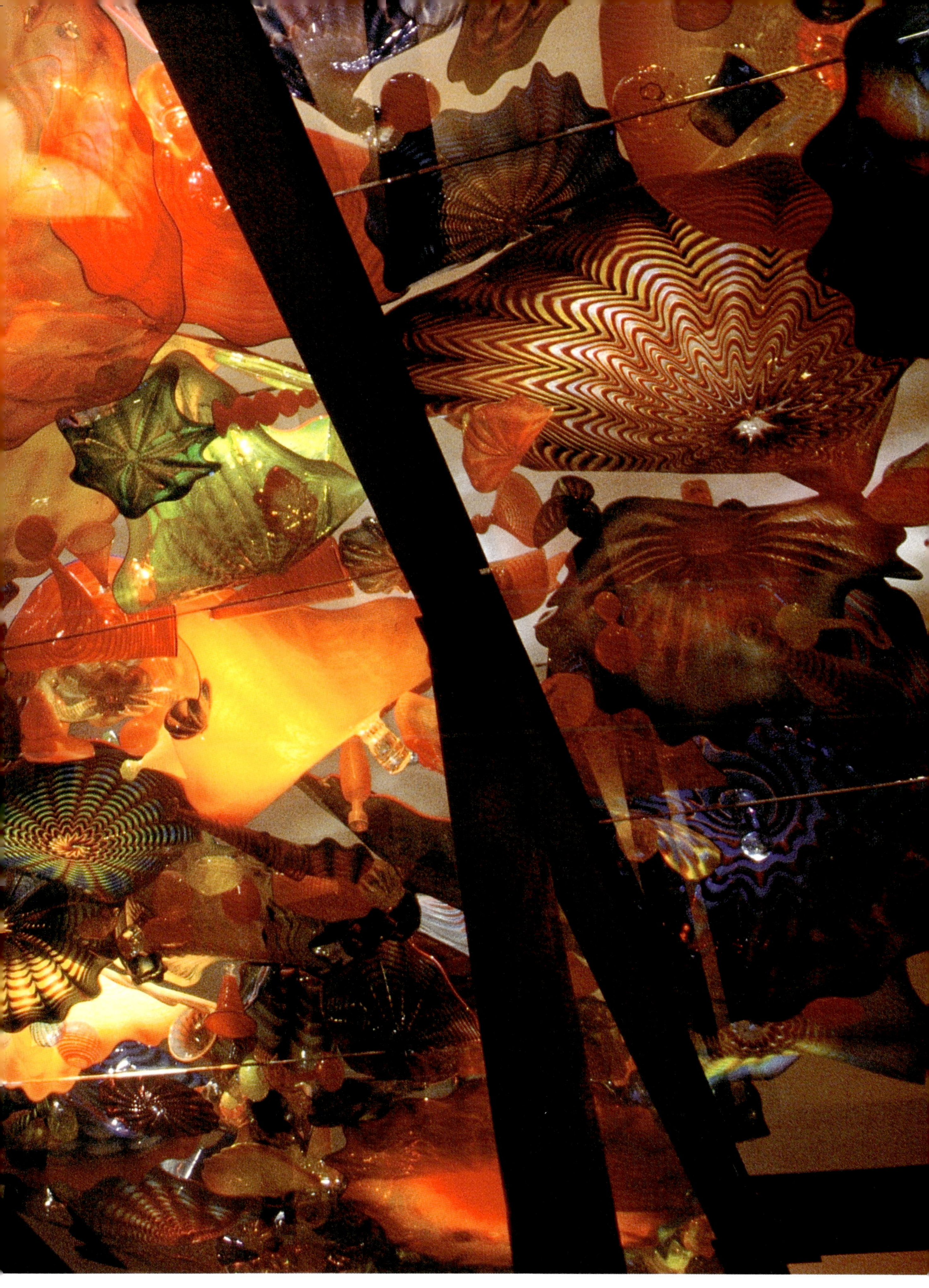

波斯棚架
“德爾.屈胡利:裝置藝術 1964-1994”
達拉斯藝術館
達拉斯，1994
攝影: S. Hagar

Persian Pergola
“Dale Chihuly: Installations 1964-1994”
Dallas Museum of Art
Dallas, 1994
photos: S. Hagar

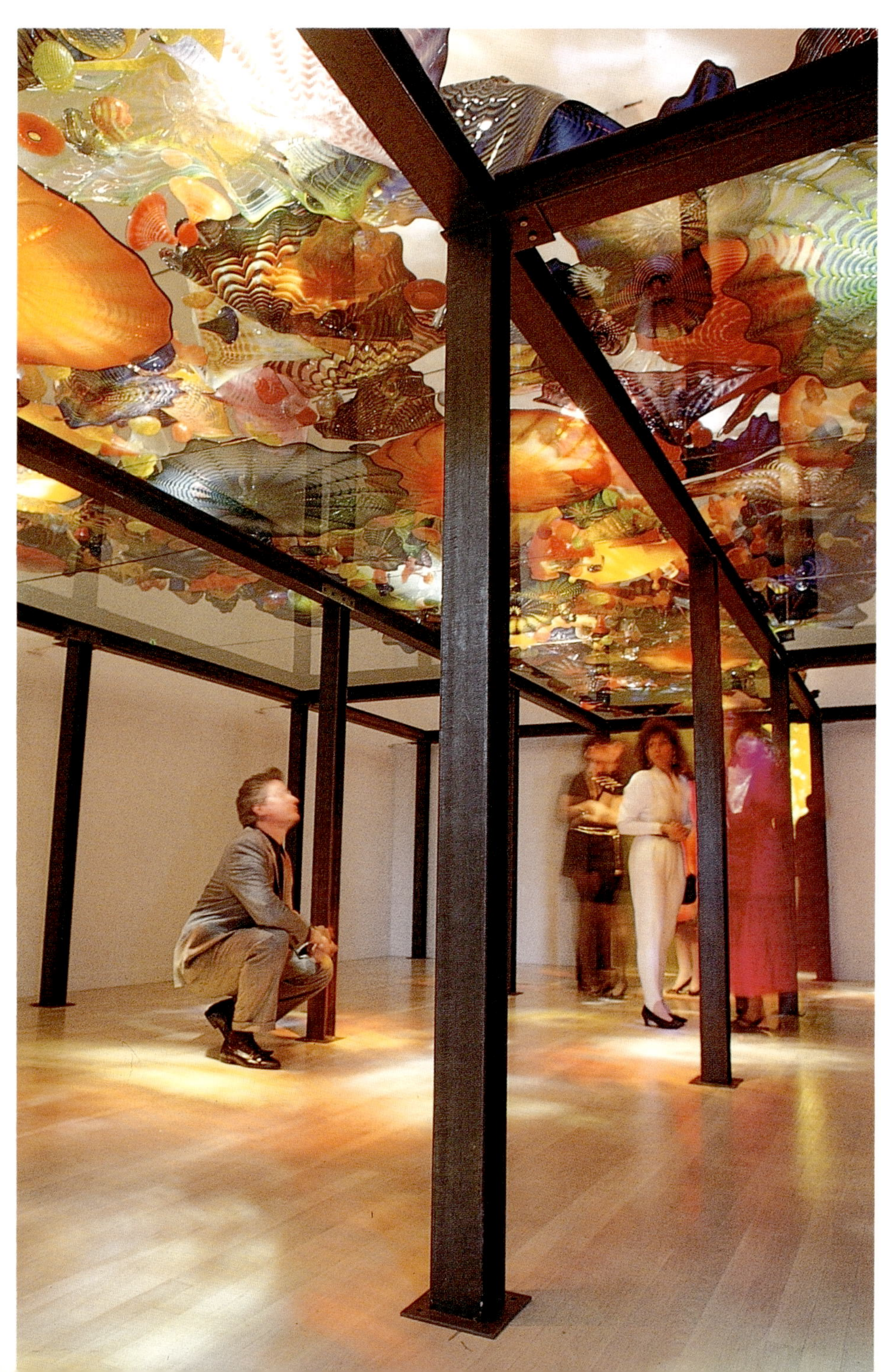

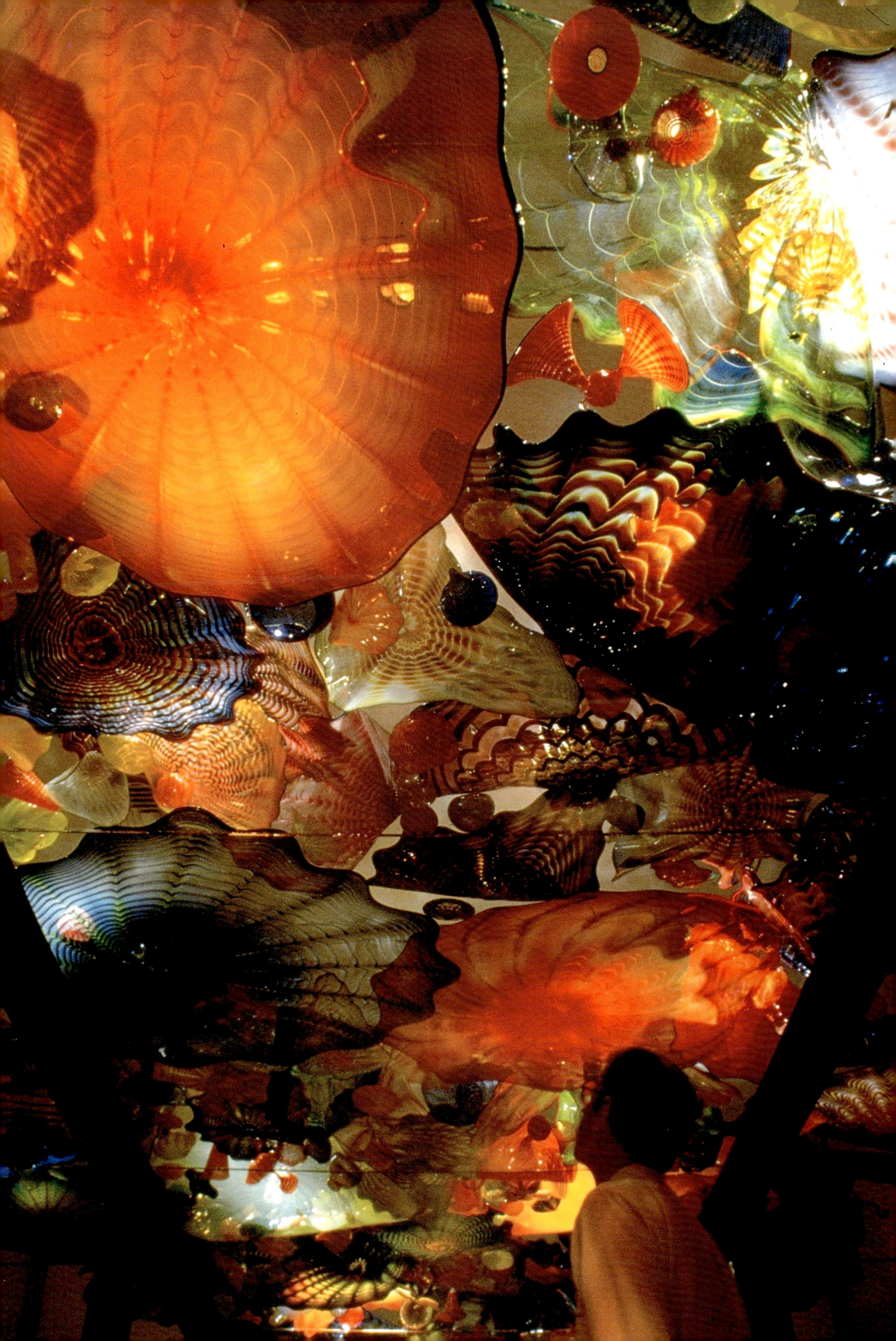

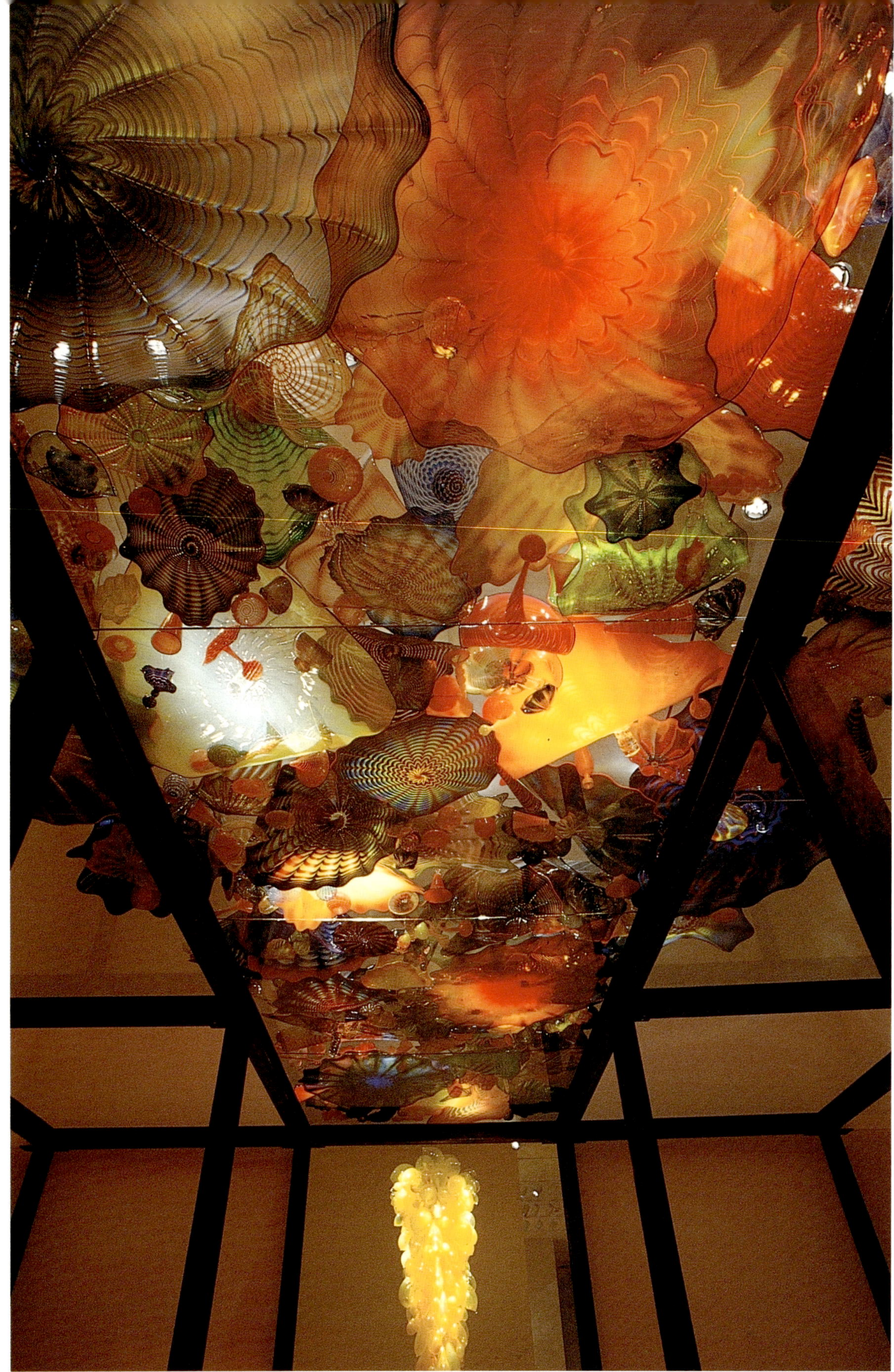

波斯棚架
“德爾.屈胡利:裝置藝術 1964-1994”
達拉斯藝術館
達拉斯，1994
攝影: S. Hagar

Persian Pergola
“Dale Chihuly: Installations 1964-1994”
Dallas Museum of Art
Dallas, 1994
photo: S. Hagar

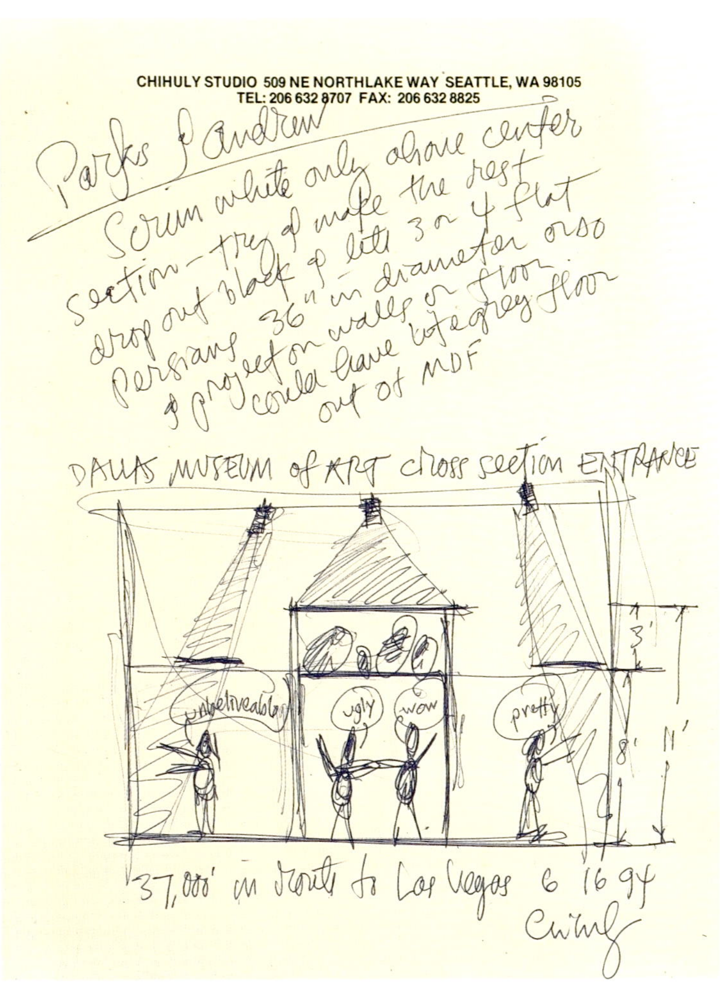

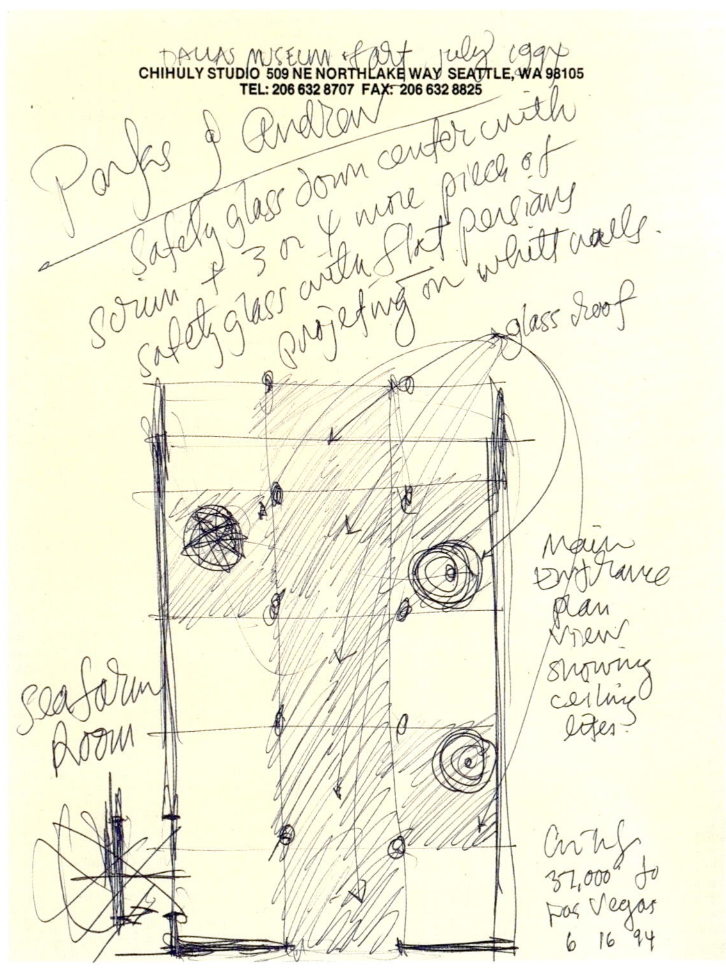

達拉斯波斯棚架之素描
8.5 x 11吋
1994
攝影：C. Garoutte

Dallas Persian Pergola Sketches
8.5 x 11"
1994
photos: C. Garoutte

太平洋路德大學
拉基斯特音樂廳素描
8.5 x 11吋
1994
攝影：C. Garoutte

Pacific Lutheran University
Lagerquist Concert Hall Sketch
8.5 x 11"
1994
photo: C. Garoutte

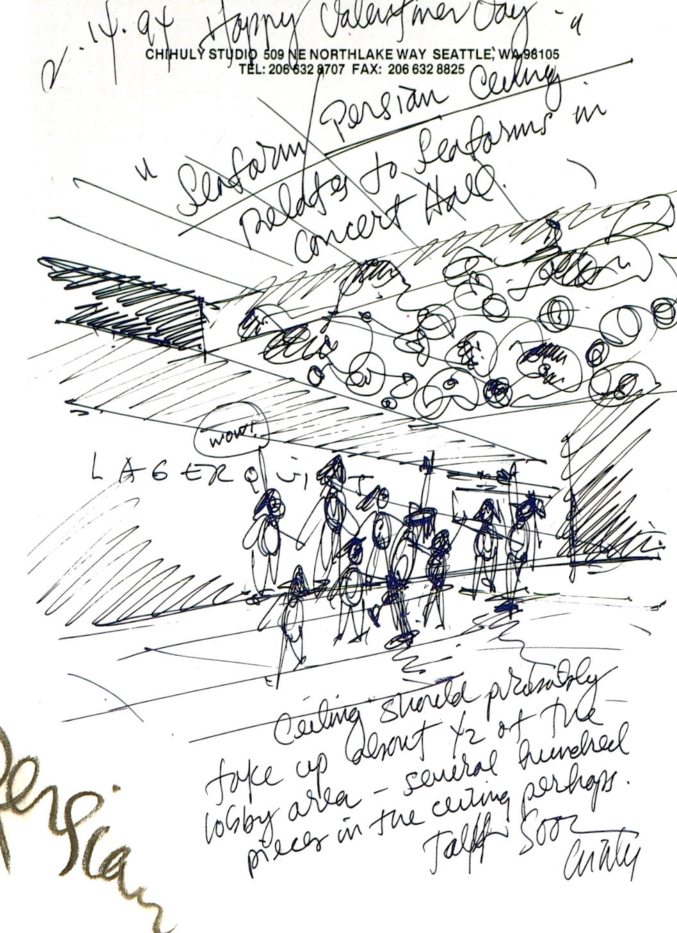

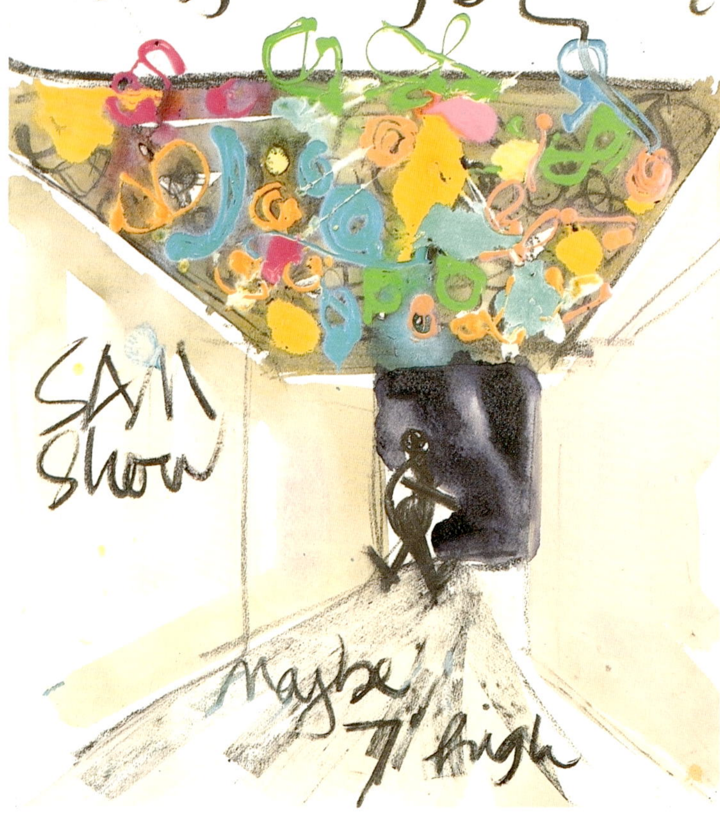

波斯棚架素描
30 x 22吋
1992
攝影：T. Rishel

Persian Pergola Drawing
30 x 22"
1992
photo: T. Rishel

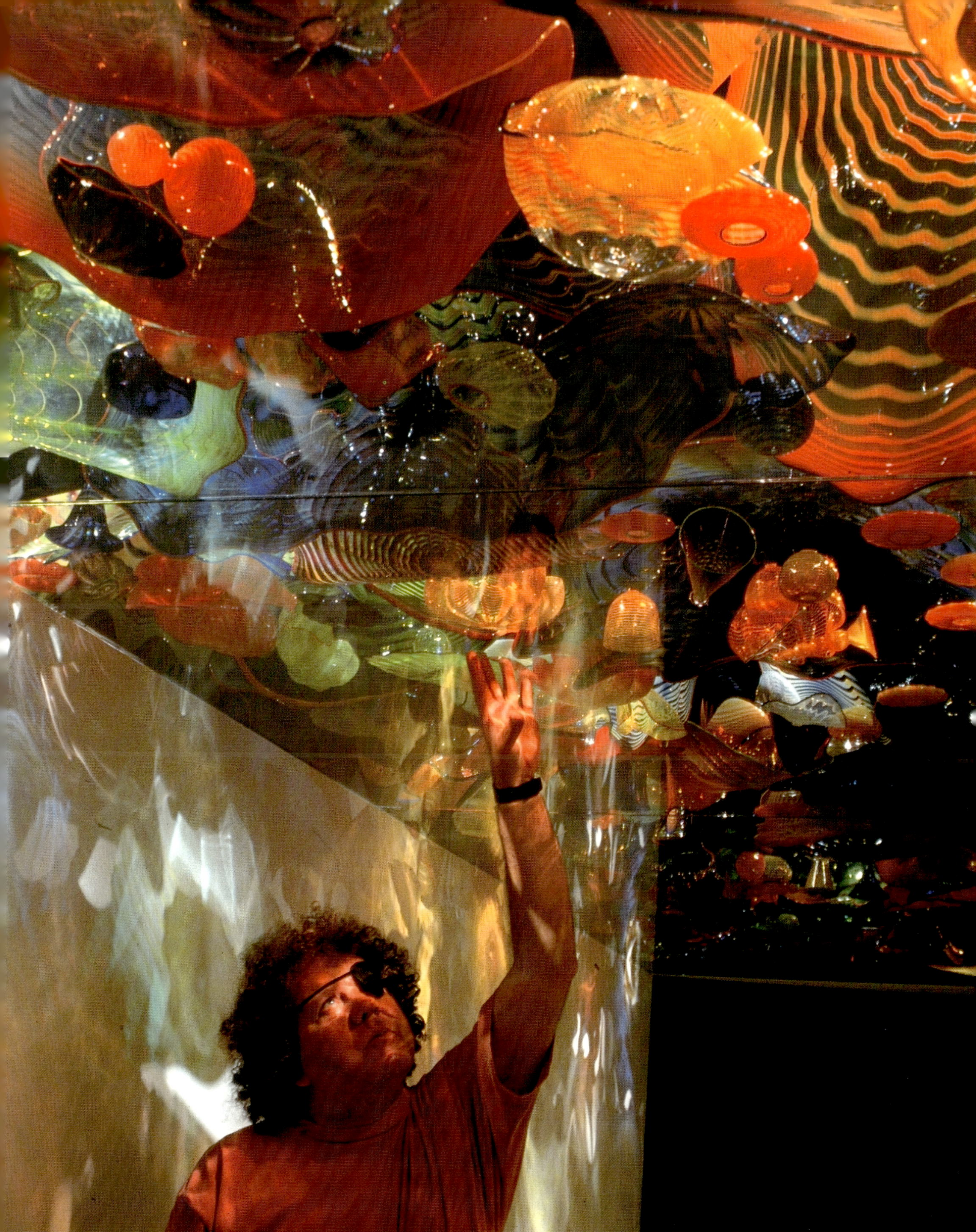

波斯棚架
7 x 5 x 24呎
“德爾．屈胡利：裝置藝術
1964-1993”
底特律藝術學院
底特律，1993
攝影：R. Johnson

Persian Pergola
7 x 5 x 24'
"Dale Chihuly: Installations 1964-1993"
The Detroit Institute of Arts
Detroit, 1993
photo: R. Johnson

niijima floats

三島浮球

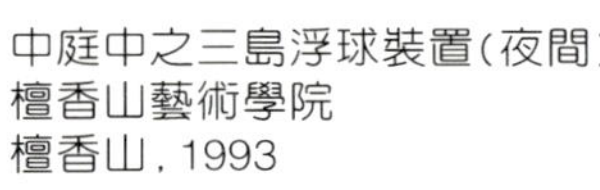

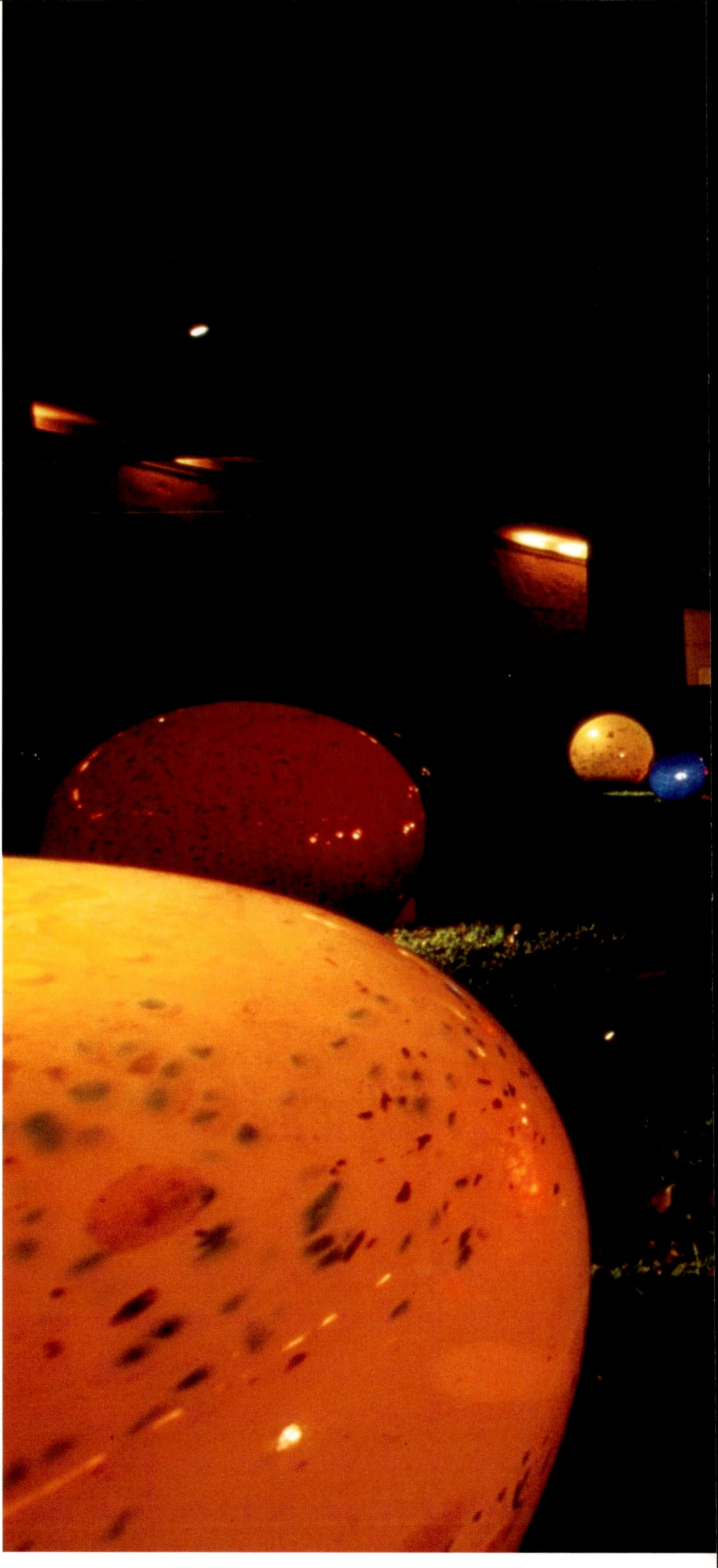

中庭中之三島浮球裝置(夜間)
檀香山藝術學院
檀香山, 1993
攝影: R. Johnson

Niijima Float Installation (at night)
in the Central Court
Honolulu Academy of Arts
Honolulu, 1993
photo: R. Johnson

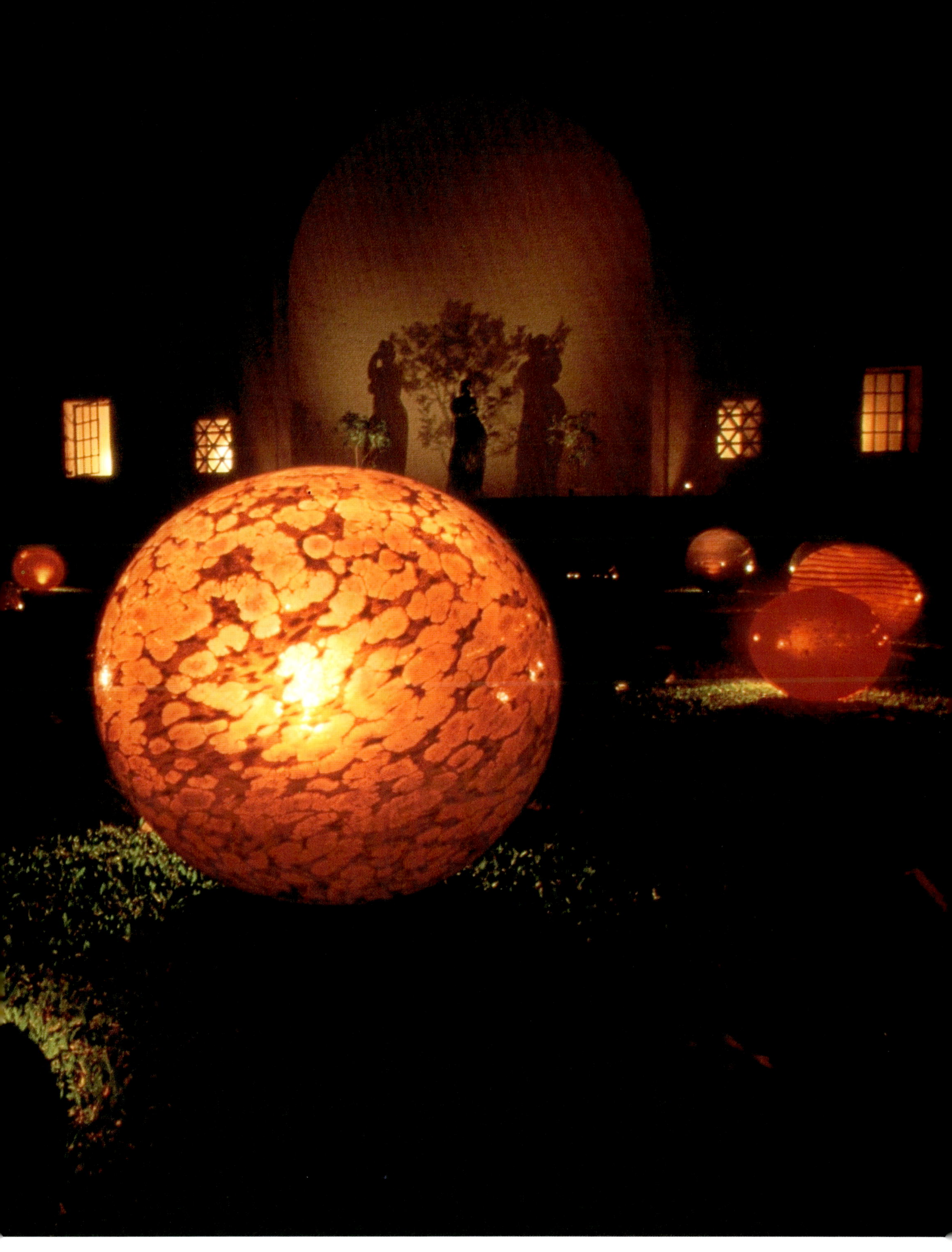

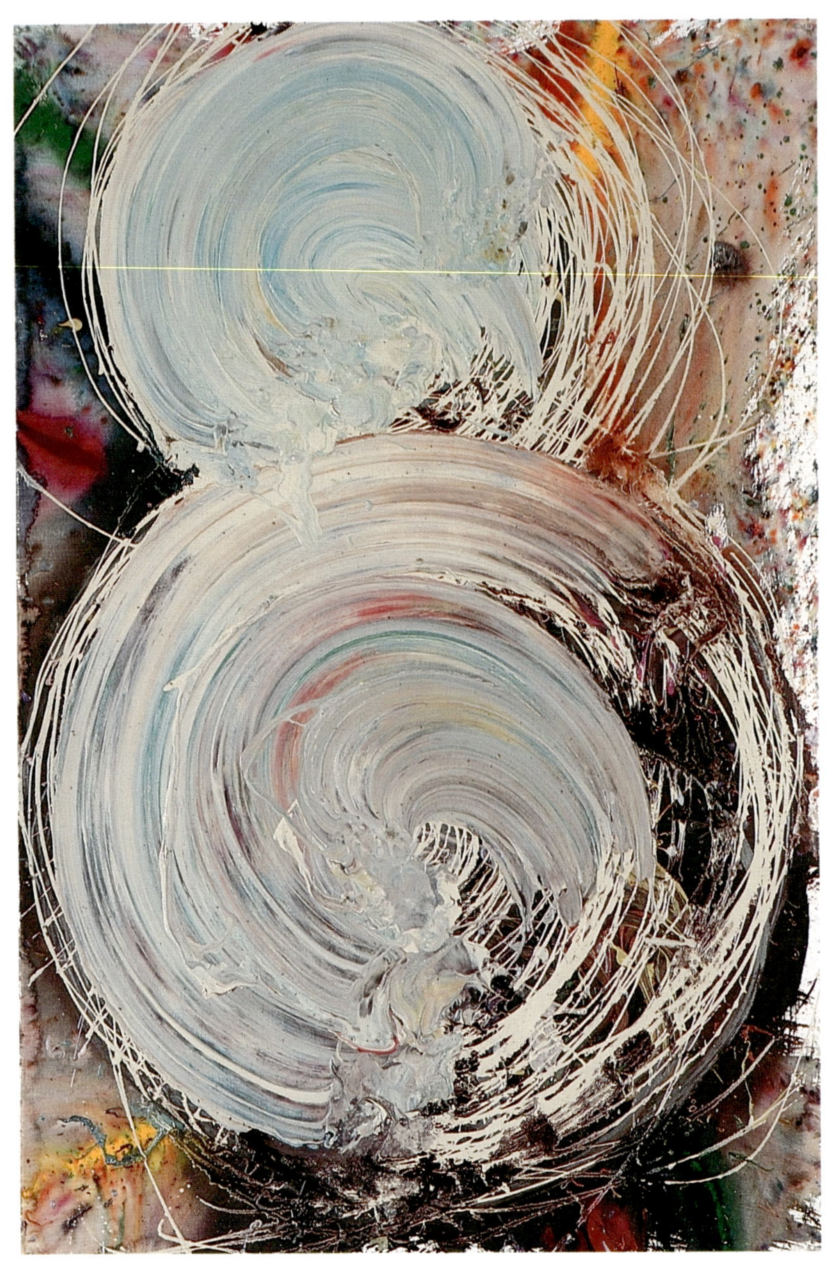

浮球素描
60 x 40吋
1991
攝影：C. Garoutte

Float Drawing
60 x 40"
1991
photo: C. Garoutte

三島浮球細部與浮球素描
船屋
西雅圖，1991
攝影：C. Garoutte

Niijima Float detail
and *Float Drawing*
The Boathouse
Seattle, 1991
photo: C. Garoutte

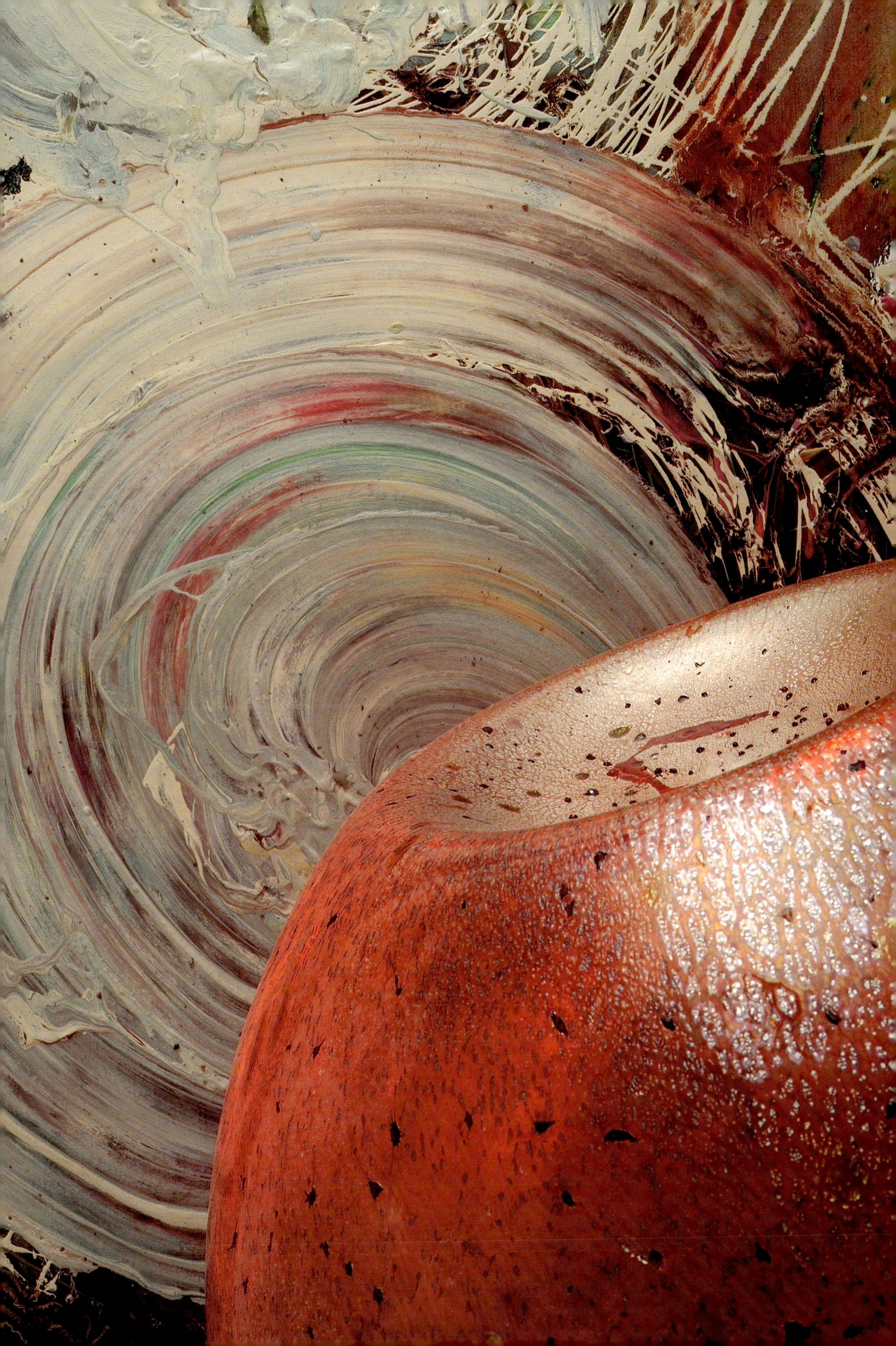

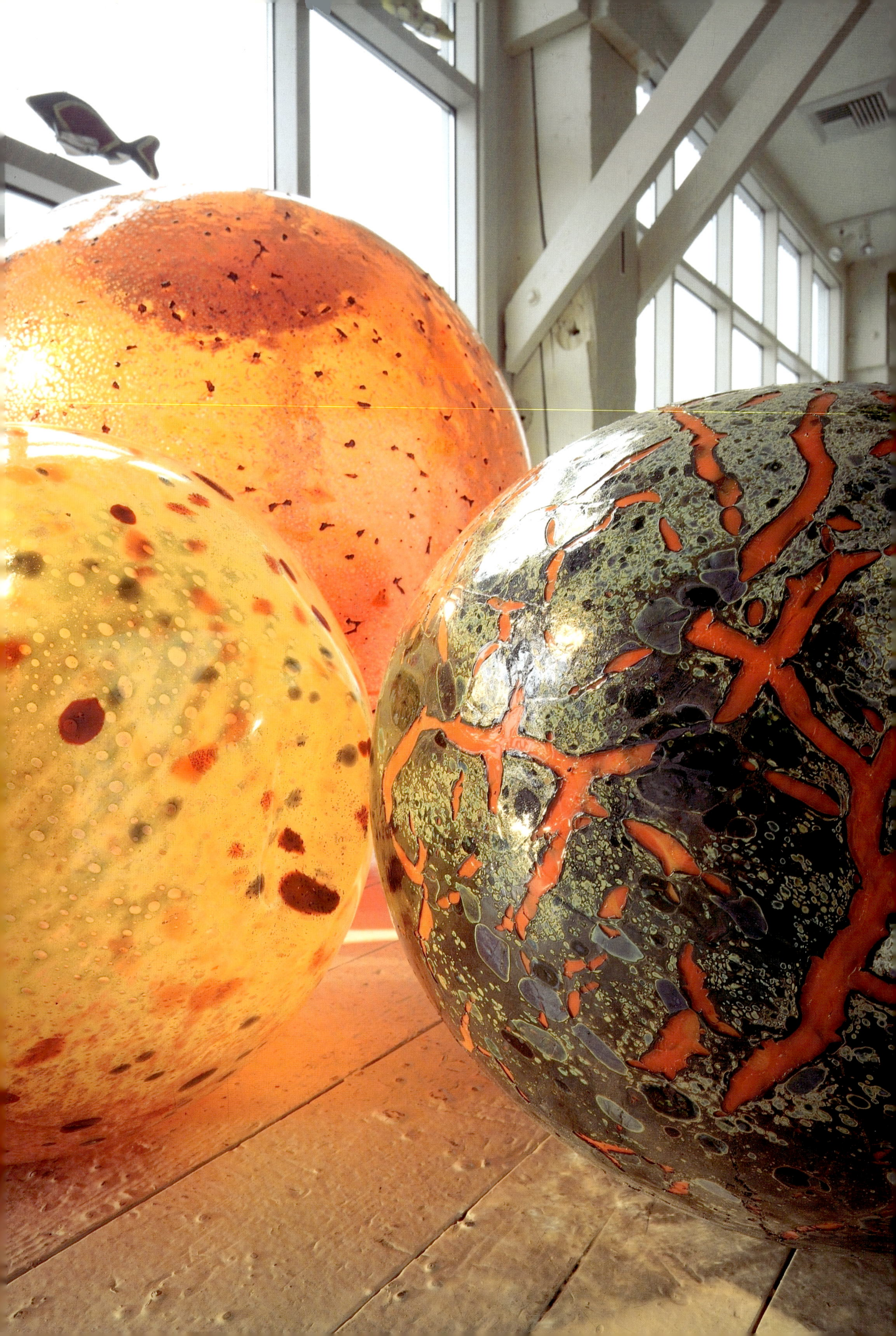

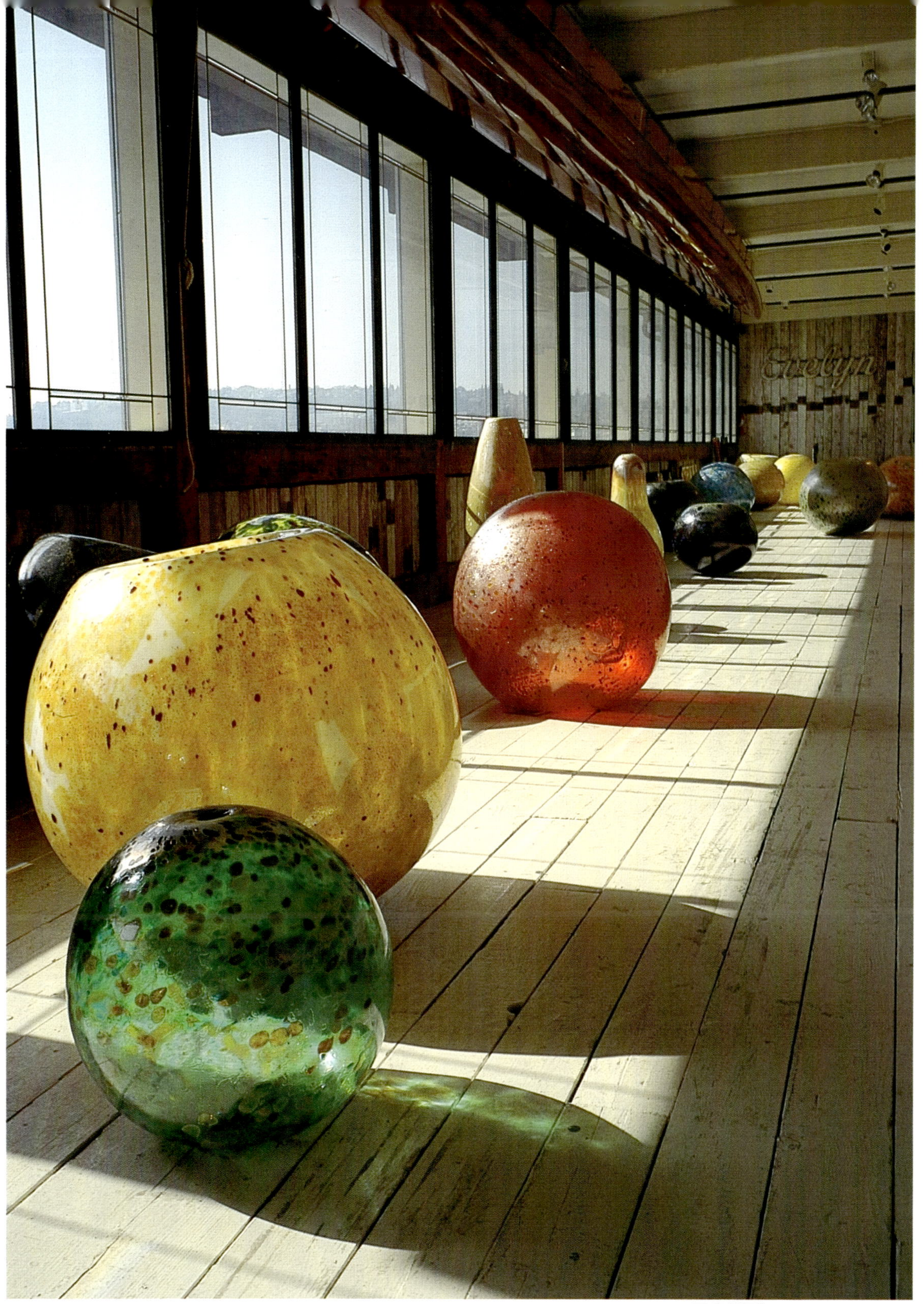

三島浮球
船屋
西雅圖, 1991
攝影: C. Garoutte

Niijima Floats
The Boathouse
Seattle, 1991
photo: C. Garoutte

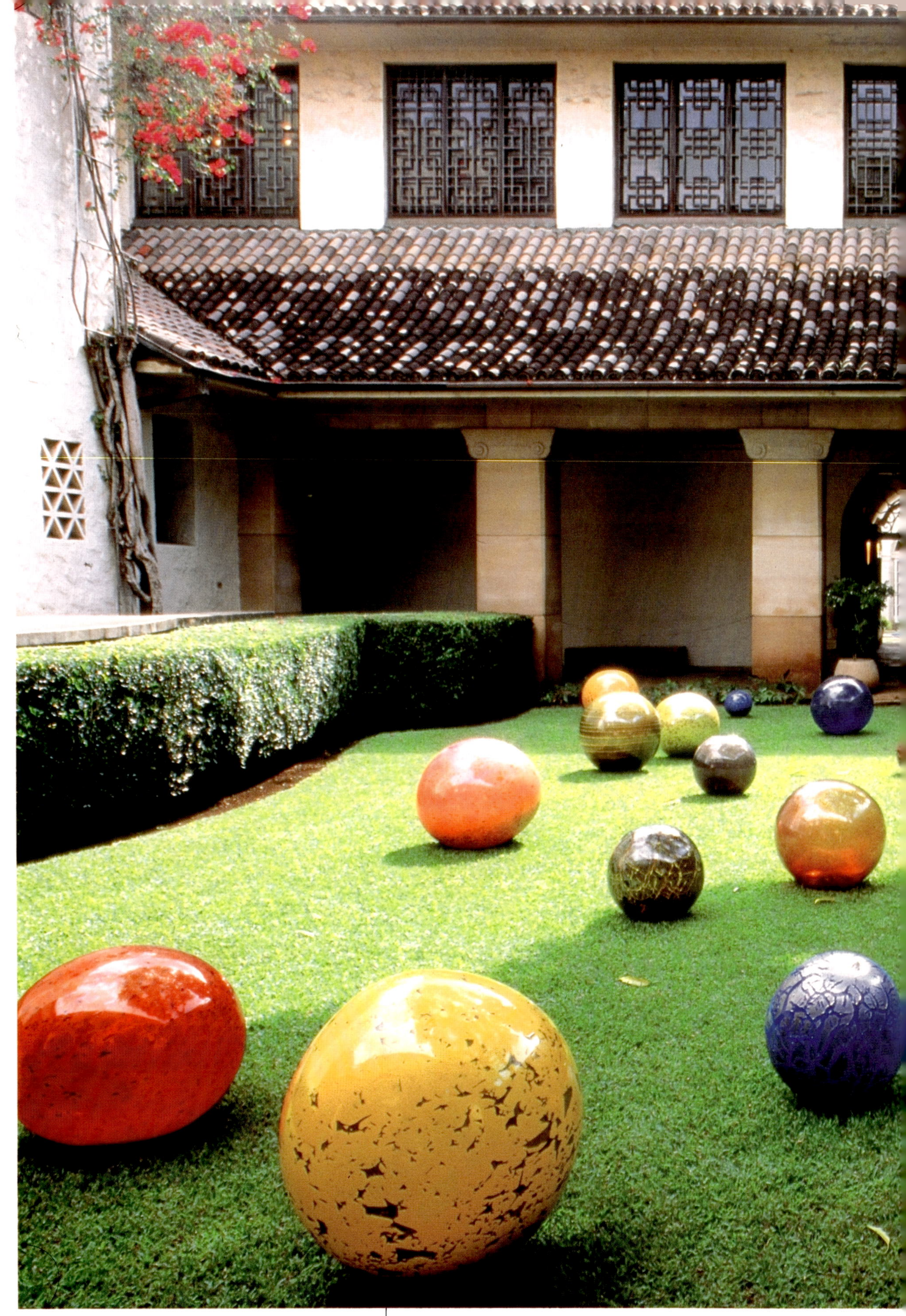

中庭中之三島浮球裝置
“屈胡利庭院展”
檀香山藝術學院
檀香山，1992
攝影：R. Johnson

Niijima Float Installation
in the Central Court
“Chihuly Courtyards”
Honolulu Academy of Arts
Honolulu, 1992
photo: R. Johnson

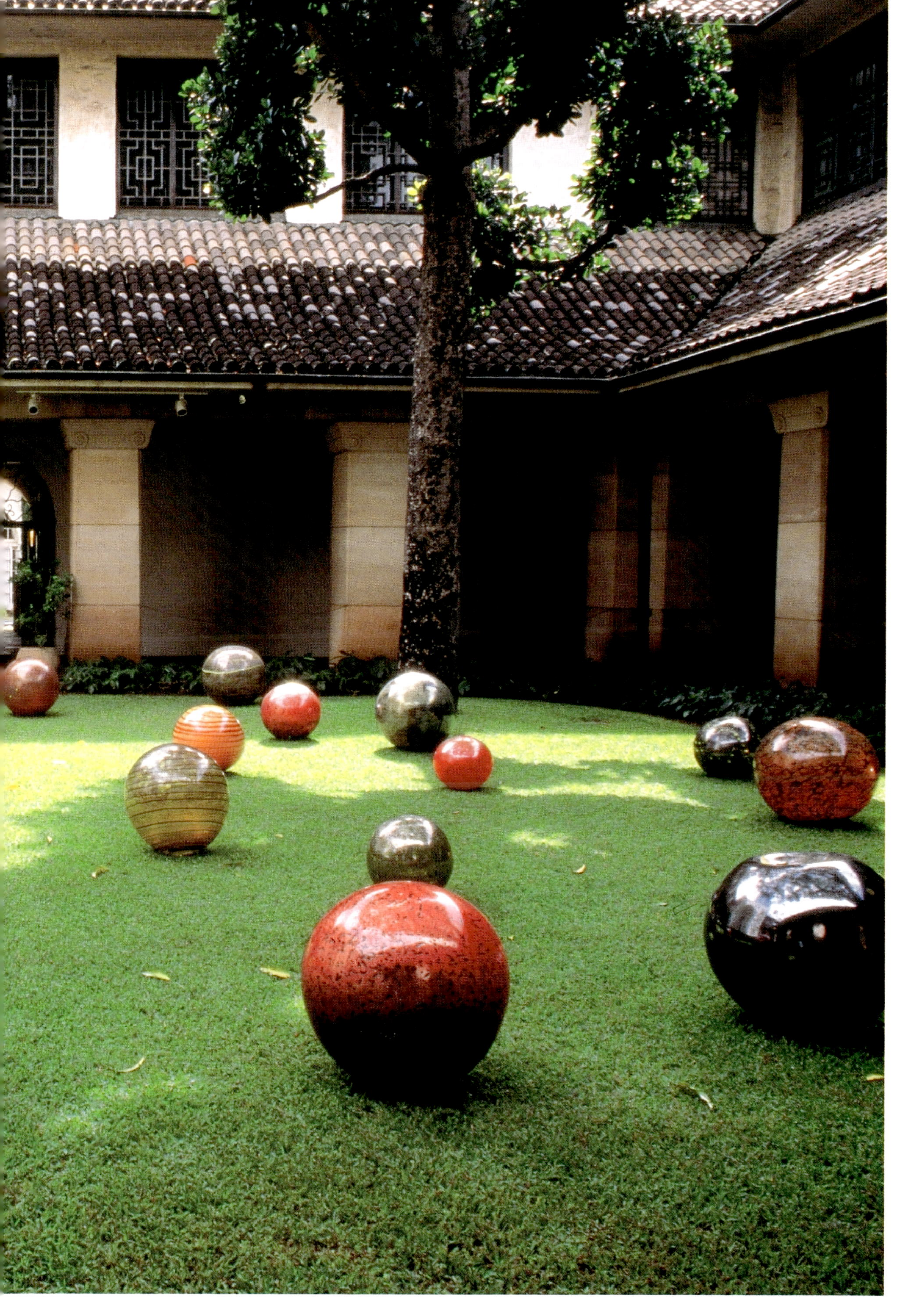

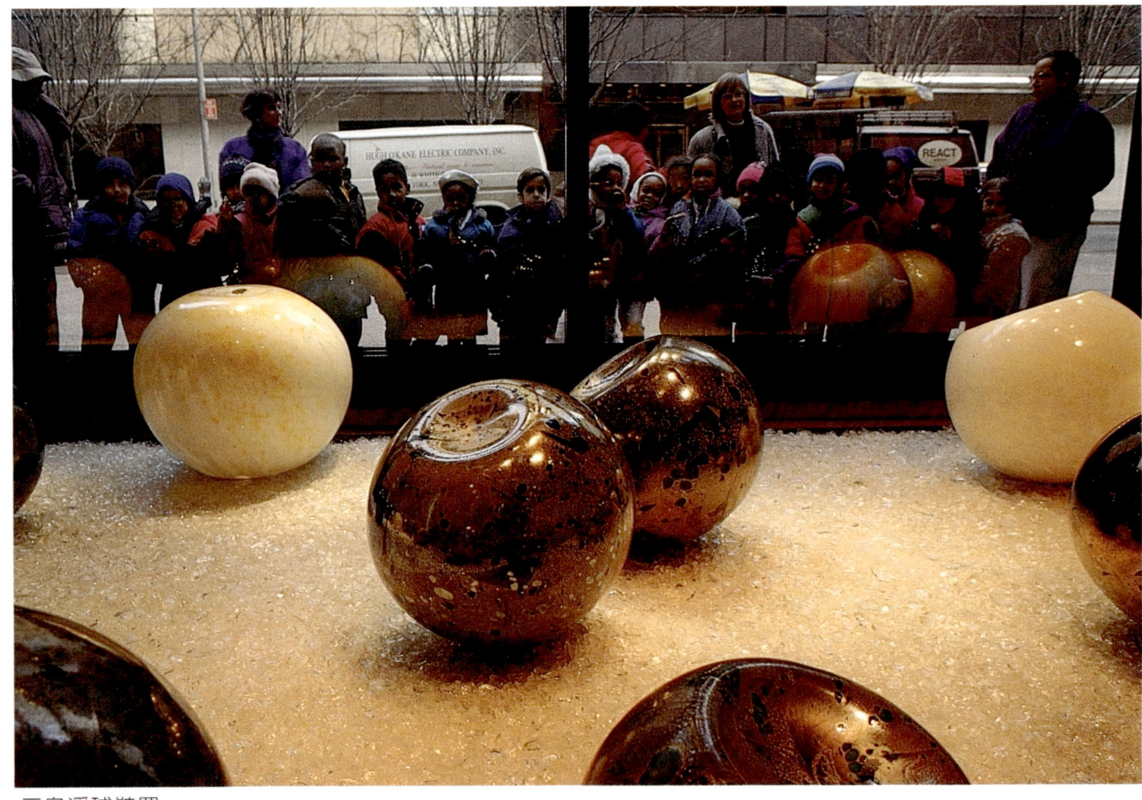

三島浮球裝置
4 x 40 x 15呎
美國手工藝博物館
紐約, 1992
攝影: G. Erml

Niijima Float Installation
4 x 40 x 15'
American Craft Museum
New York, 1992
photo: G. Erml

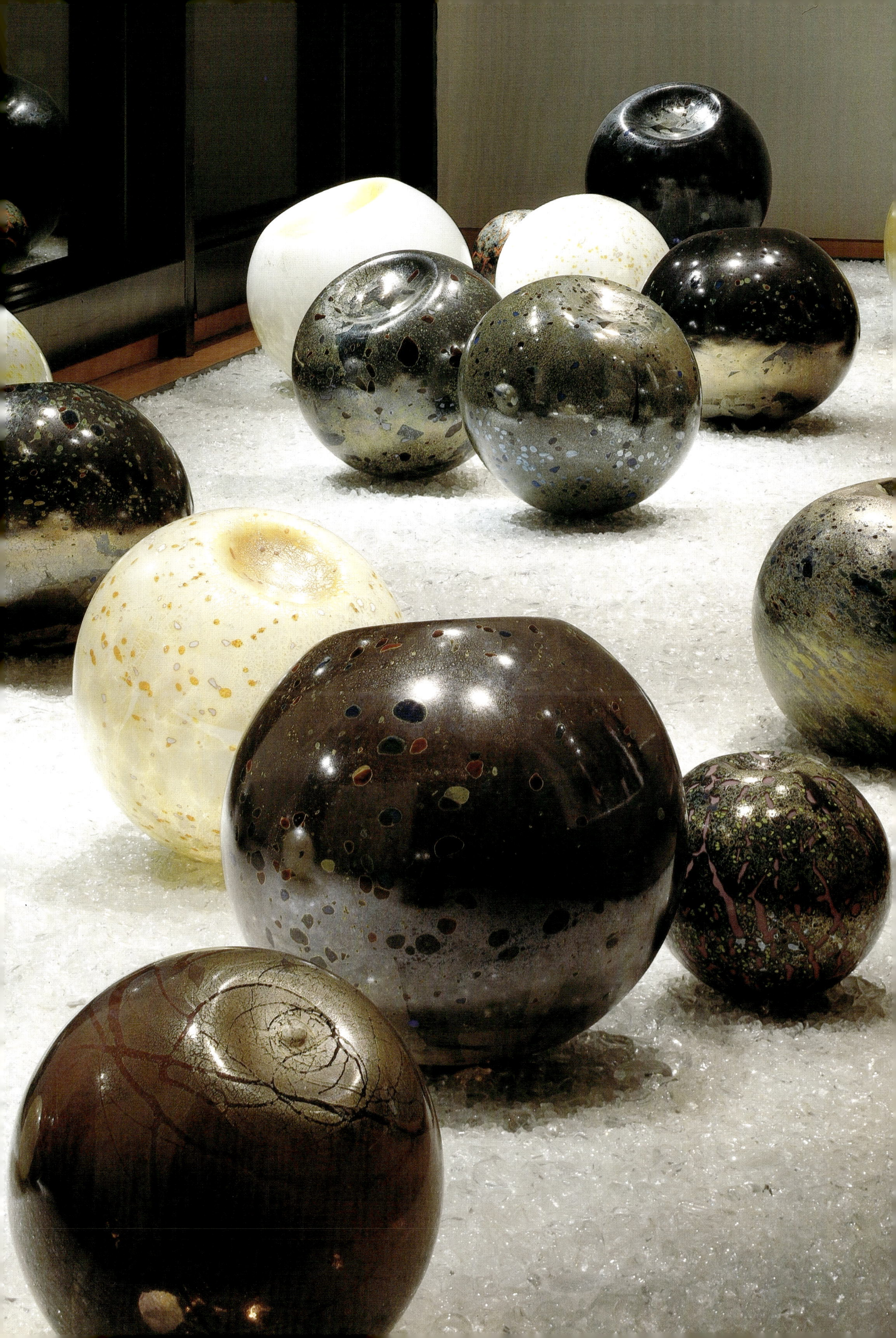

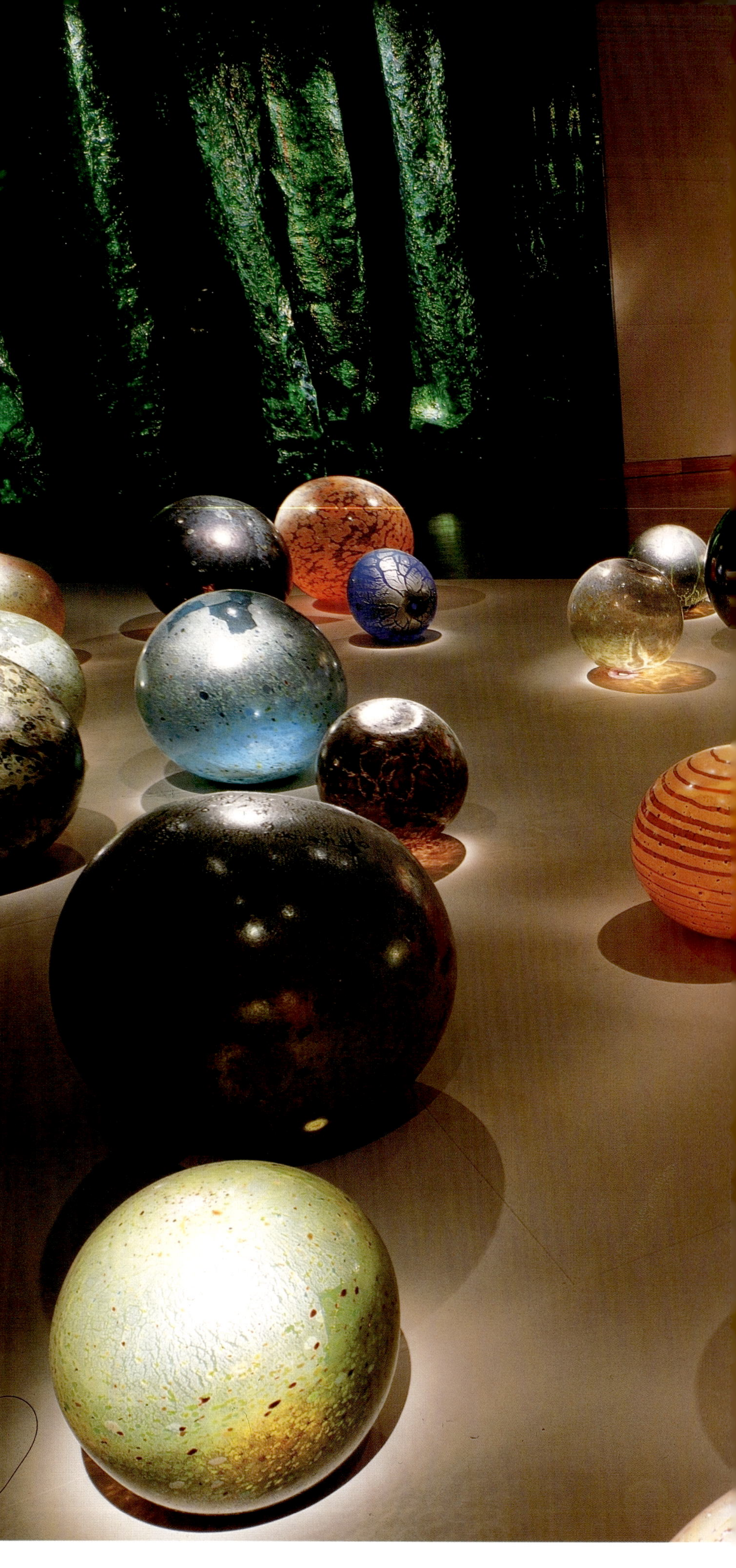

三島浮球
“德爾.屈胡利:裝置藝術
1964-1992”
西雅圖藝術館
西雅圖, 1992
攝影: E. Calderon

Niijima Floats
“Dale Chihuly:
Installations 1964-1992”
Seattle Art Museum
Seattle, 1992
photo: E. Calderon

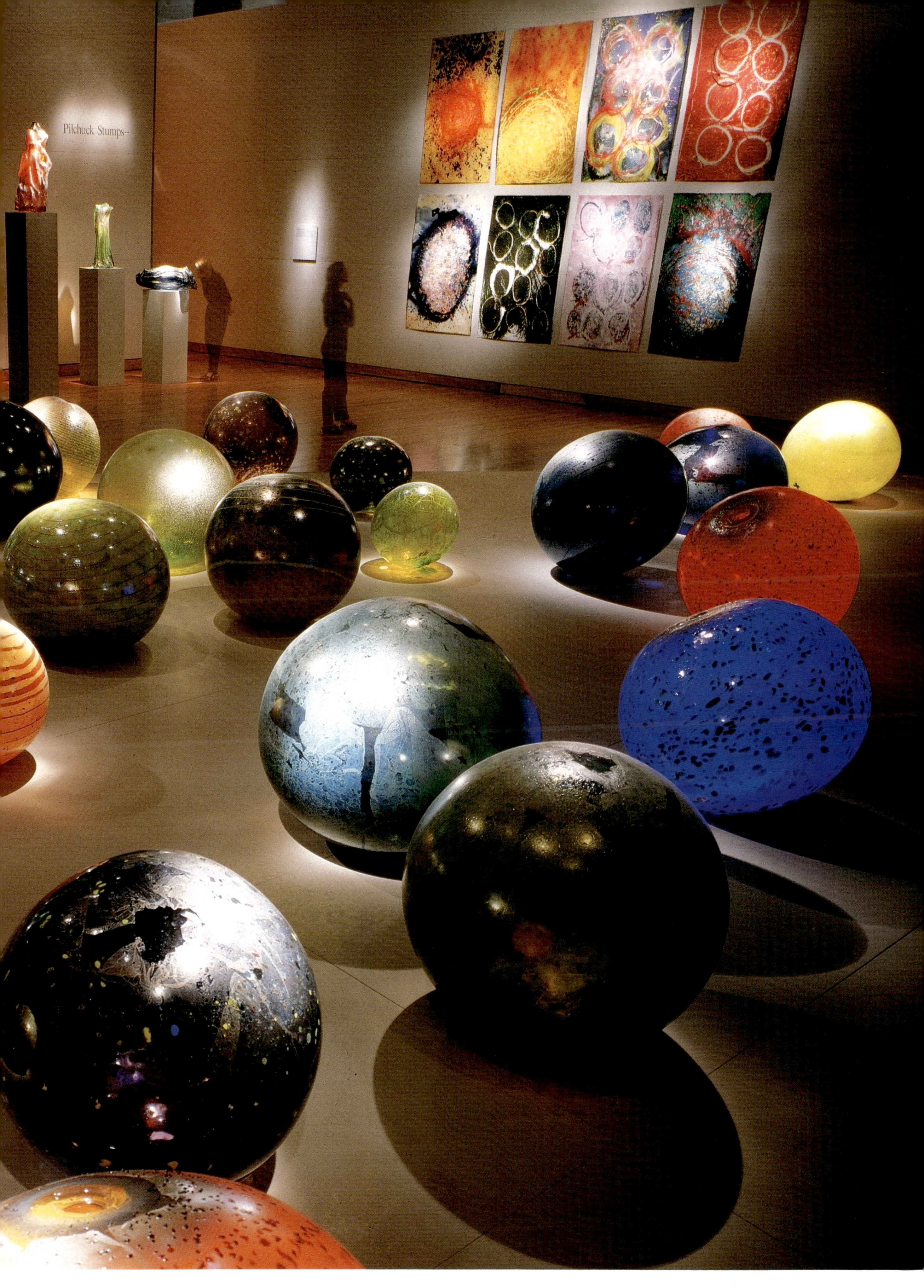
Pilchuck Stumps

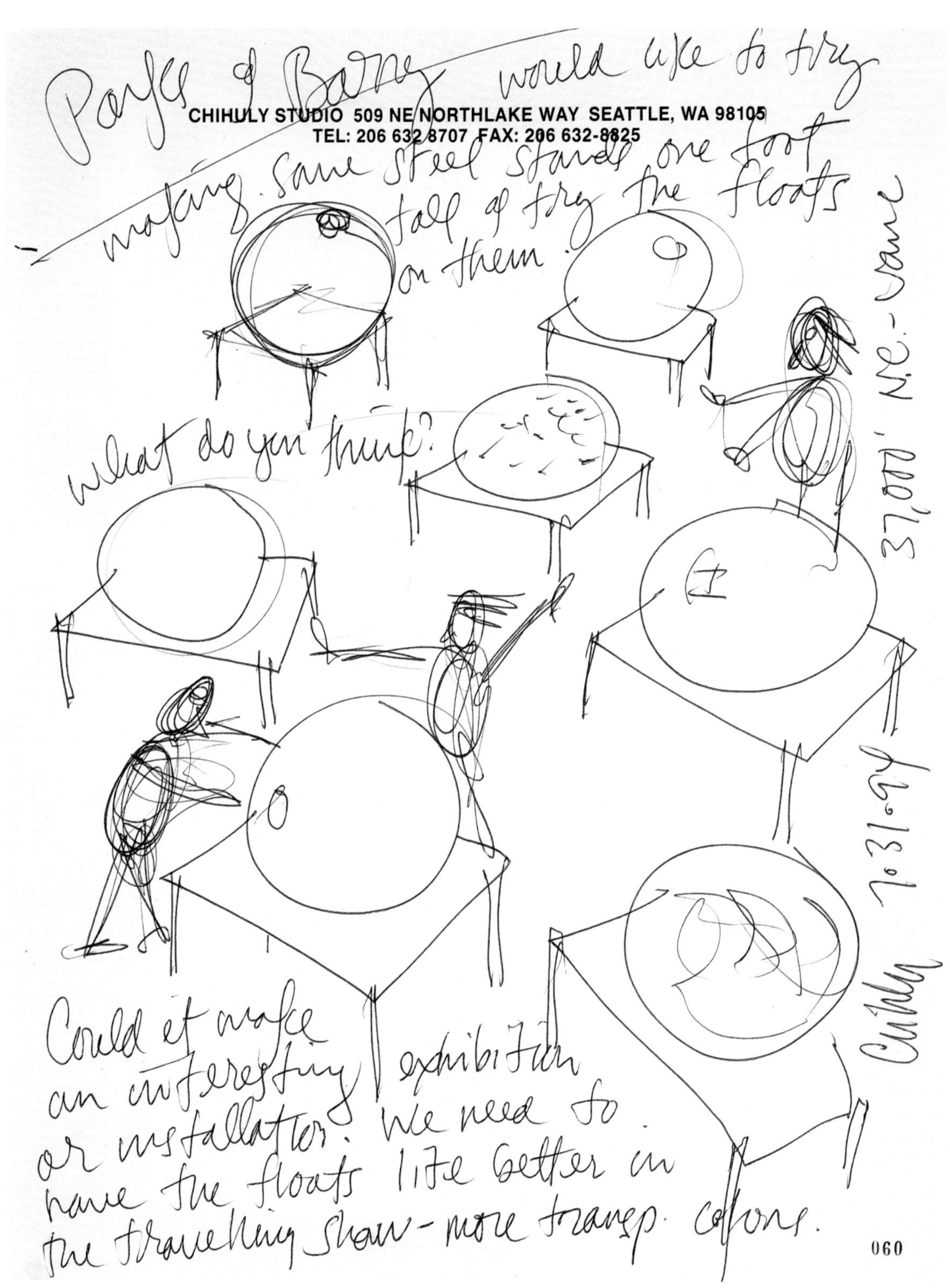

三島浮球裝置之素描
8.5 x 11吋
1994
攝影: C. Garoutte

Niijima Float Installation Sketch
8.5 x 11"
1994
photo: C. Garoutte

三島浮球裝置之素描
8.5 x 11吋
1994
攝影：C. Garoutte

Niijima Float
Installation Sketch
8.5 x 11"
1994
photo: C. Garoutte

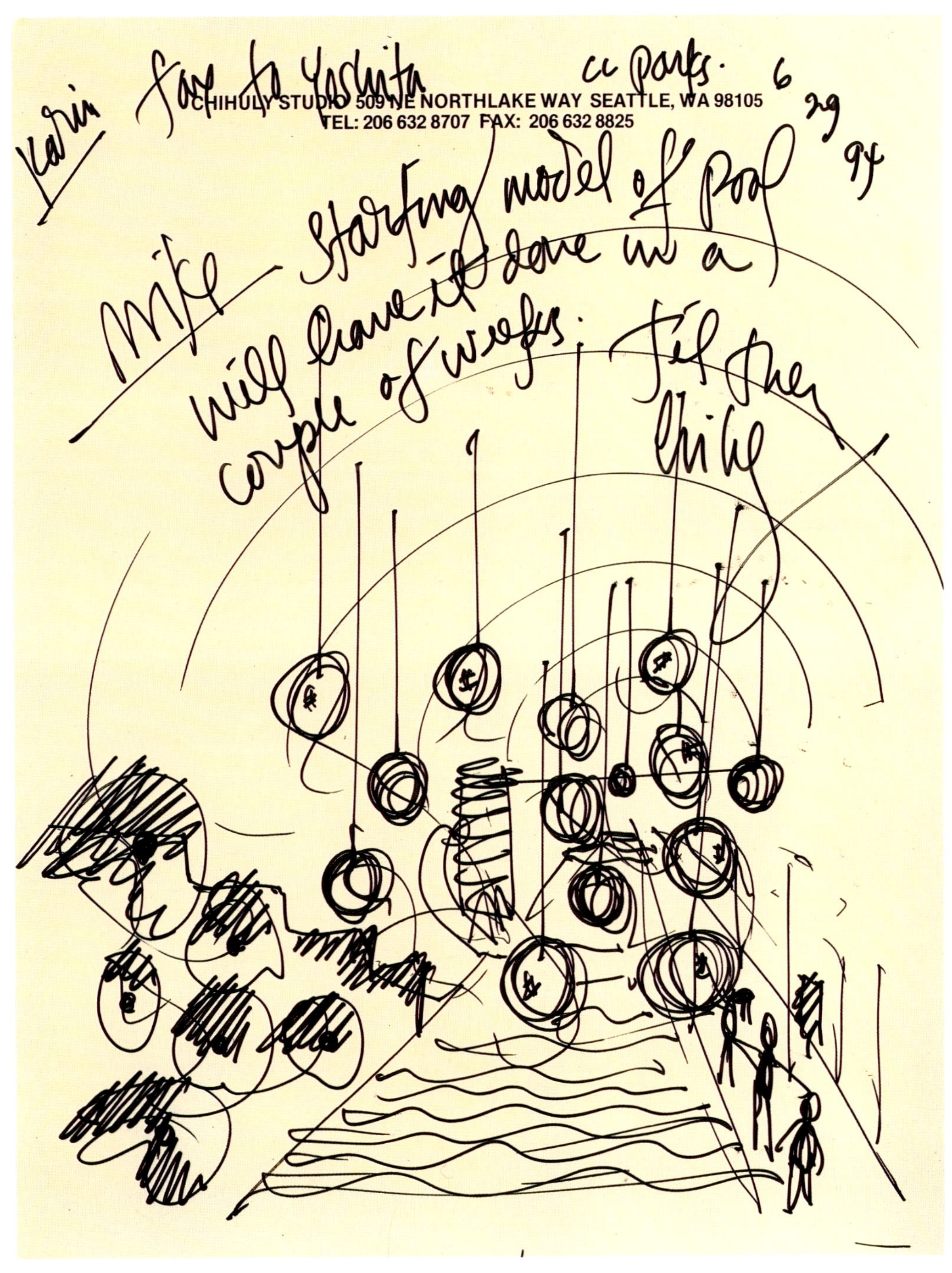

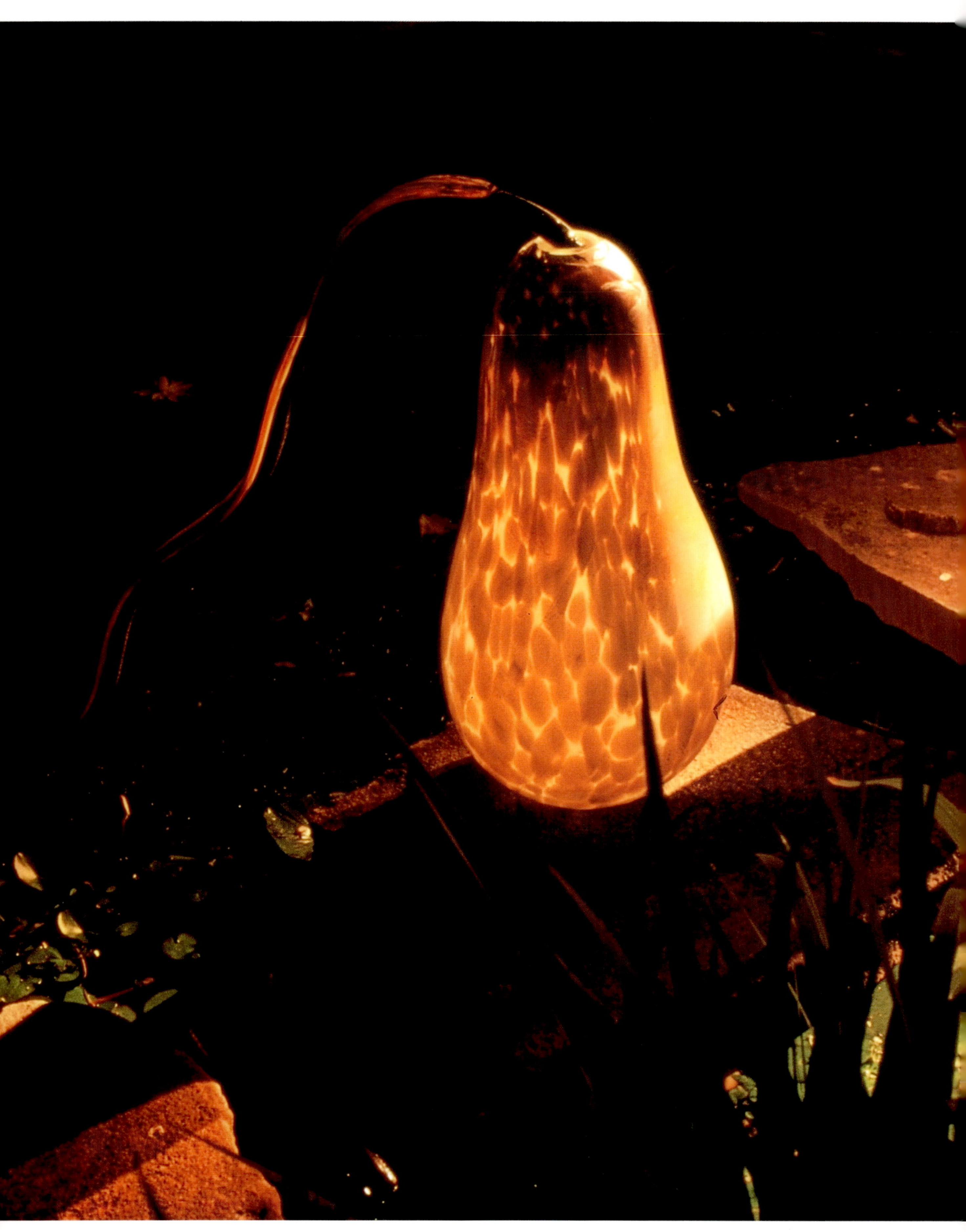

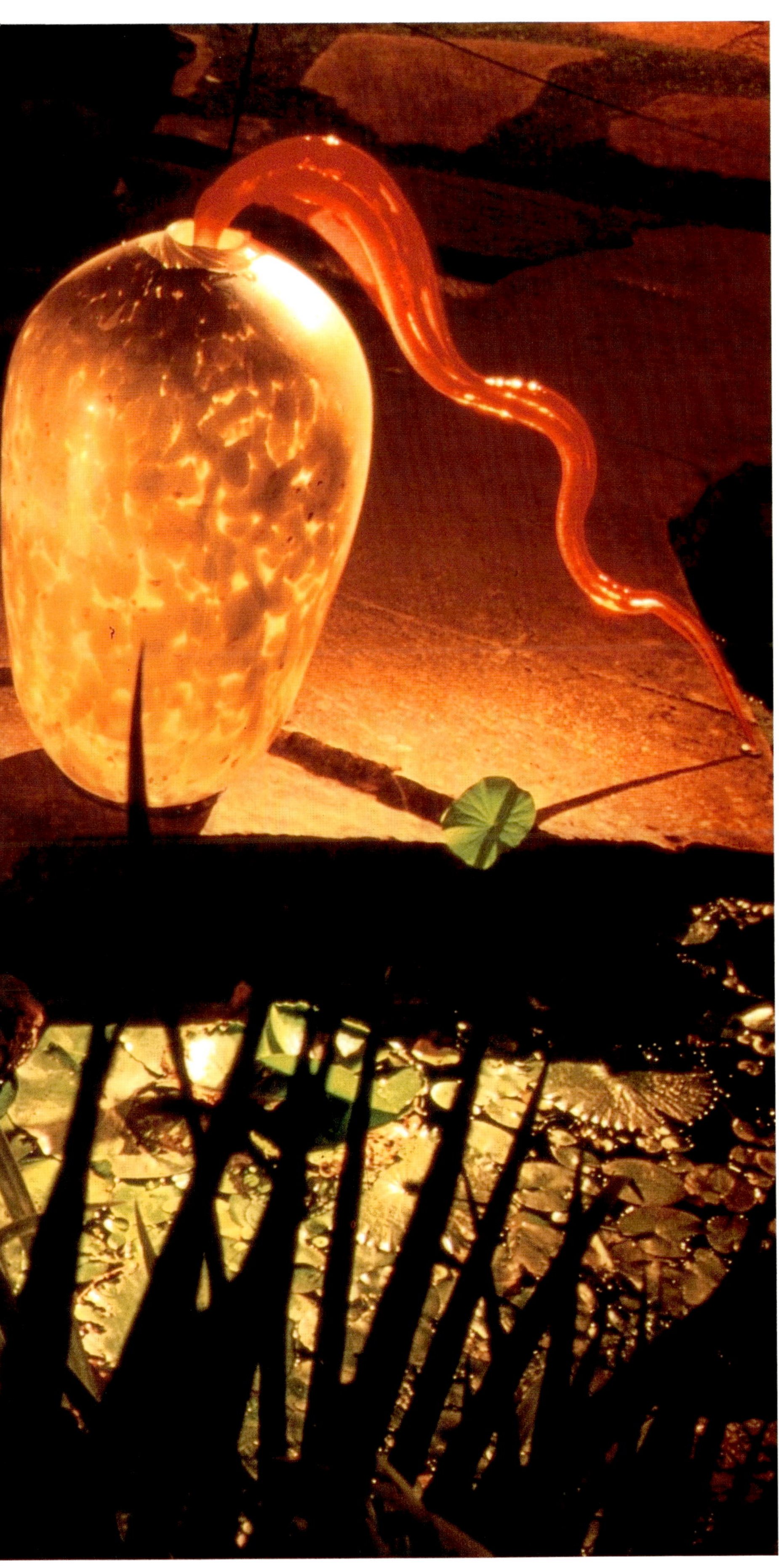

ikebana

花道

亞洲庭院中的花道
"屈胡利庭院展"
檀香山藝術學院
檀香山, 1992
攝影: R. Johnson

Ikebana Pair
in the Asian Court
"Chihuly Courtyards"
Honolulu Academy of Arts
Honolulu, 1992
photo: R. Johnson

亞洲庭院中的黃葉梨形花道(細部)
"屈胡利庭院展"
檀香山藝術學院
檀香山, 1992
攝影: R. Johnson

Pear Ikebana with Yellow Leaf (detail)
in the Asian Court
"Chihuly Courtyards"
Honolulu Academy of Arts
Honolulu, 1992
photo: R. Johnson

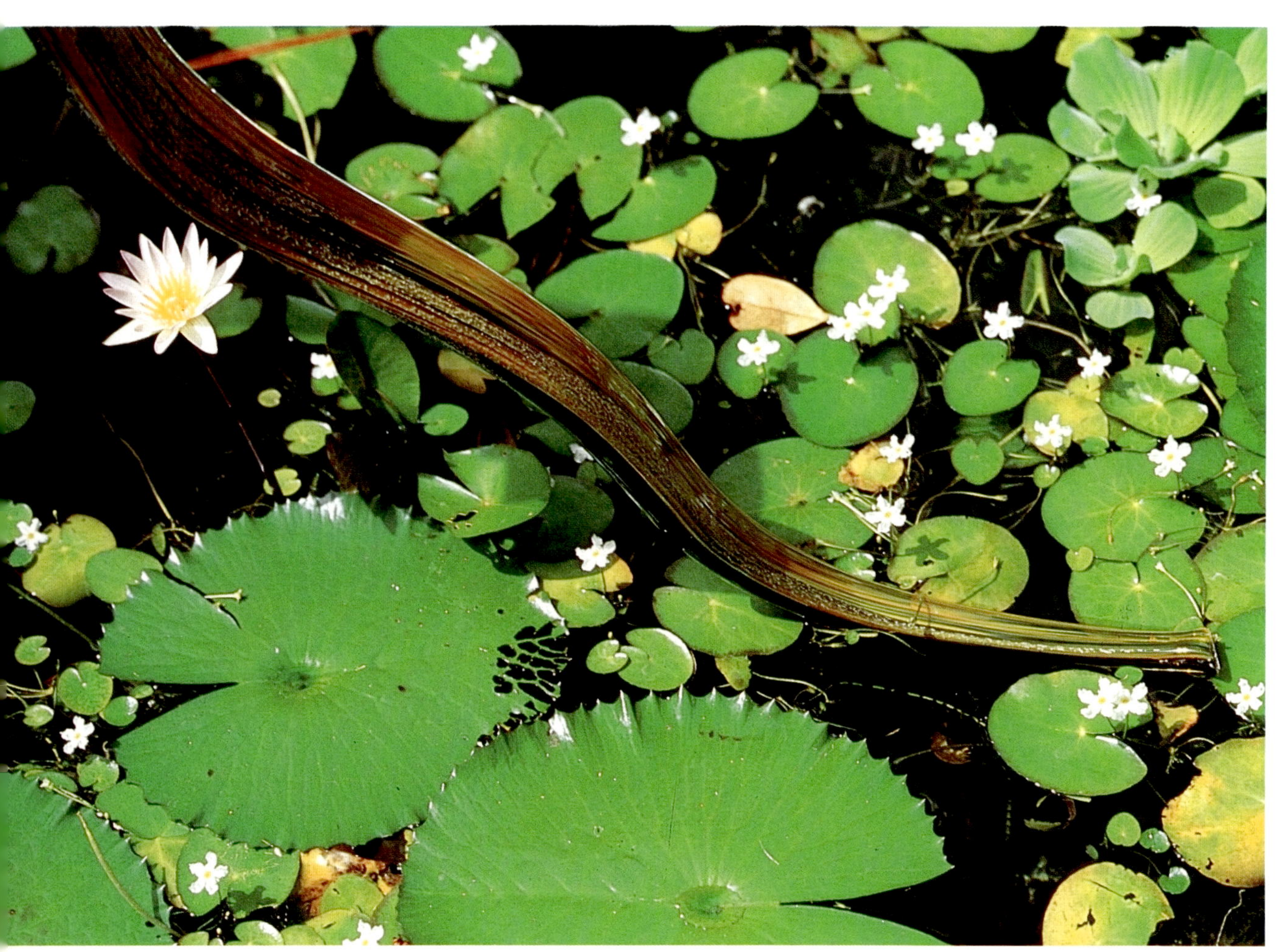

亞洲庭院中的花道
"屈胡利庭院展"
檀香山藝術學院
檀香山, 1992
攝影: R. Johnson

Ikebana Courtyard
in the Asian Court
"Chihuly Courtyards"
Honolulu Academy of Arts
Honolulu, 1992
photo: R. Johnson

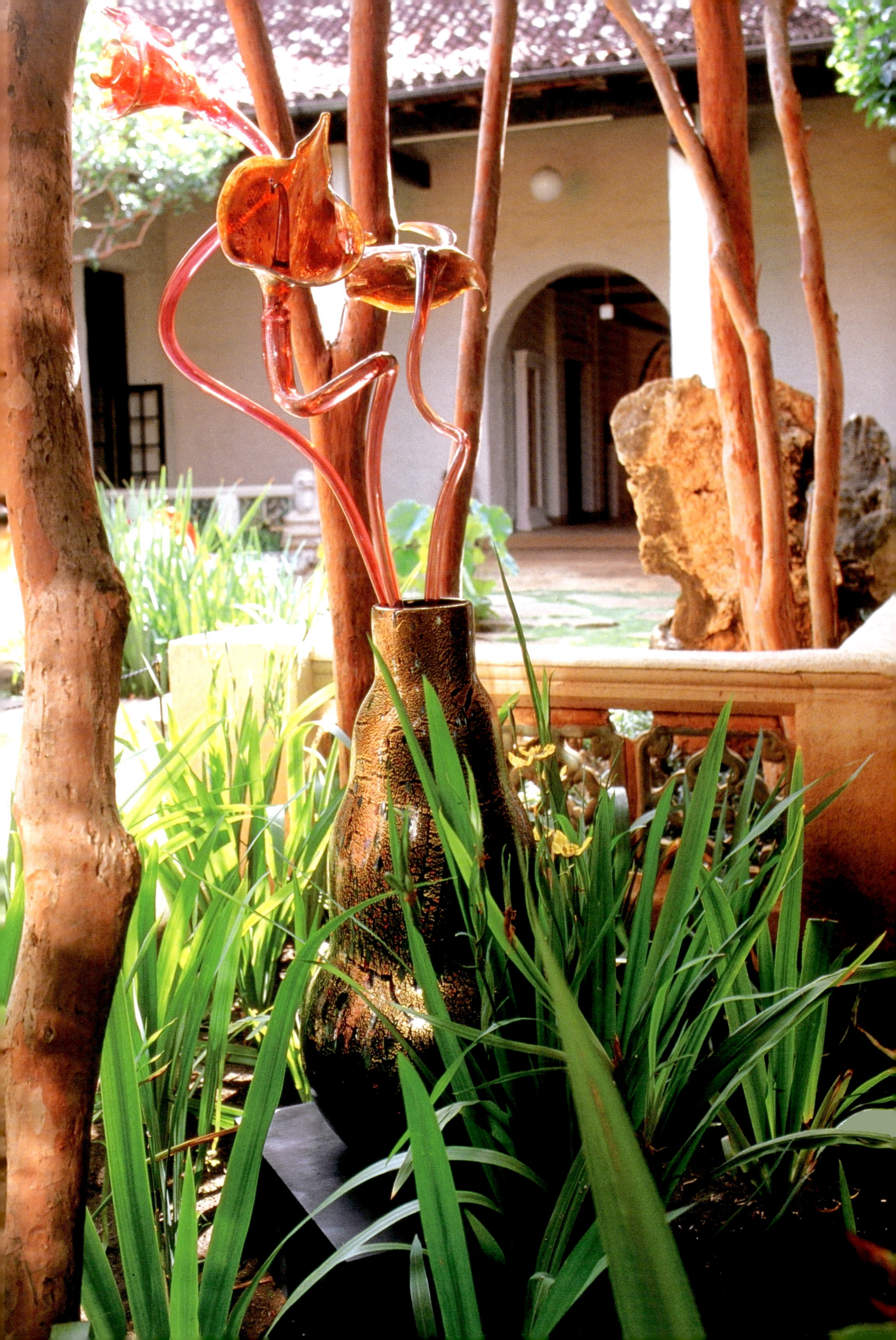

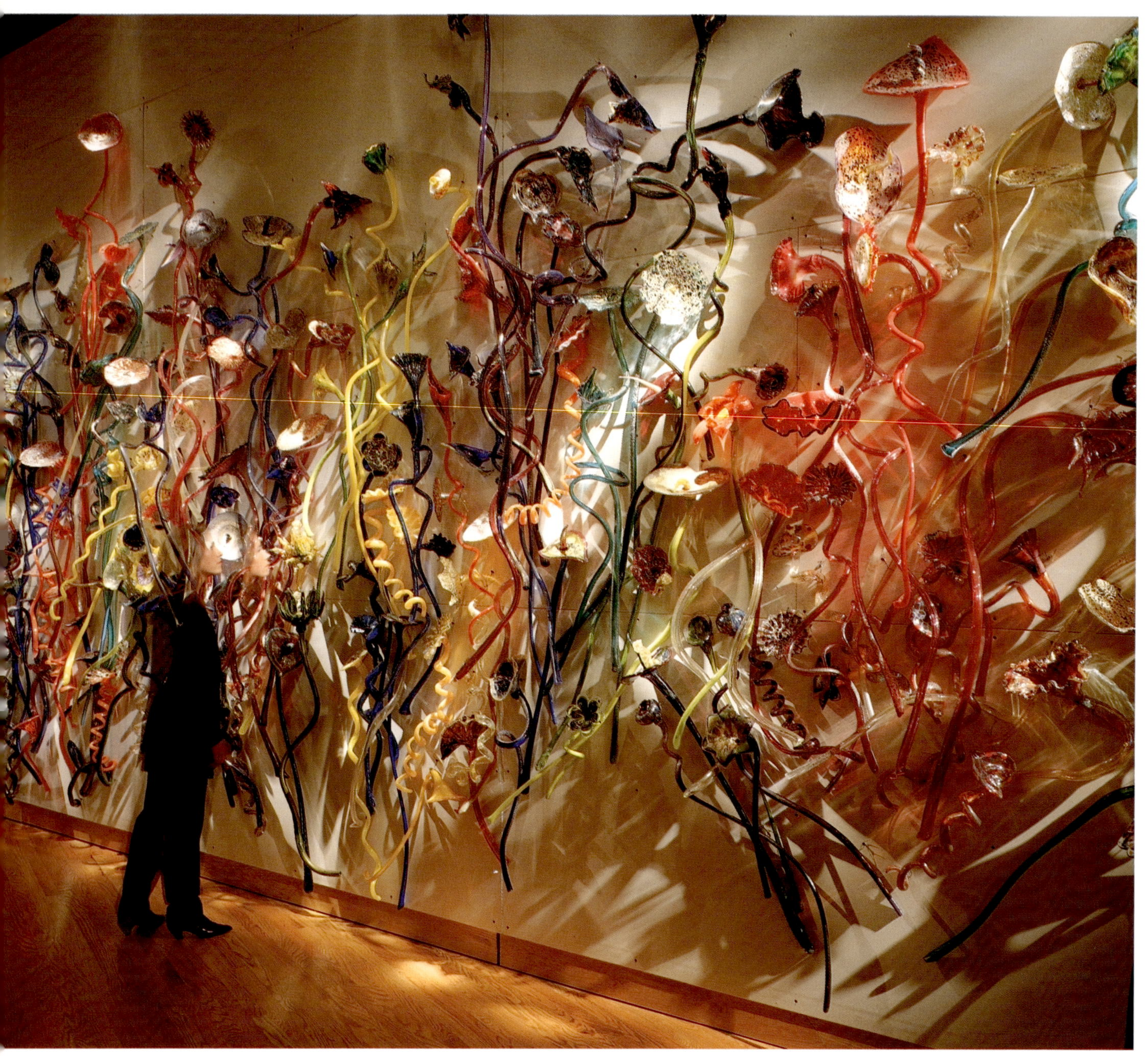

花道牆
“德爾.屈胡利:裝置藝術 1964-1992”
西雅圖藝術館
西雅圖, 1993
攝影: E. Calderon

Ikebana Wall
“Dale Chihuly: Installations: 1964-1992”
Seattle Art Museum
Seattle, 1993
photo: E. Calderon

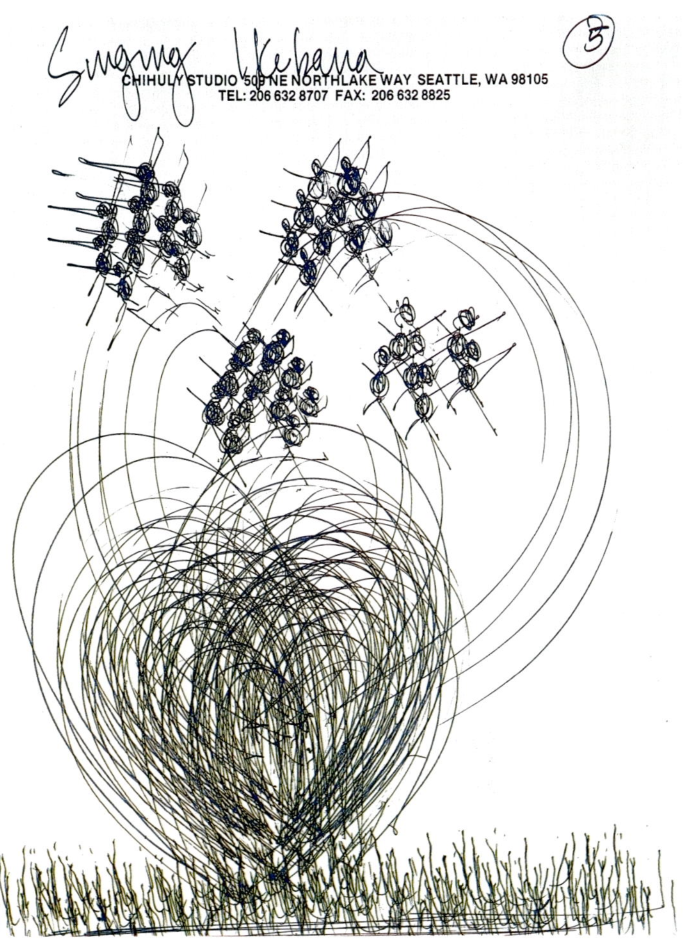

歡唱花道素描
8.5 x 11吋
1994
攝影：M. Seidl

Singing Ikebana Sketch
8.5 x 11"
1994
photo: M. Seidl

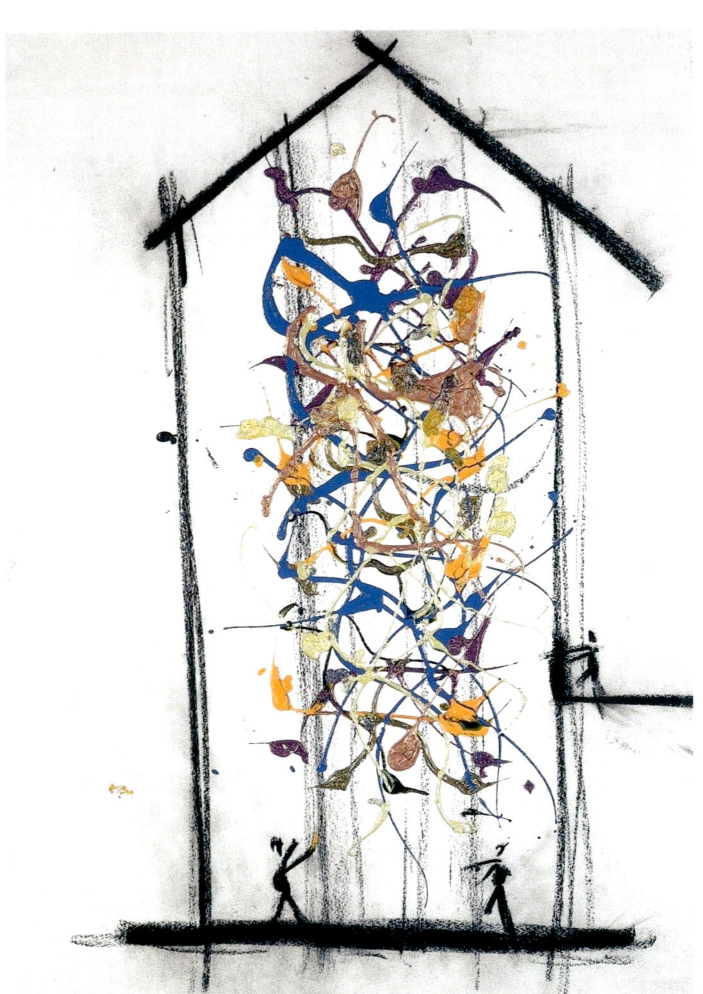

佛瑞德.哈契森之花道素描
30 x 22吋
1993
攝影：T. Rishel

Fred Hutchinson Ikebana Sketch
30 x 22"
1993
photo: T. Rishel

小天使花道
船屋
西雅圖，1991
攝影：R. Johnson

Putti Ikebana
The Boathouse
Seattle, 1991
photo: R. Johnson

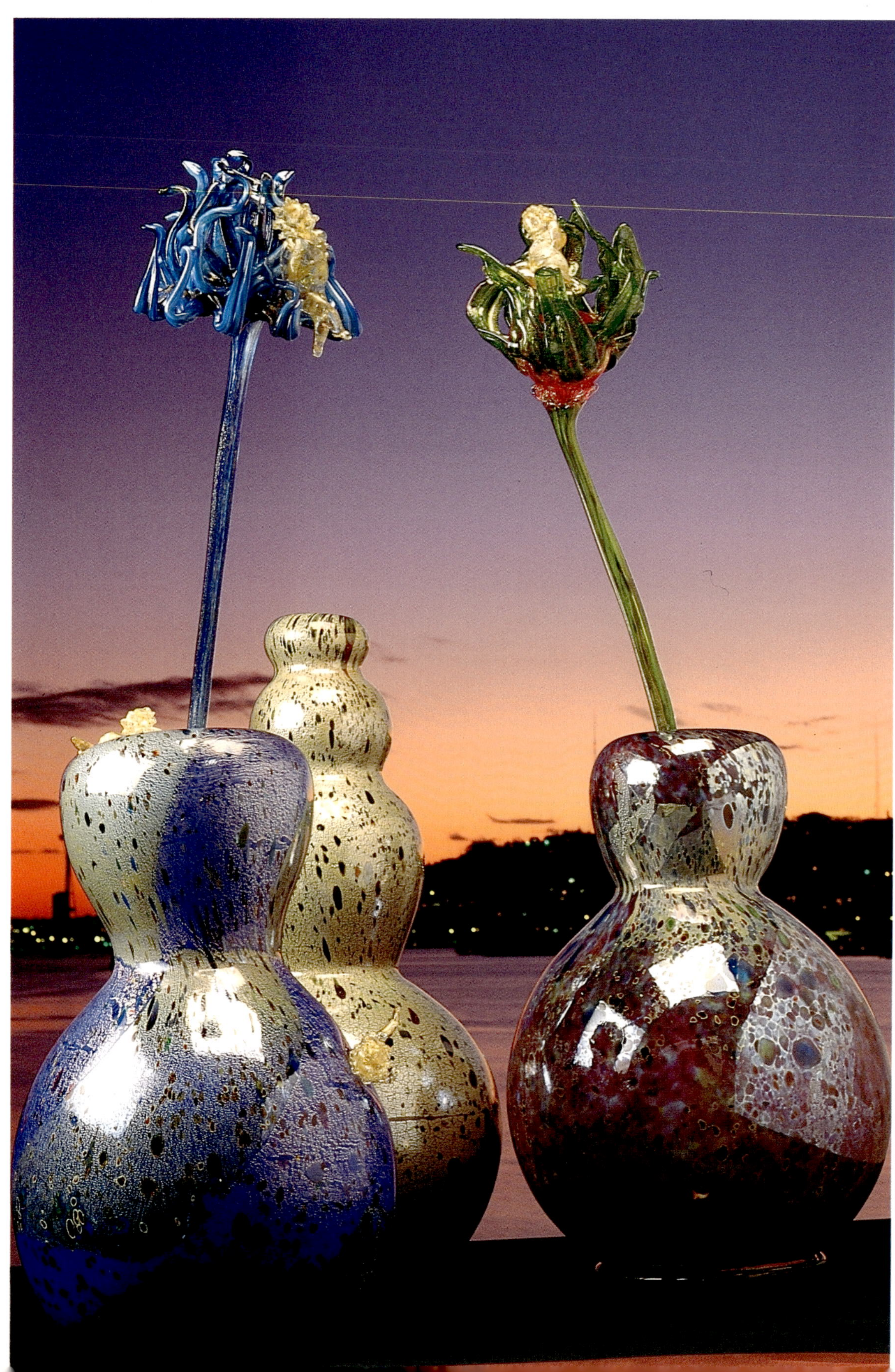

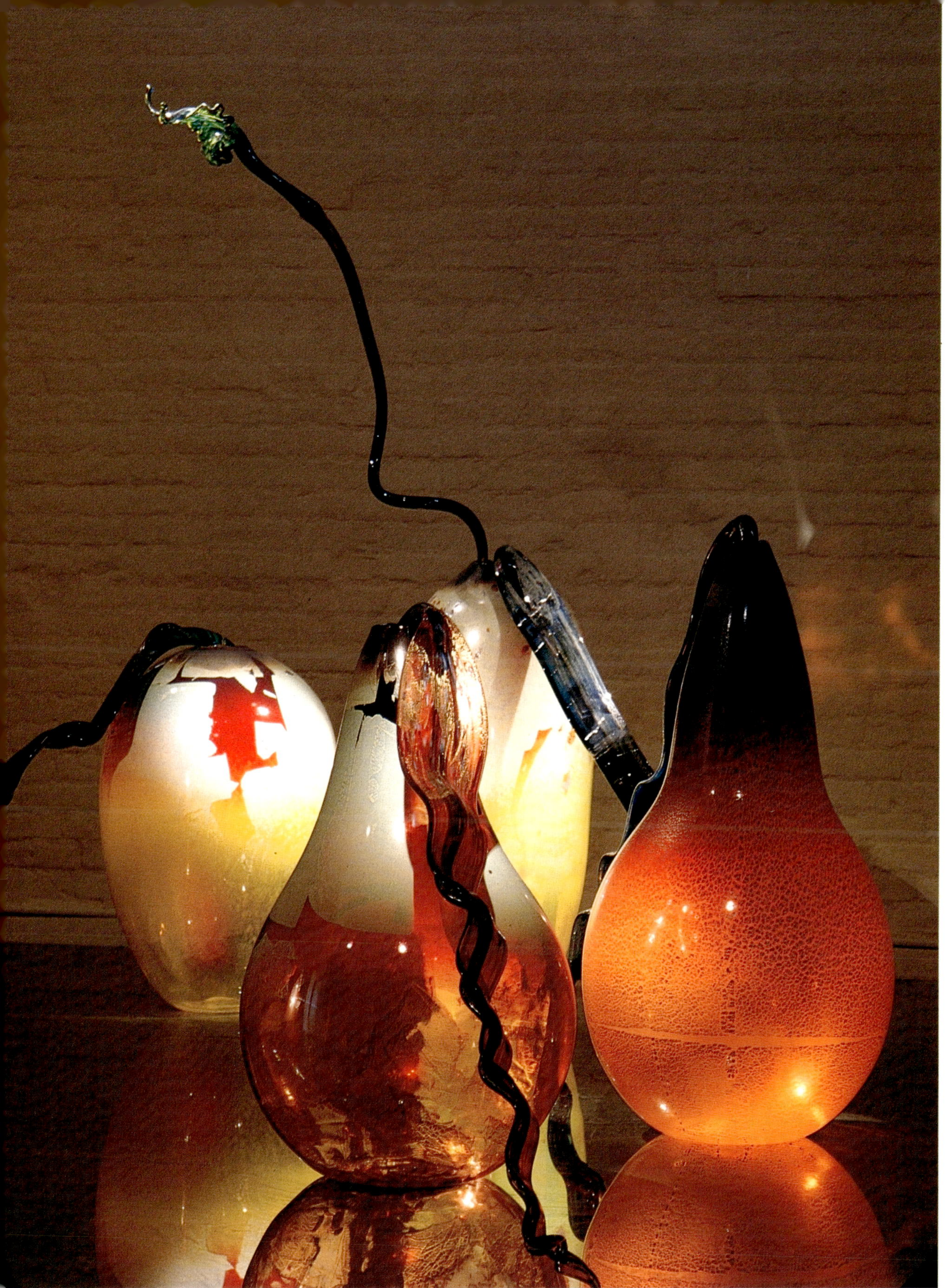

花道
弗斯特.懷特陳列館
西雅圖, 1993
攝影: R. Johnson

Ikebana
Foster White Gallery
Seattle, 1993
photo: R. Johnson

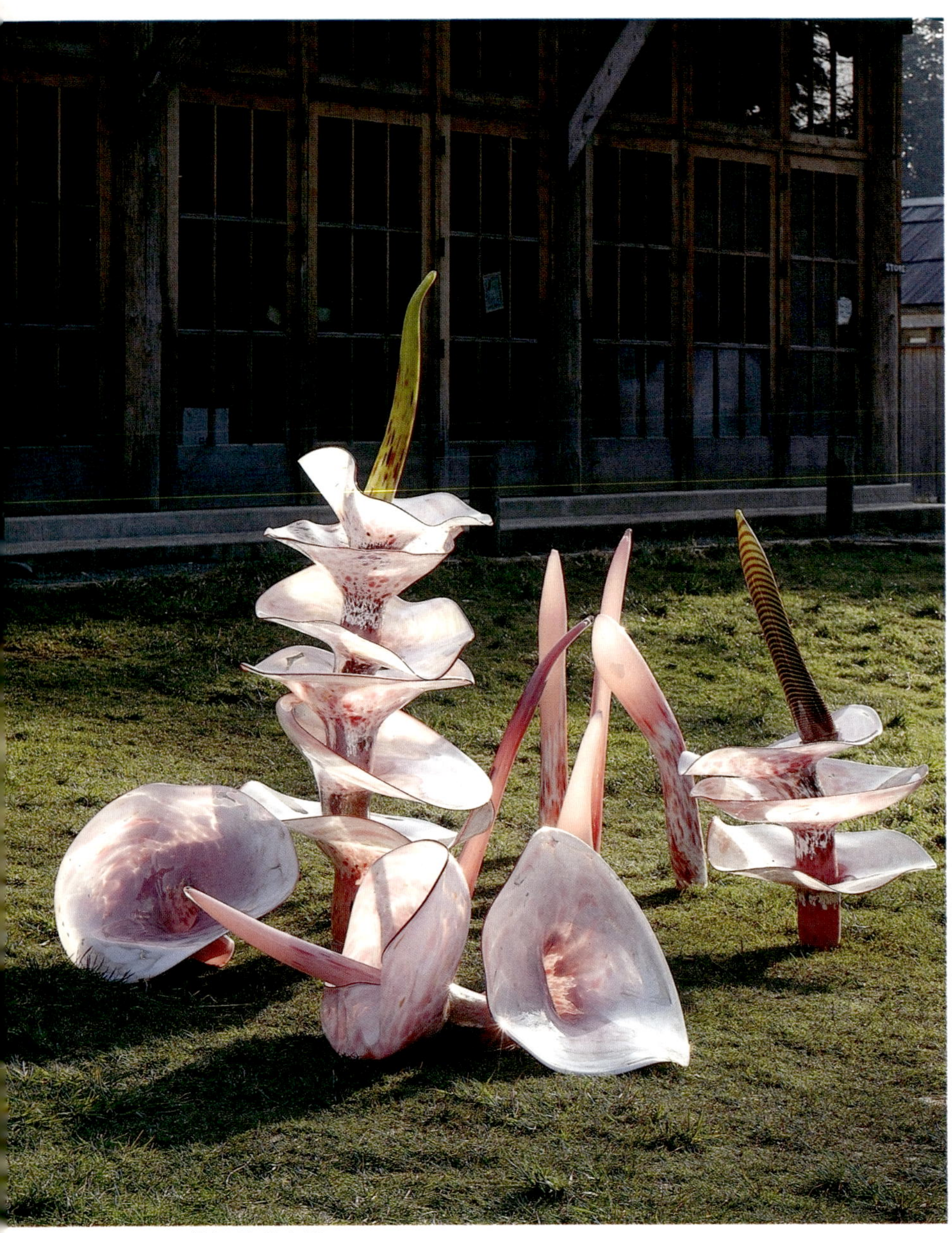

粉紅色花之形
44 x 84 x 62吋
比恰克玻璃學校
史坦伍德，1985
攝影：R. Schreiber

Pink Flower Forms
44 x 84 x 62"
Pilchuck Glass School
Stanwood, 1985
photo: R. Schreiber

花之形（細部）
5 x 6 x 3呎
喜來登飯店
西雅圖，1986
攝影：D. Busher

Flower Forms (detail)
5 x 6 x 3'
Sheraton Hotel
Seattle, 1986
photo: D. Busher

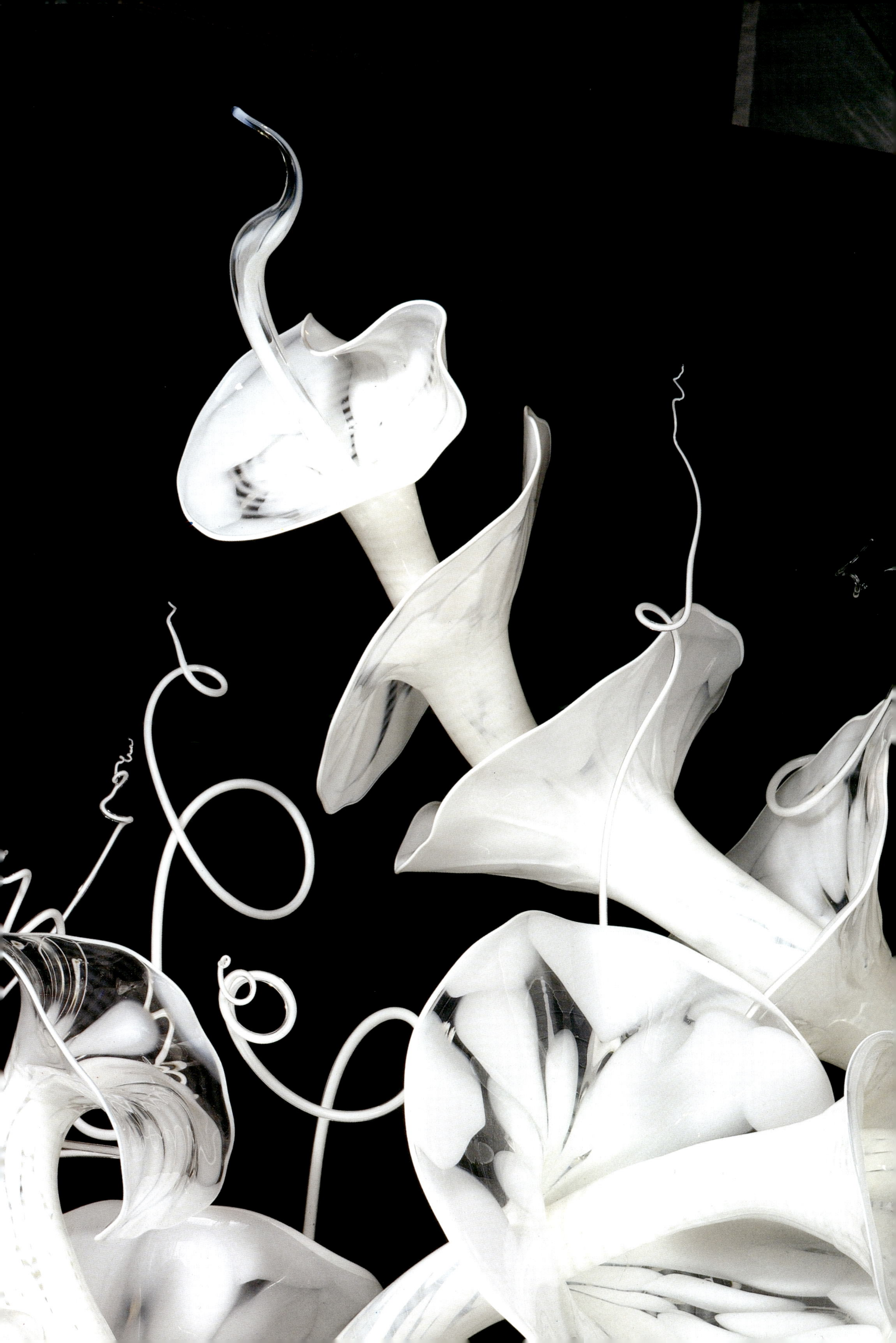

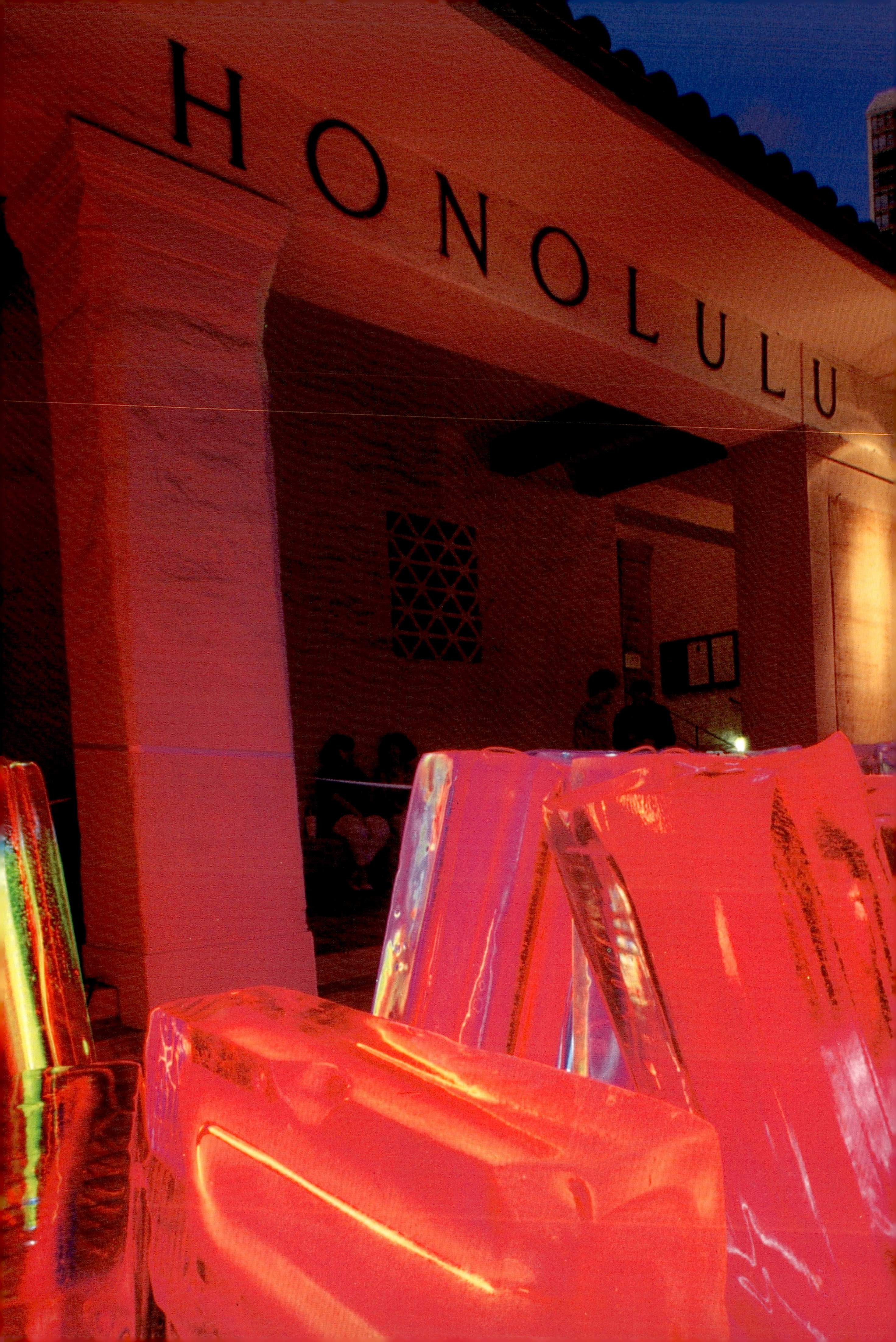
HONOLULU

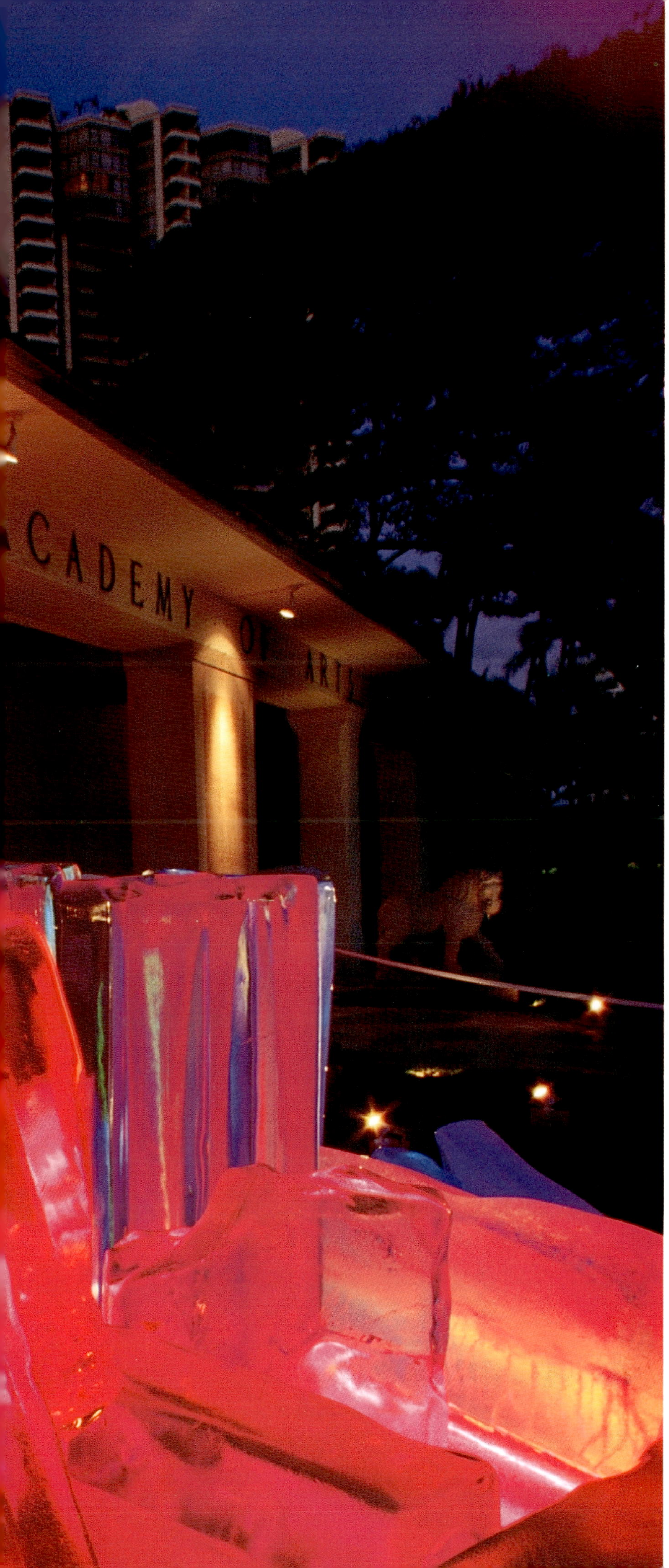

neon & ice

霓虹與冰

檀香山之霓虹與冰
"屈胡利庭院展"
檀香山藝術學院
檀香山, 1992
攝影: R. Johnson

Honolulu Neon and Ice
"Chihuly Courtyards"
Honolulu Academy of Arts
Honolulu, 1992
photo: R. Johnson

2萬磅的霓虹與冰
冰屋中之模型
1992
攝影：R. Johnson

20,000 pounds of Ice and Neon
Mock-up in the ice house
1992
photo: R. Johnson

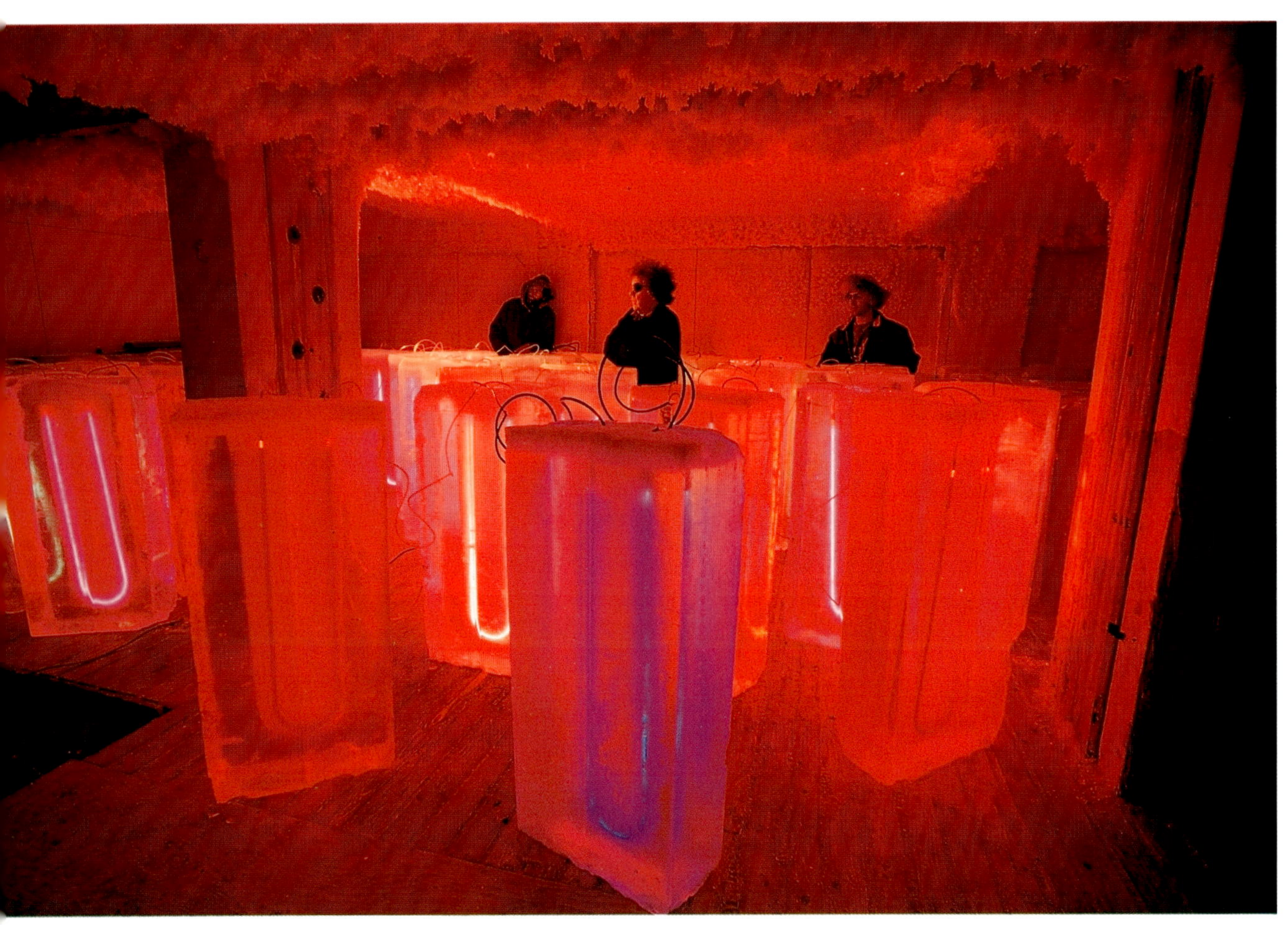

十萬磅的霓虹與冰之素描
8.5 x 11吋
1993
攝影：M. Seidl

100,000 pounds of
Ice and Neon *Sketch*
8.5 x 11"
1993
photo: M. Seidl

page 2

Marriott
HOTELS · RESORTS · SUITES

8.27.1993

Tacoma Dome

[illegible]
100,000 Ice [illegible]
Free Sept 2 & 3

Keep off the ice!

wow

stupid!

Let's go

awesome

I'M COLD

groovy

KOOL

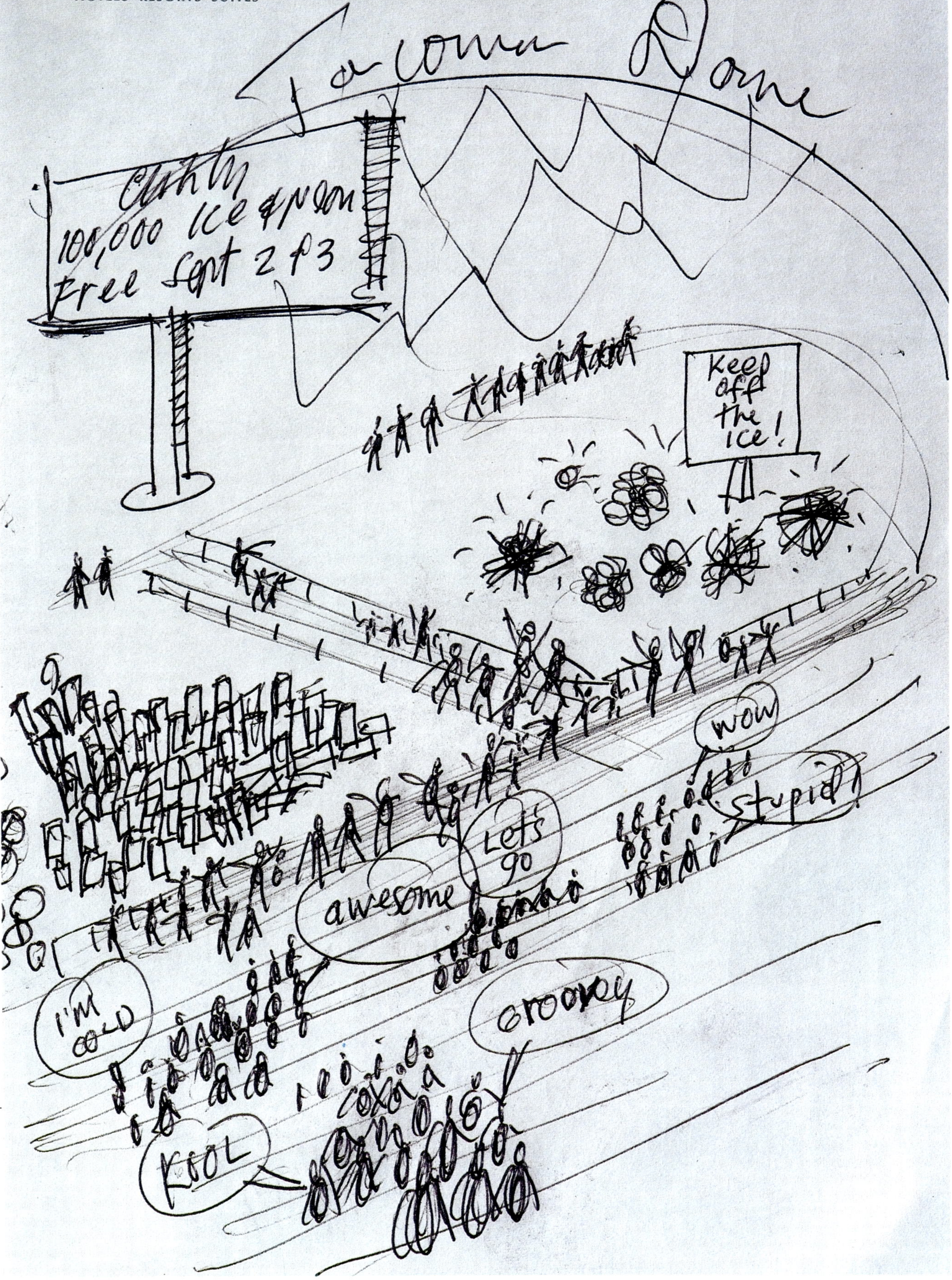

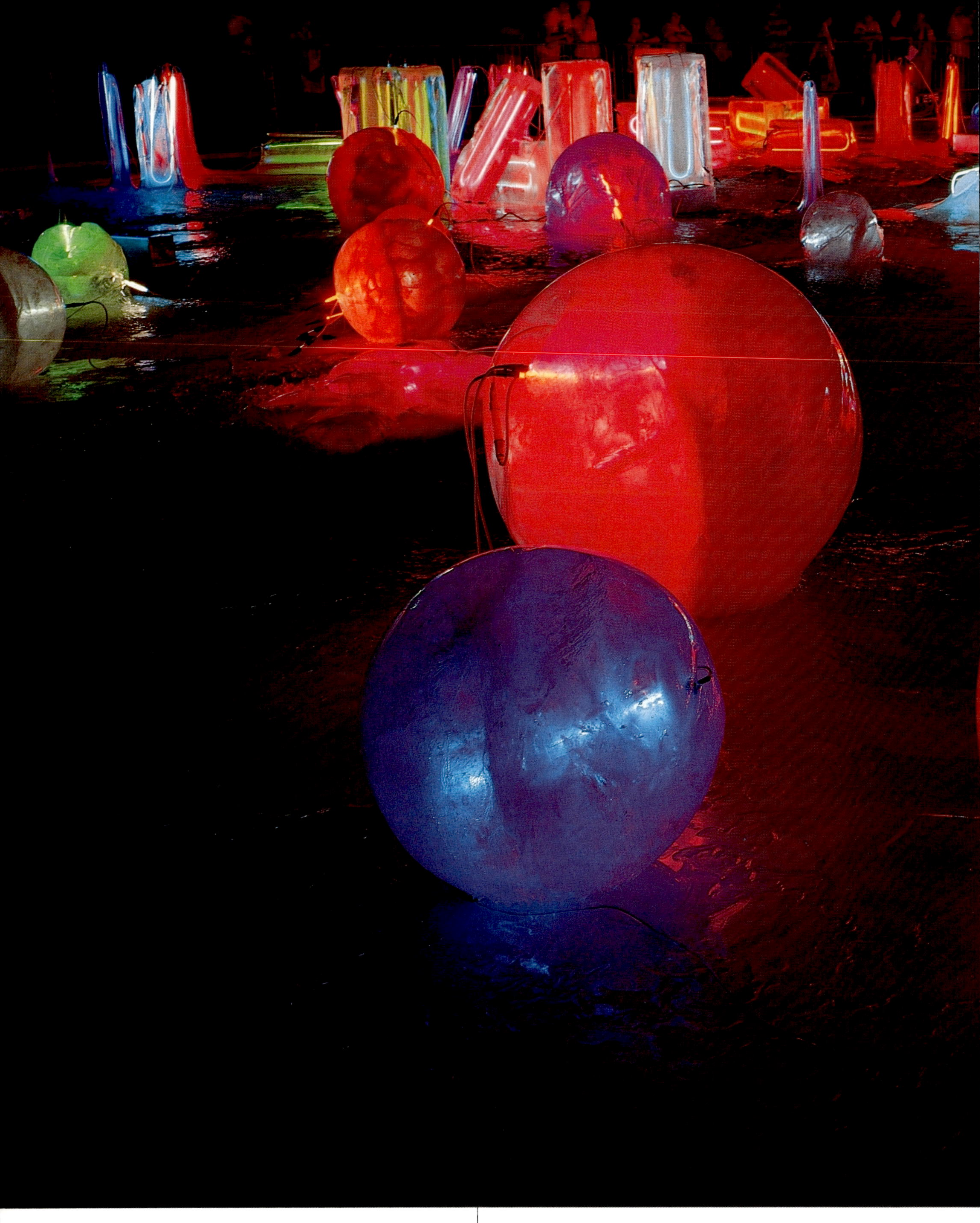

"十萬磅的霓虹與冰"展覽
塔科馬圓頂華夏
塔科馬, 1993
攝影: T. Rishel

"100,000 pounds of Ice and Neon"
The Tacoma Dome
Tacoma, 1993
photo: T. Rishel

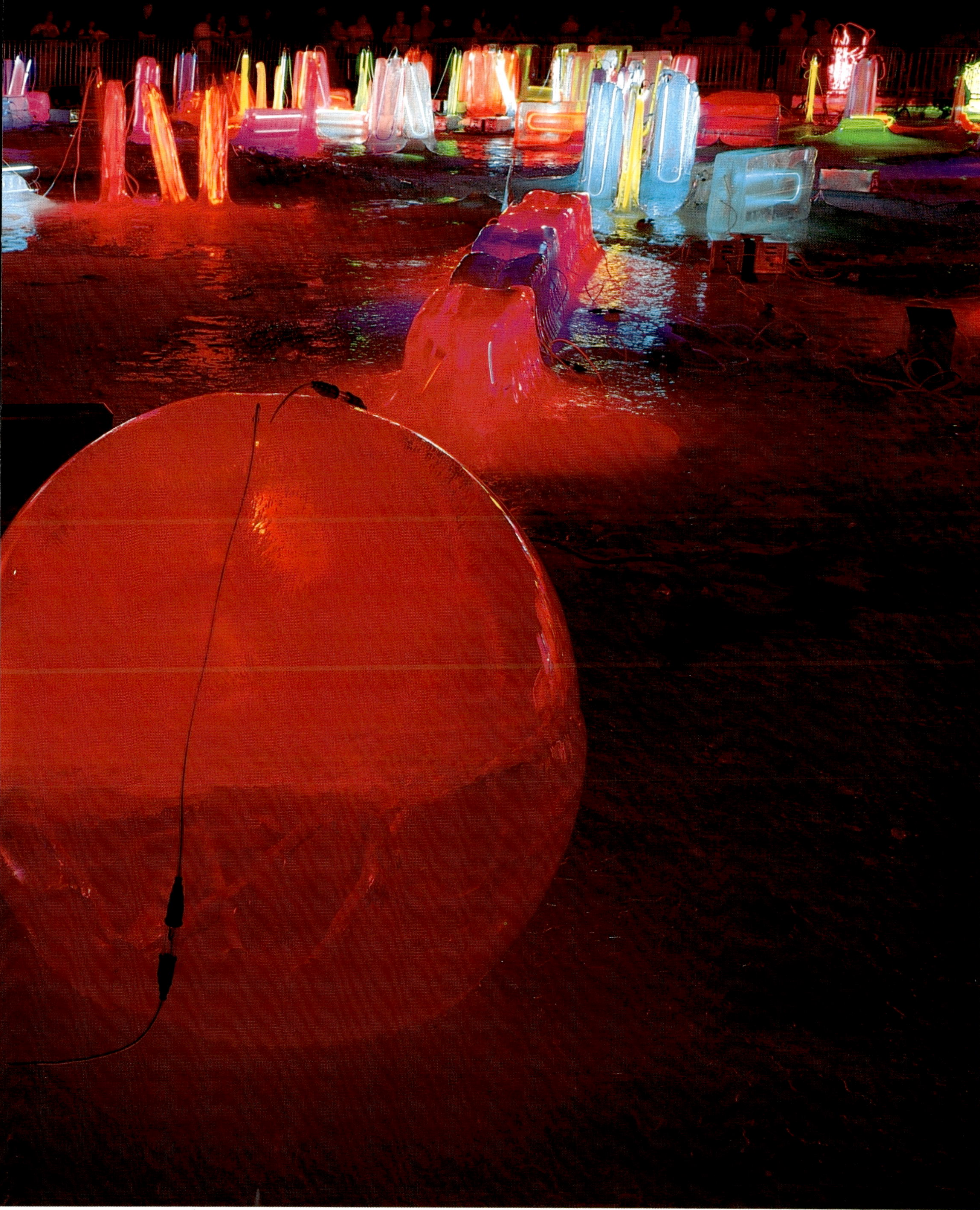

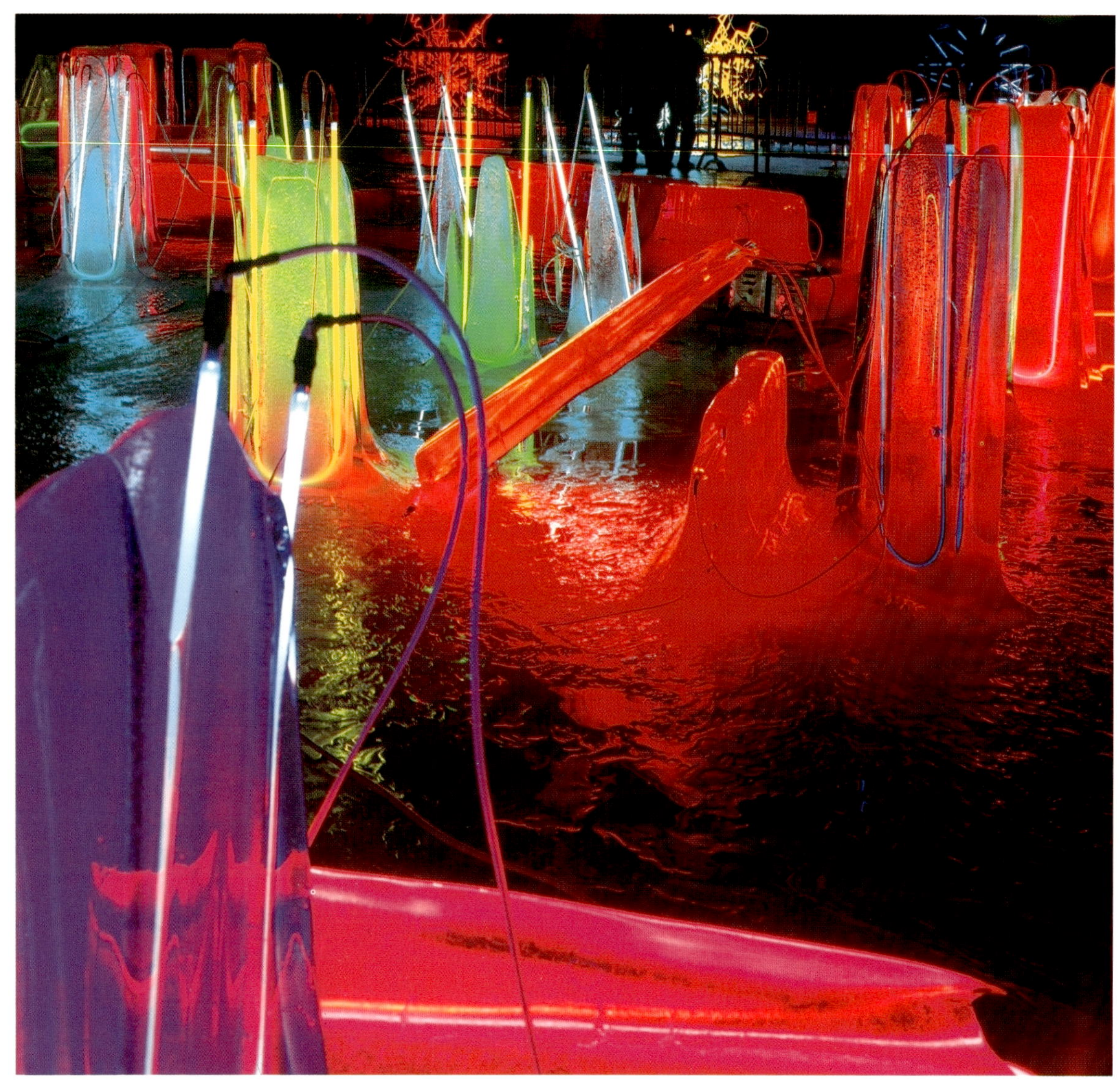

"十萬磅的霓虹與冰"展覽
塔科馬圓頂華廈
塔科馬, 1993
攝影: T. Rishel

"100,000 pounds of Ice and Neon"
The Tacoma Dome
Tacoma, 1993
photo: T. Rishel

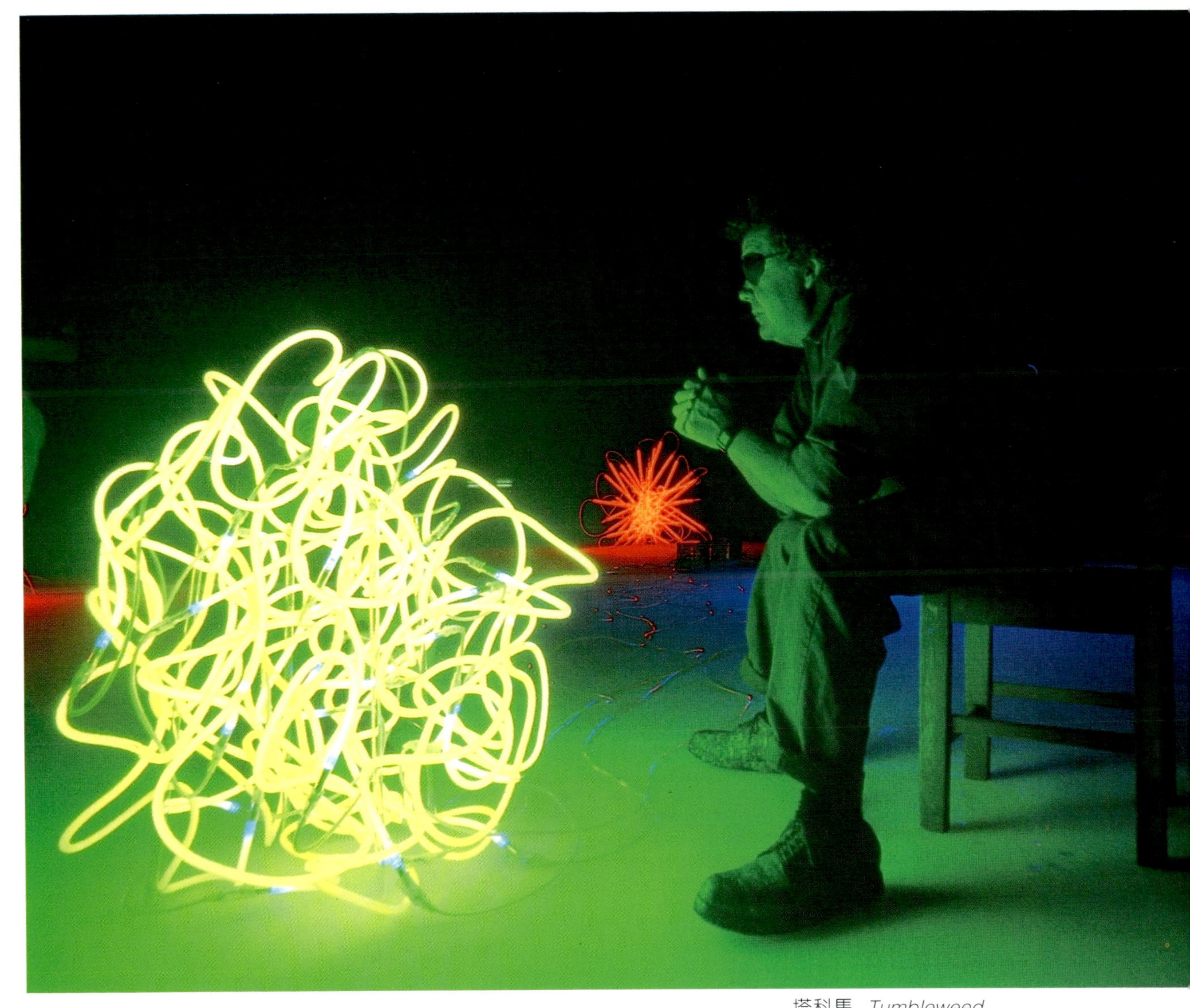

塔科馬 *Tumbleweed*
"十萬磅的霓虹與冰"展覽
塔科馬圓頂華廈
塔科馬, 1993
攝影: R. Johnson

Tacoma Tumbleweed
"100,000 pounds
of Ice and Neon"
The Tacoma Dome
Tacoma, 1993
photo: R. Johnson

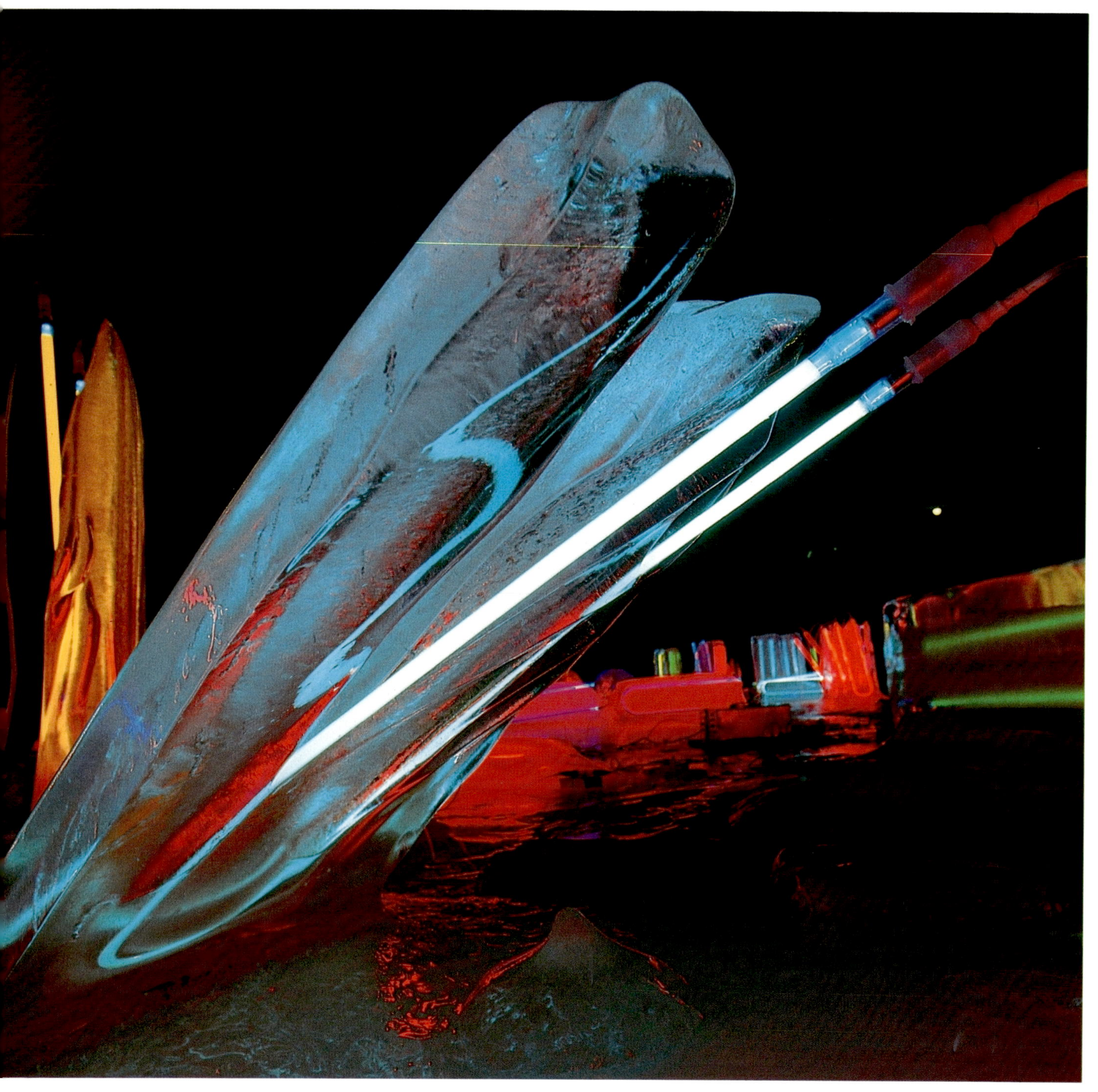

"十萬磅的霓虹與冰"展覽
塔科馬圓頂華廈
塔科馬, 1993
攝影: T. Rishel

"100,000 pounds of Ice and Neon"
The Tacoma Dome
Tacoma, 1993
photo: T. Rishel

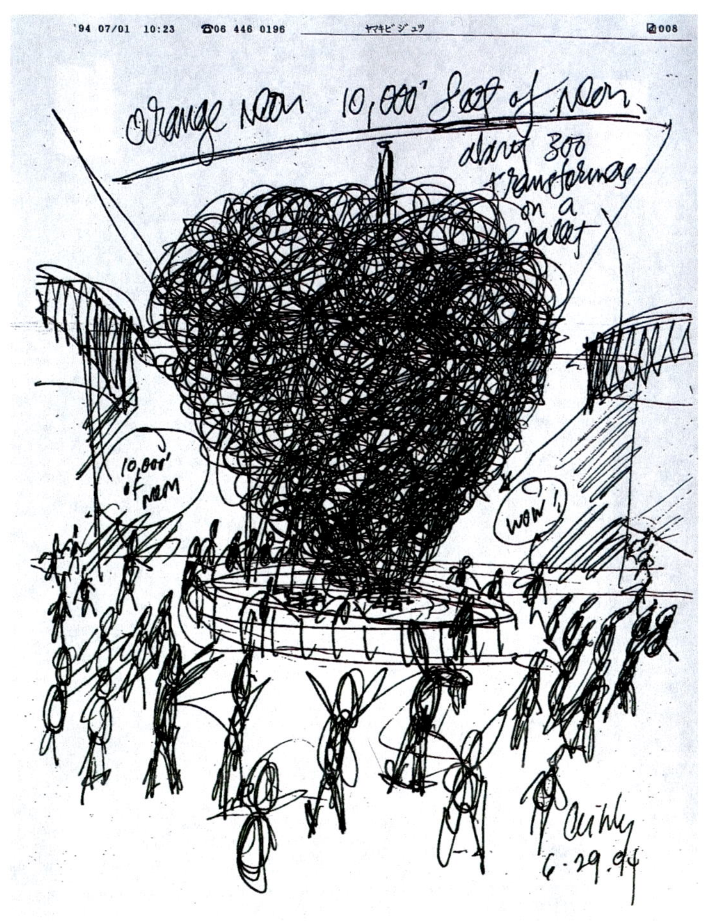

橘色霓虹裝置素描
8.5 x 11吋
1994
攝影：M. Seidl

Orange Neon Installation Sketch
8.5 x 11"
1994
photo: M. Seidl

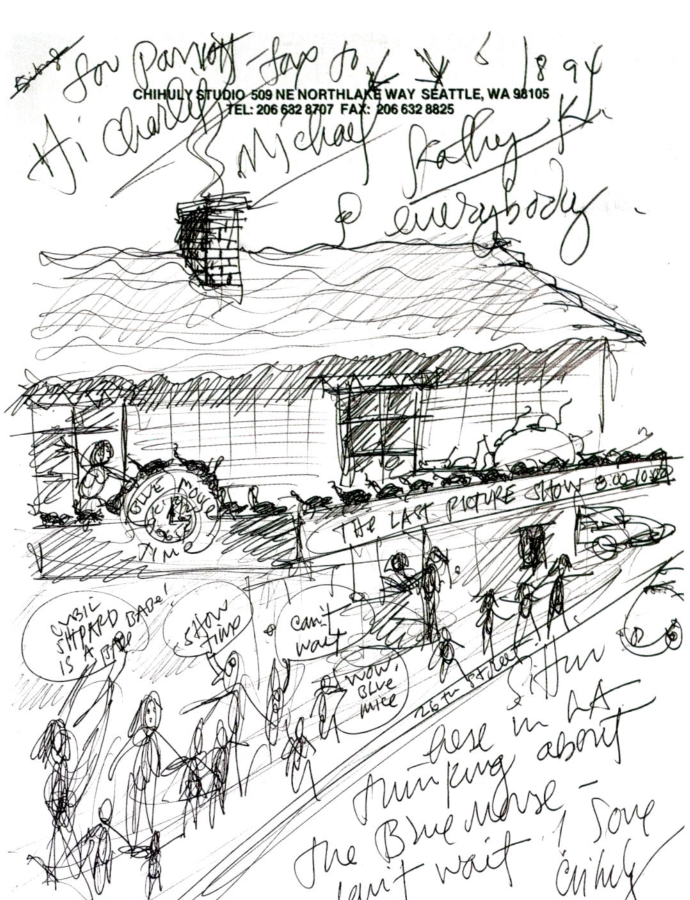

藍色博物館劇院之霓虹裝置素描
8.5 x 11吋
1994
攝影：M. Seidl

Blue Mouse Theatre Neon Installation Sketch
8.5 x 11"
1994
photo: M. Seidl

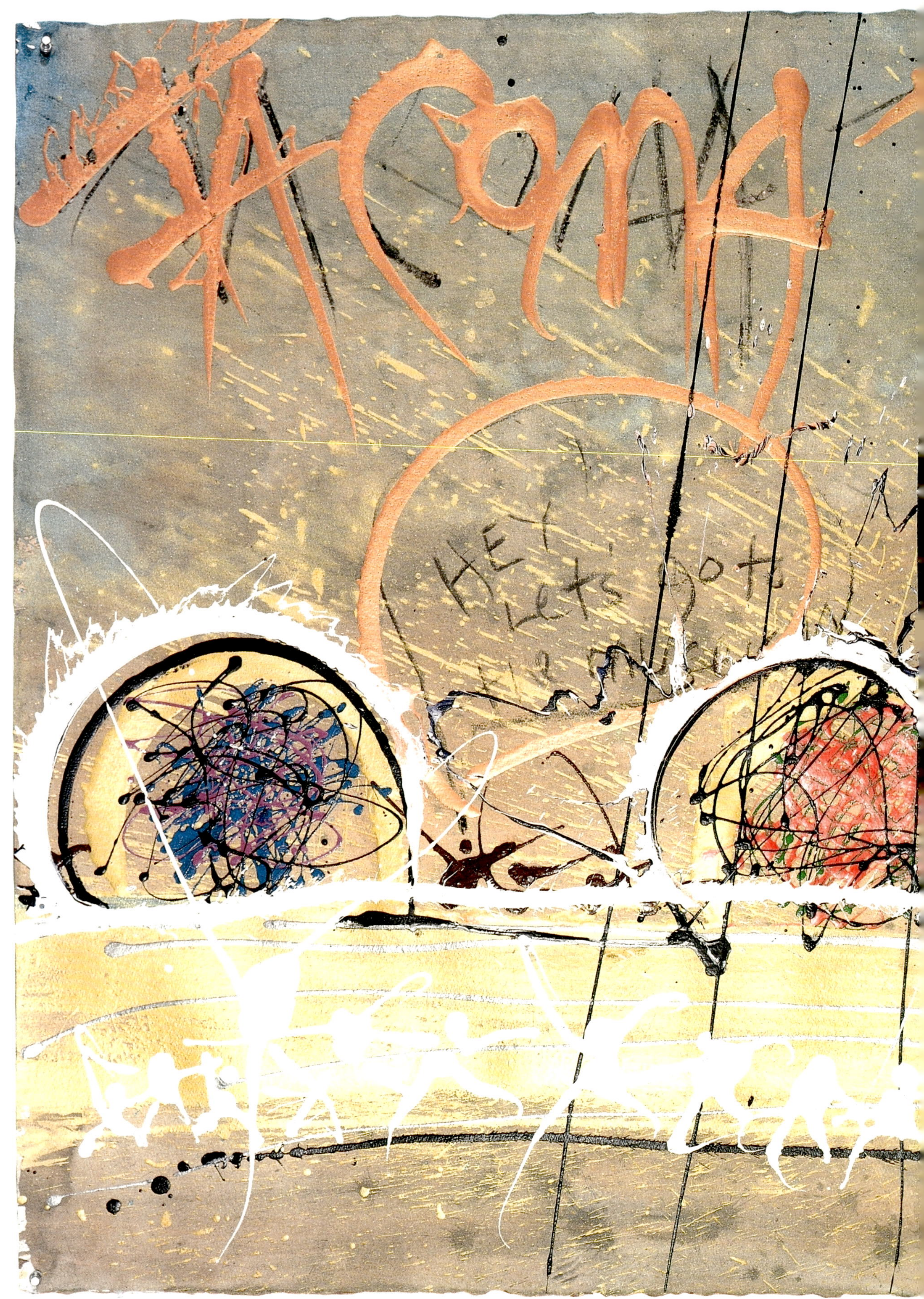

塔科馬 *Tumbleweed* 素描
40 x 60吋
1993
攝影: C. Garoutte

Tacoma Tumbleweed Drawing
40 x 60"
1993
photo: C. Garoutte

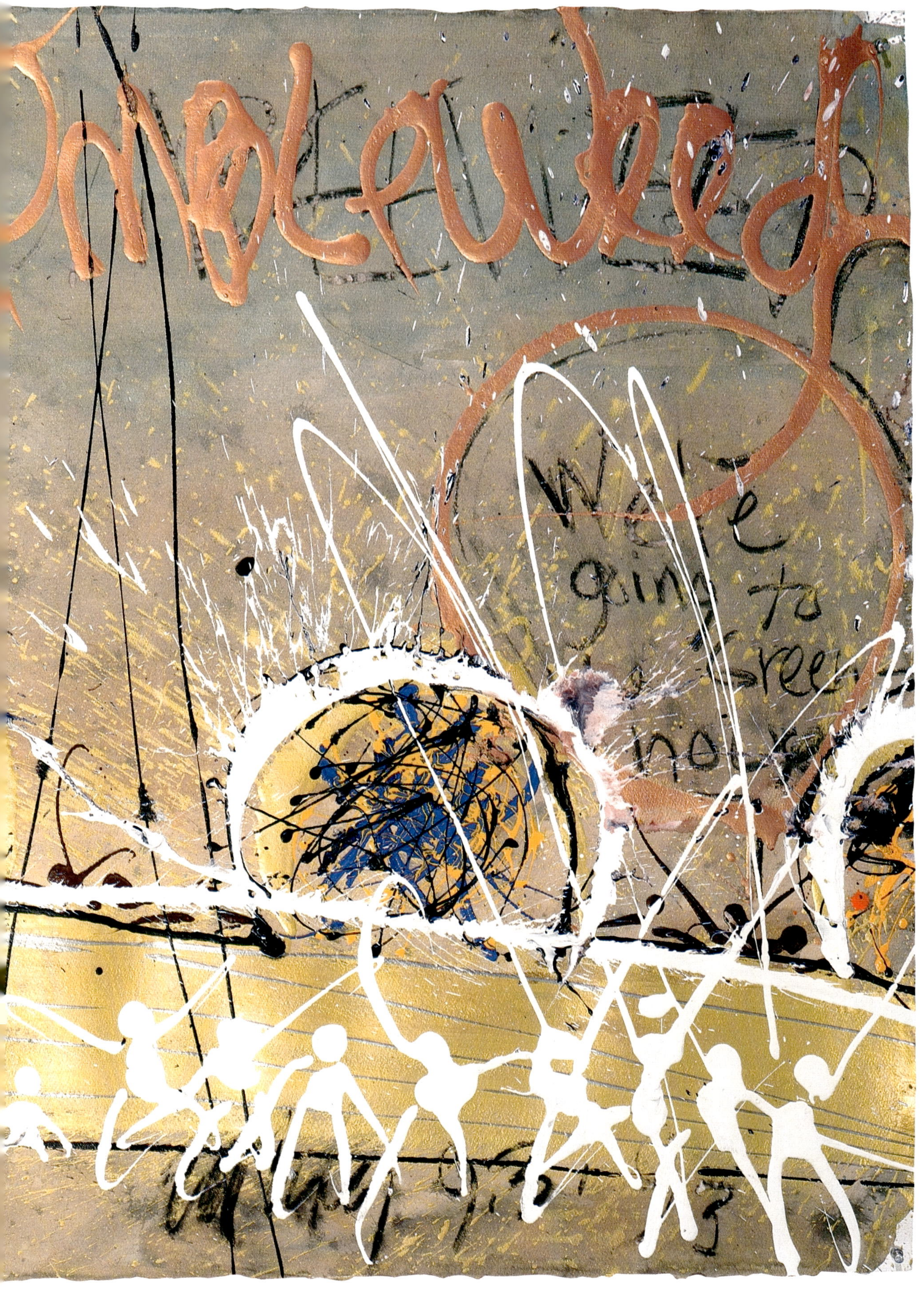
going to

chandeliers

吊燈

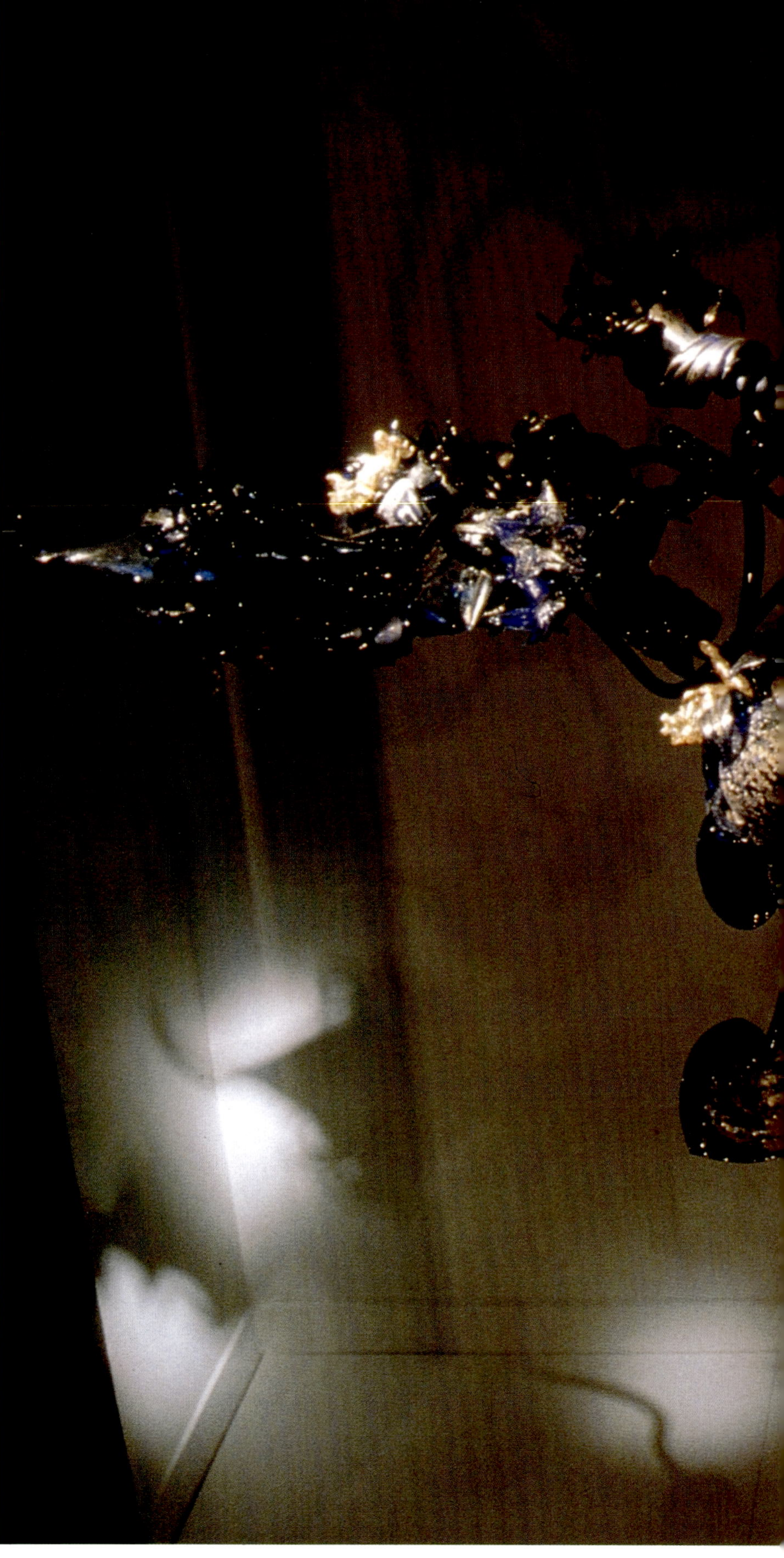

小天使吊燈
39 x 108吋
"德爾.屈胡利:裝置藝術
1964-1993"
底特律藝術學院
底特律, 1993
攝影: R. Johnson

Putti Chandelier
39 x 108" diameter
"Dale Chihuly:
Installations 1964-1993"
The Detroit Institute of Arts
Detroit, 1993
photo: R. Johnson

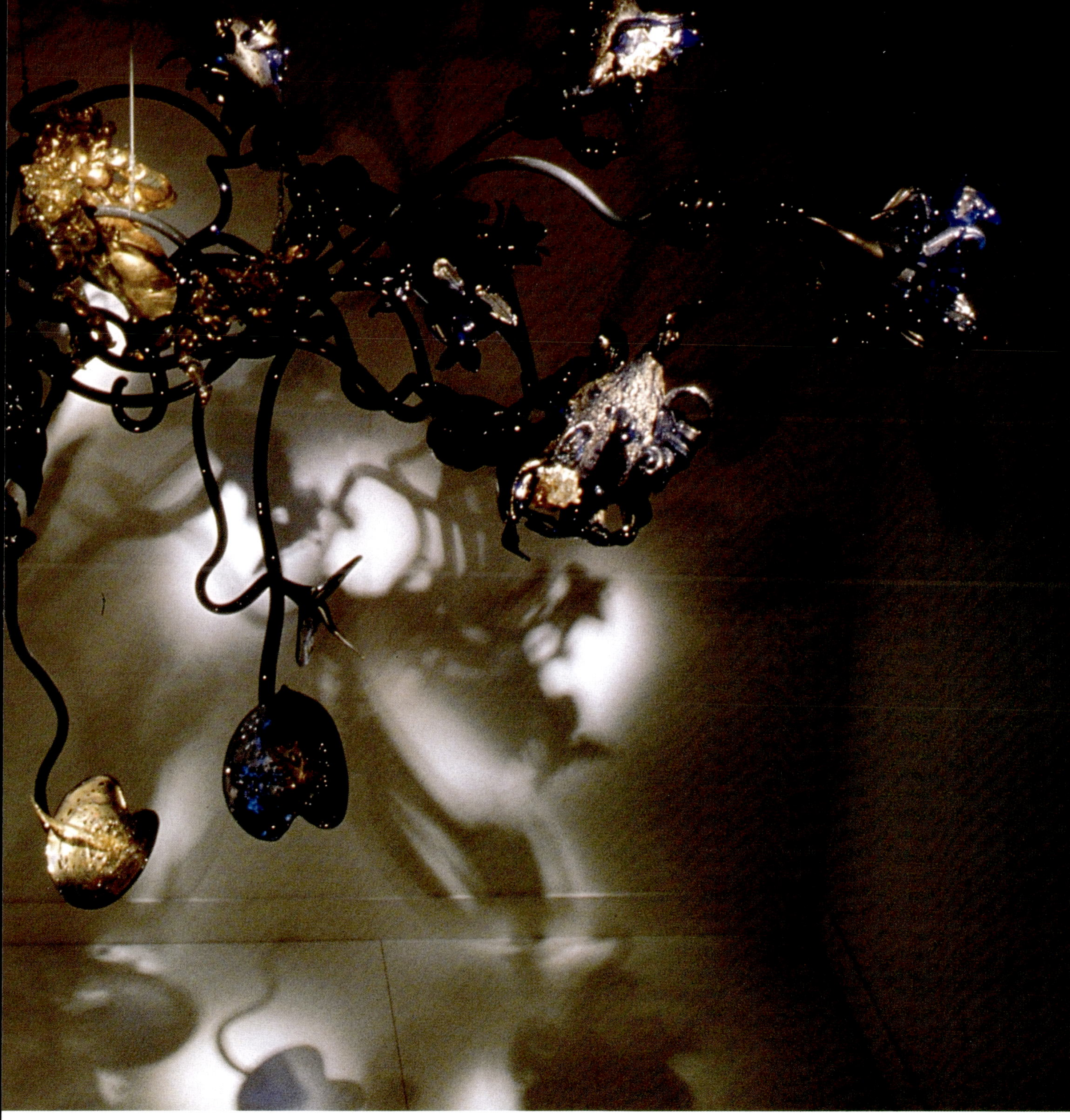

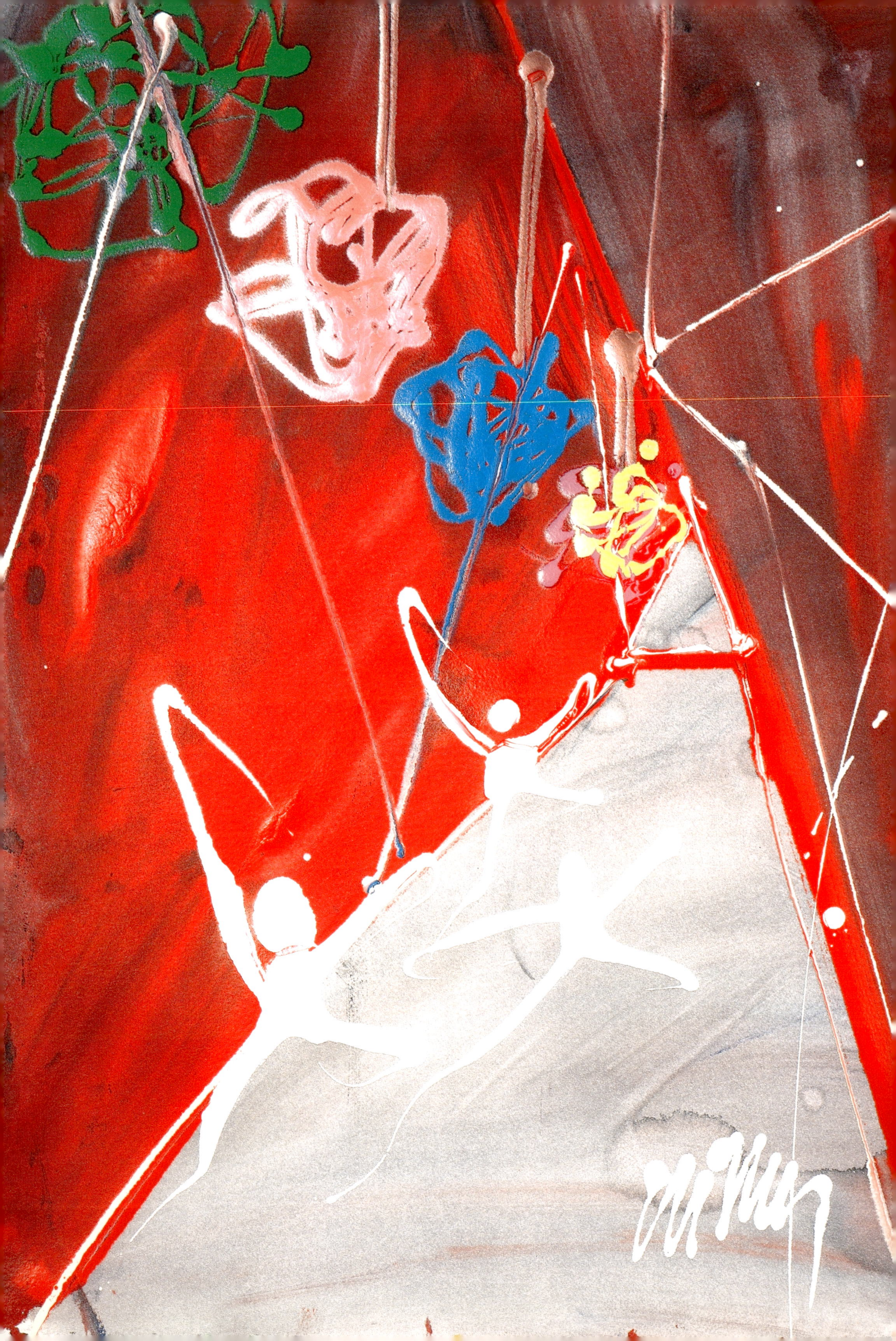

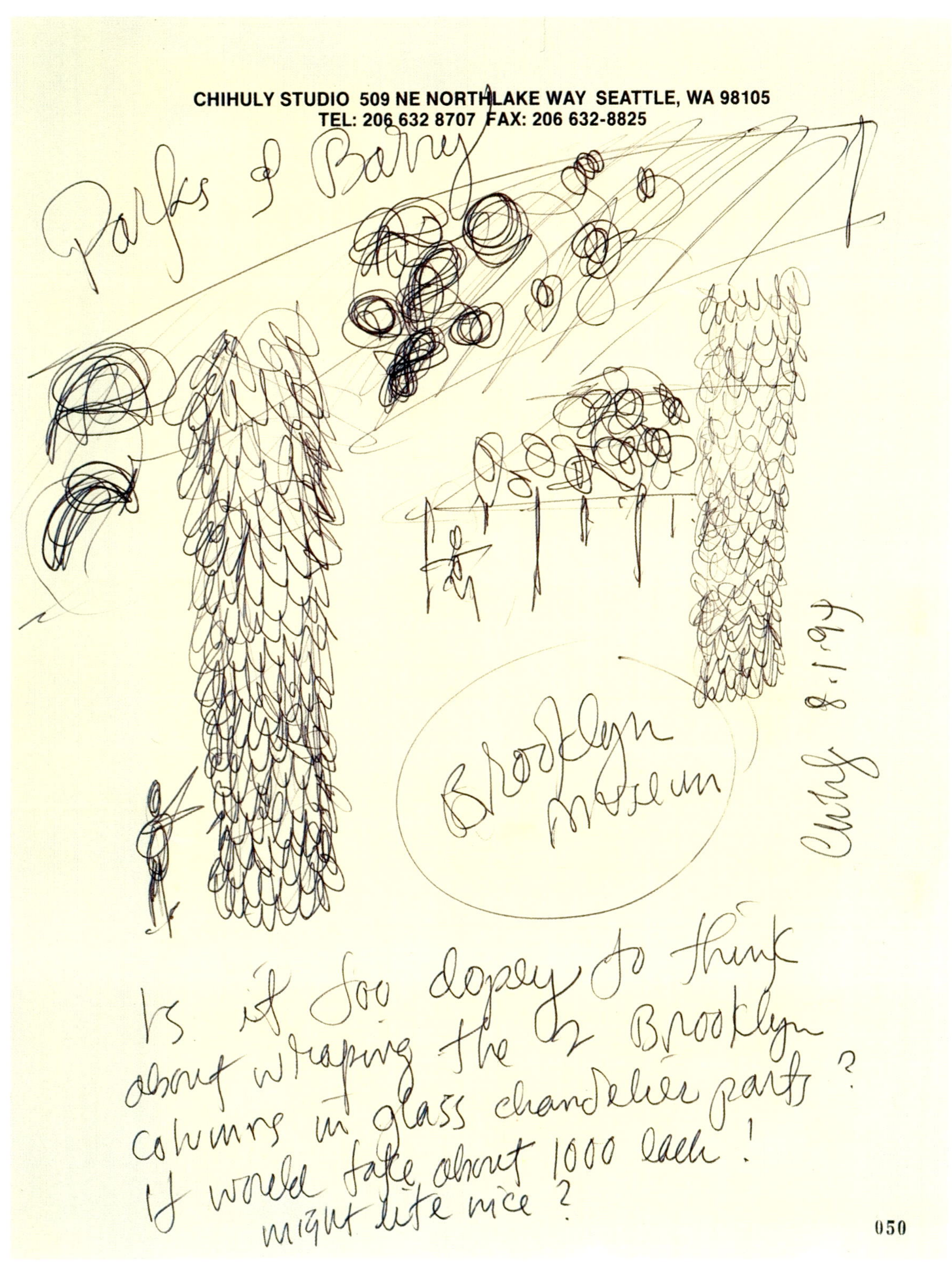

布魯克萊博物館之裝置素描
8.5 x 11吋
1994
攝影：C. Garoutte

Brooklyn Museum
Installation Sketch
8.5 x 11"
1994
photo: C. Garoutte

塔科馬橋之素描
41 x 29吋
1994
攝影：M. Seidl

Tacoma Bridge Drawing
41 x 29"
1994
photo: M. Seidl

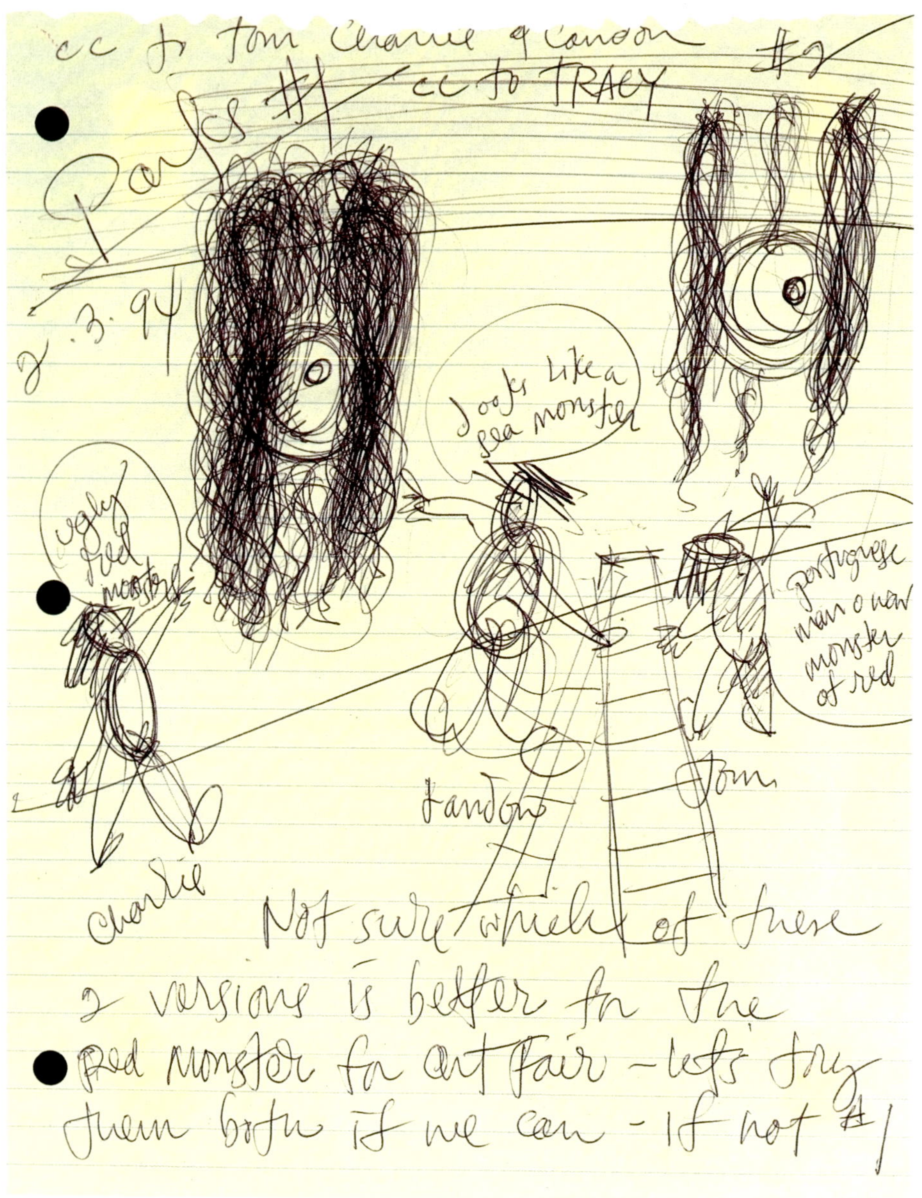

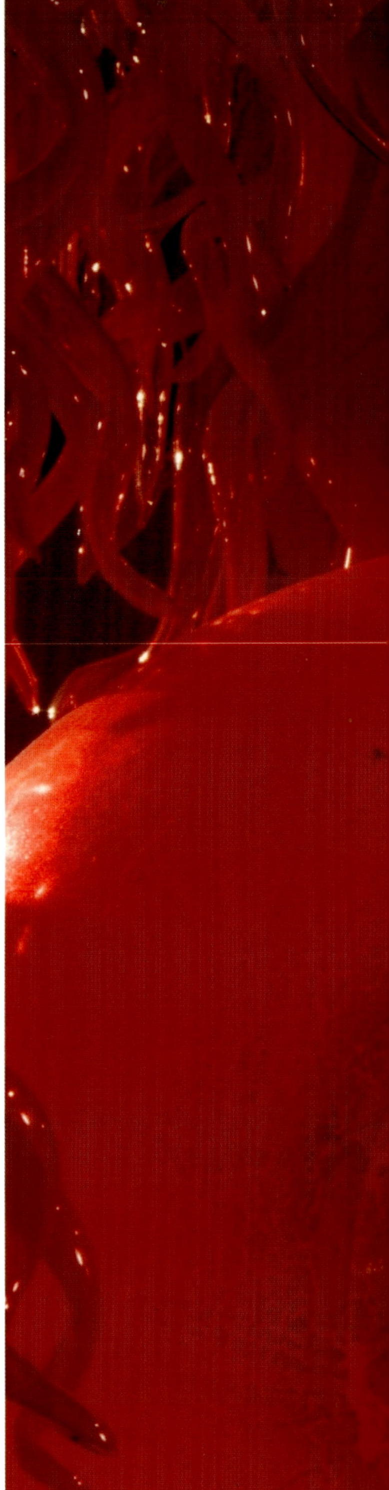

鎘紅色三島浮球吊燈素描
8.5 x 11吋
1994
攝影：M. Seidl

Cadmium Red Niijima Float Chandelier Sketch
8.5 x 11"
1994
photo: M. Seidl

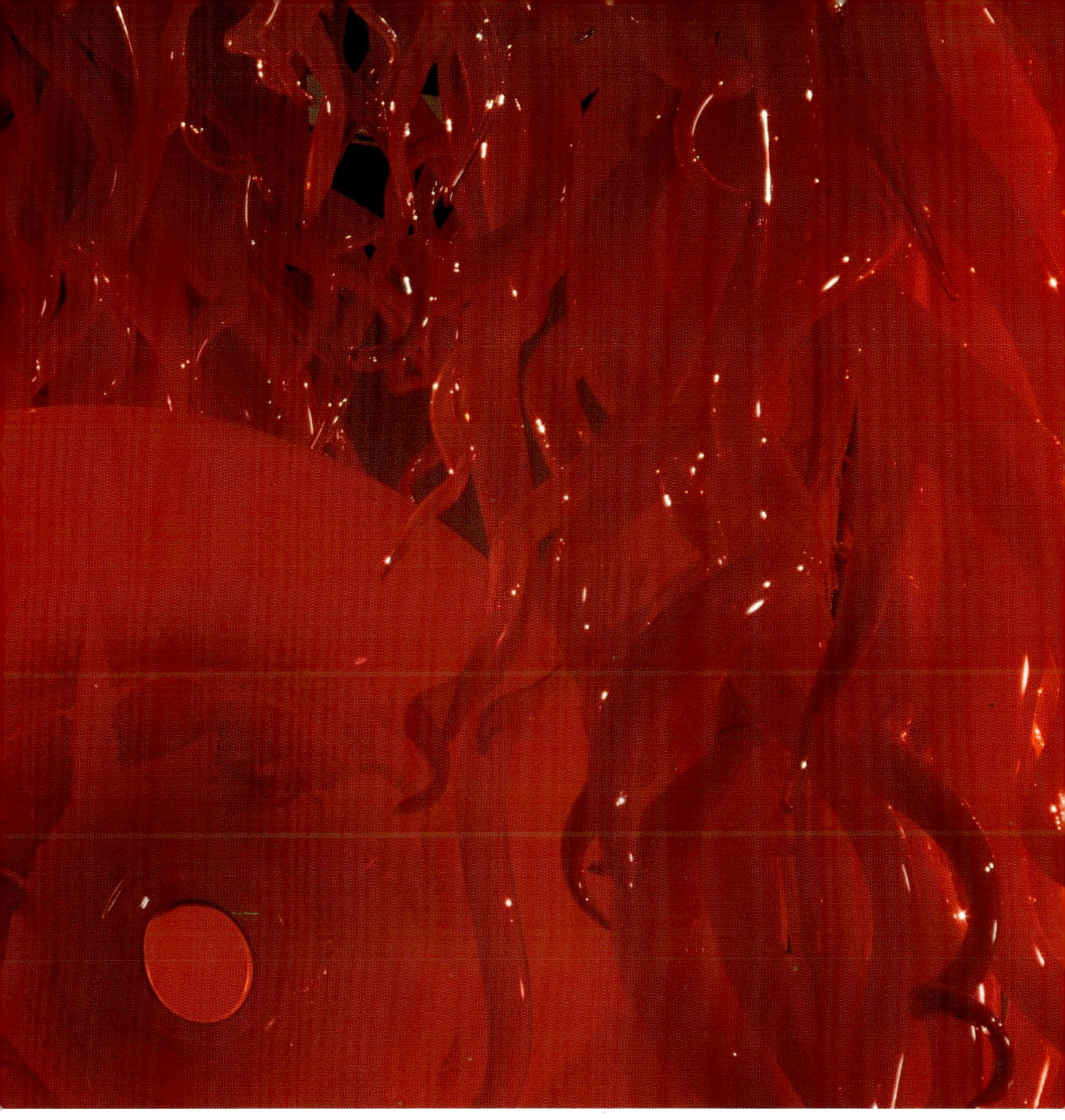

鎘紅色三島浮球吊燈(細部)
72 x 60 x 60吋
西雅圖藝術博覽會
西雅圖, 1994
攝影: C. Garoutte

Cadmium Red Niijima Float Chandelier (detail)
72 x 60 x 60"
Art/fair Seattle
Seattle, 1994
photo: C. Garoutte

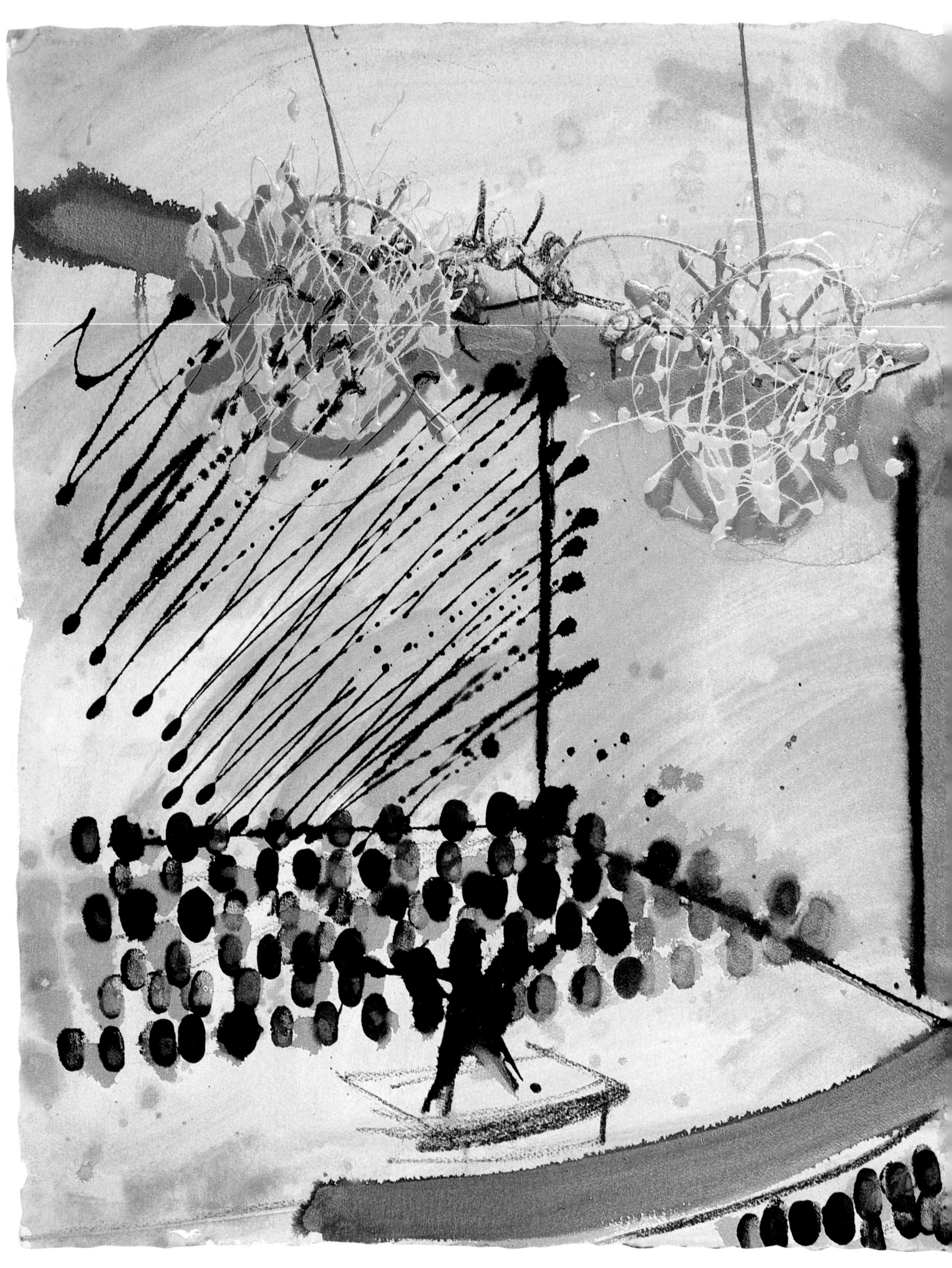

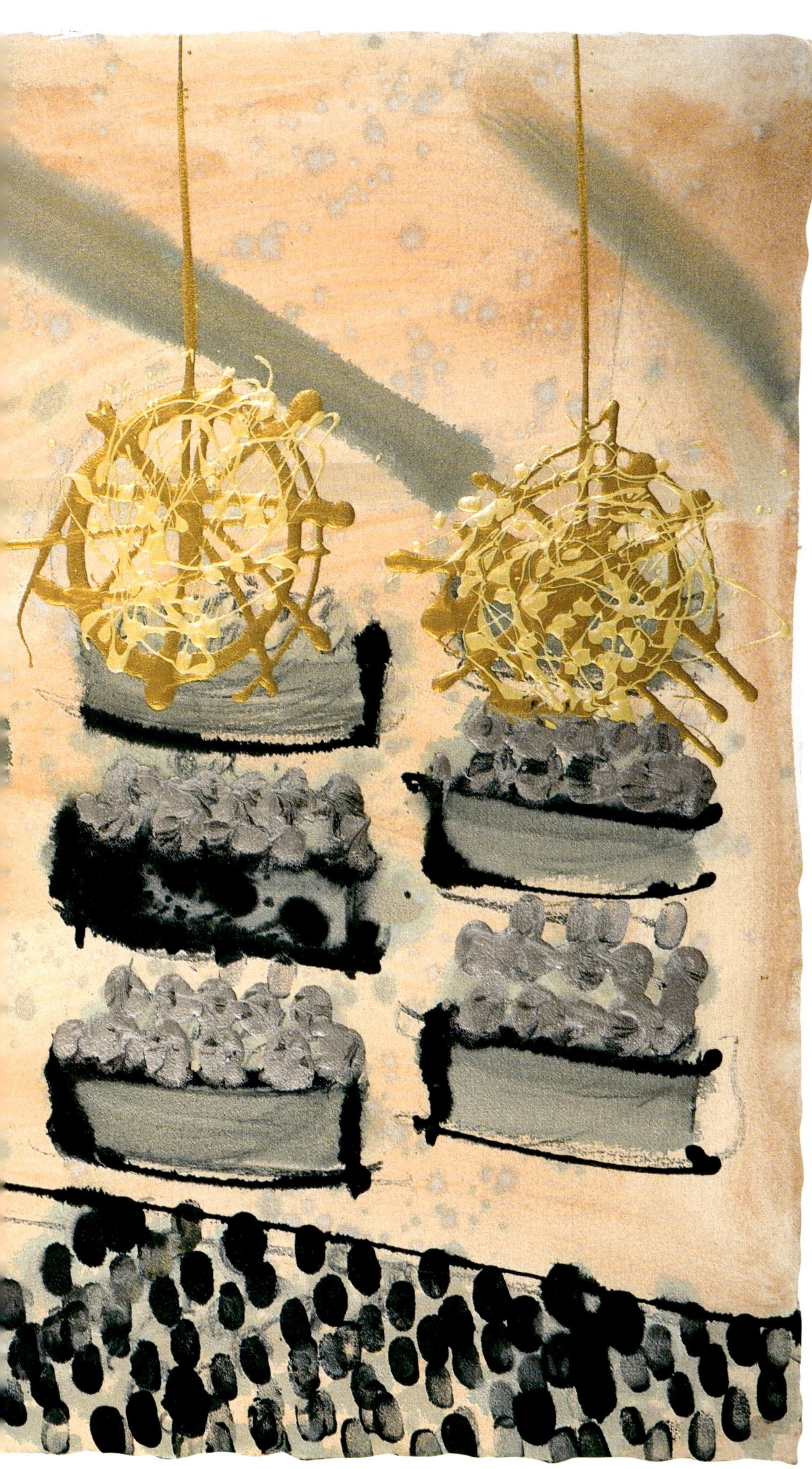

貝那瑞雅音樂廳之吊燈素描
29 x 41吋
1993
攝影：C. Garoutte

Benaroya Concert Hall Chandelier Drawing
29 x 41"
1993
photo: C. Garoutte

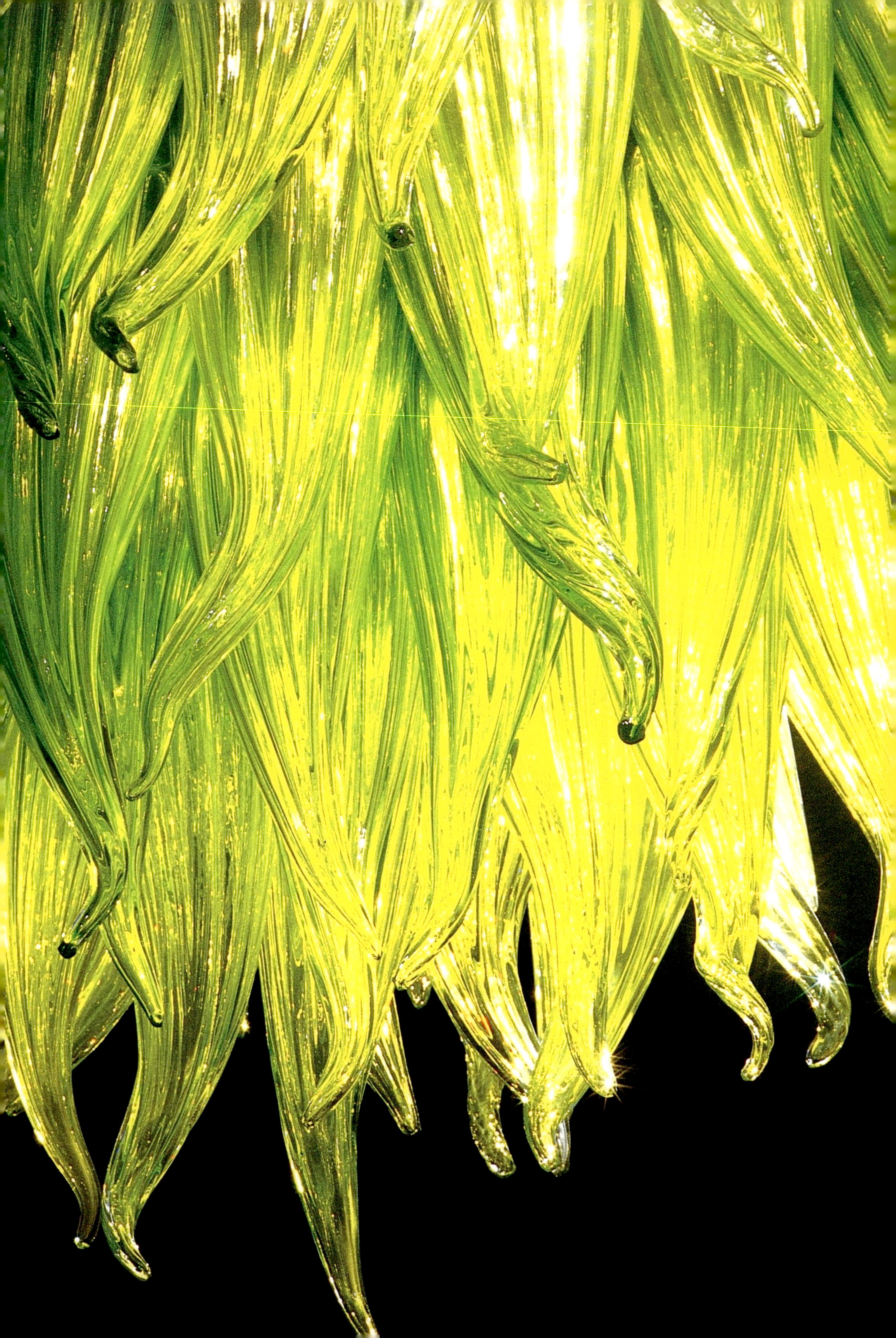

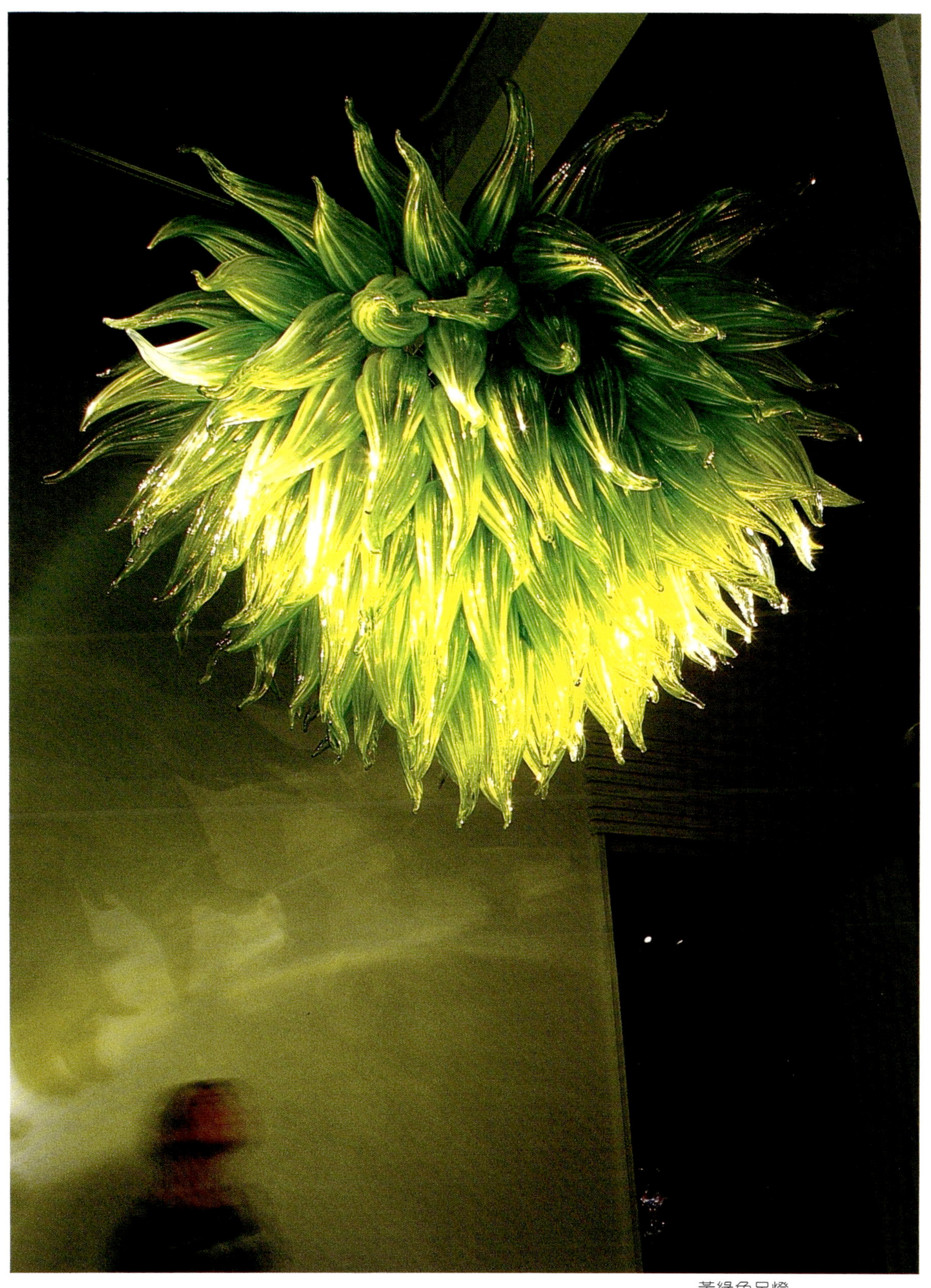

黃綠色吊燈
38 x 64 x 64吋
弗斯特.懷特陳列館
西雅圖, 1993
攝影: R. Johnson

Chartreuse Chandelier
38 x 64 x 64"
Foster White Gallery
Seattle, 1993
photo: R. Johnson

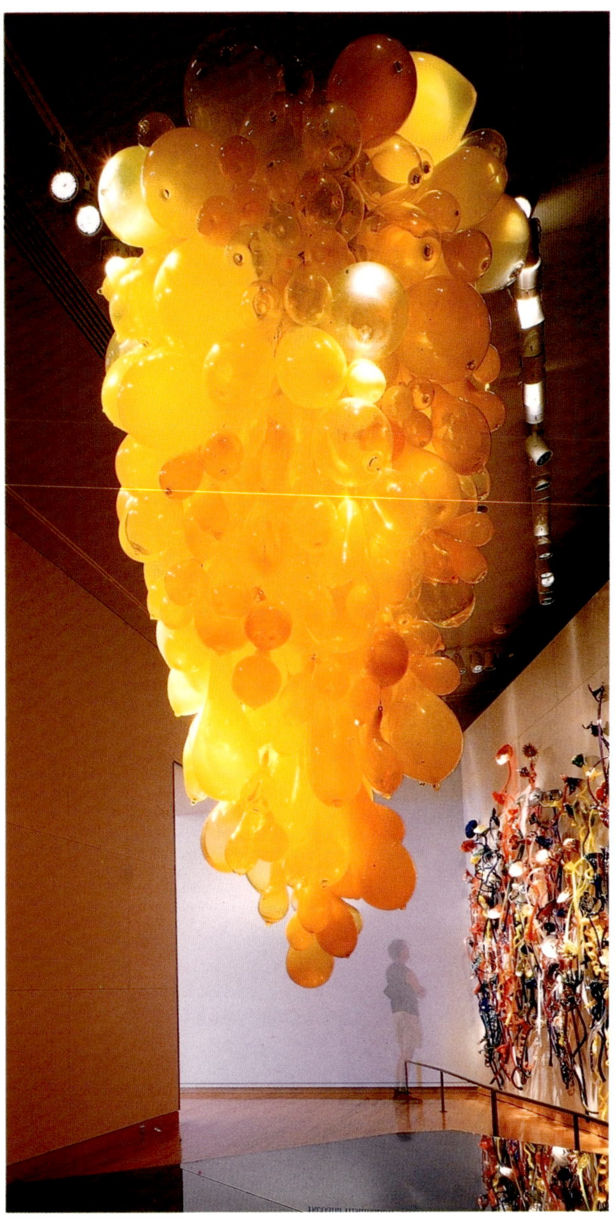

西雅圖藝術館之吊燈
96 x 48 x 48吋
"德爾.屈胡利:裝置藝術
1964-1992"
西雅圖藝術館
西雅圖, 1992
攝影: E. Calderon

Seattle Art Museum Chandelier
96 x 48 x 48"
"Dale Chihuly: Installations 1964-1992"
Seattle Art Museum
Seattle, 1992
photo: E. Calderon

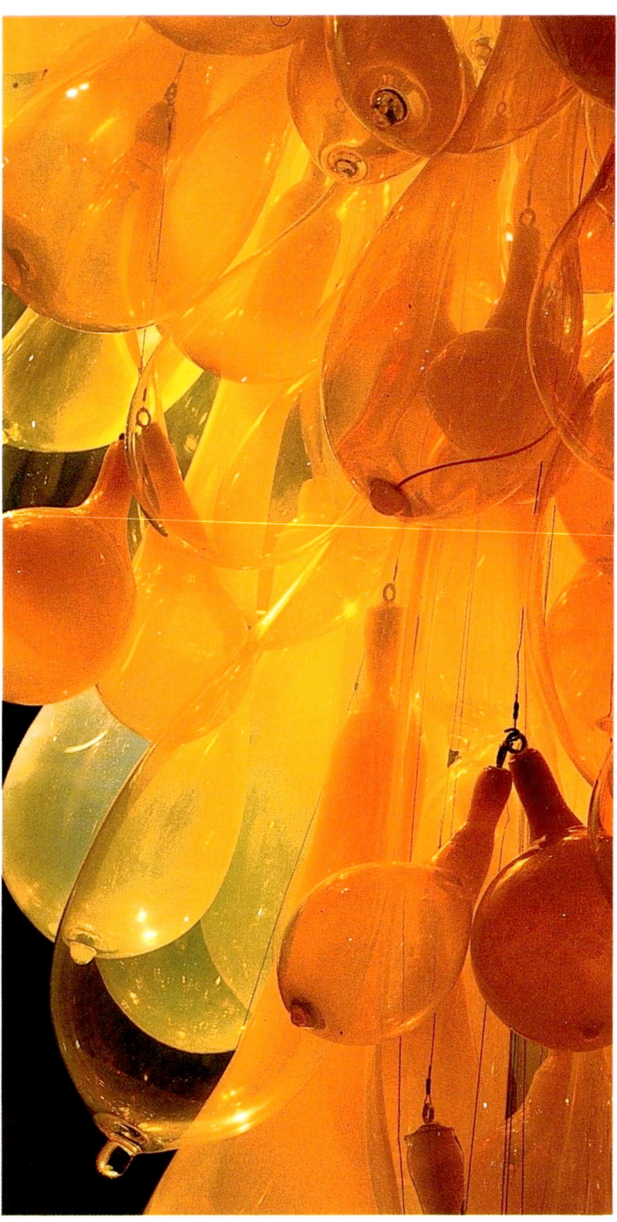

吊燈細部
"德爾.屈胡利:裝置藝術
1964-1992"
當代藝術中心
辛辛那提, 1992
攝影: R. Johnson

Chandelier detail
"Dale Chihuly: Installations 1964-1992"
The Contemporary Arts Center
Cincinnati, 1992
photo: R. Johnson

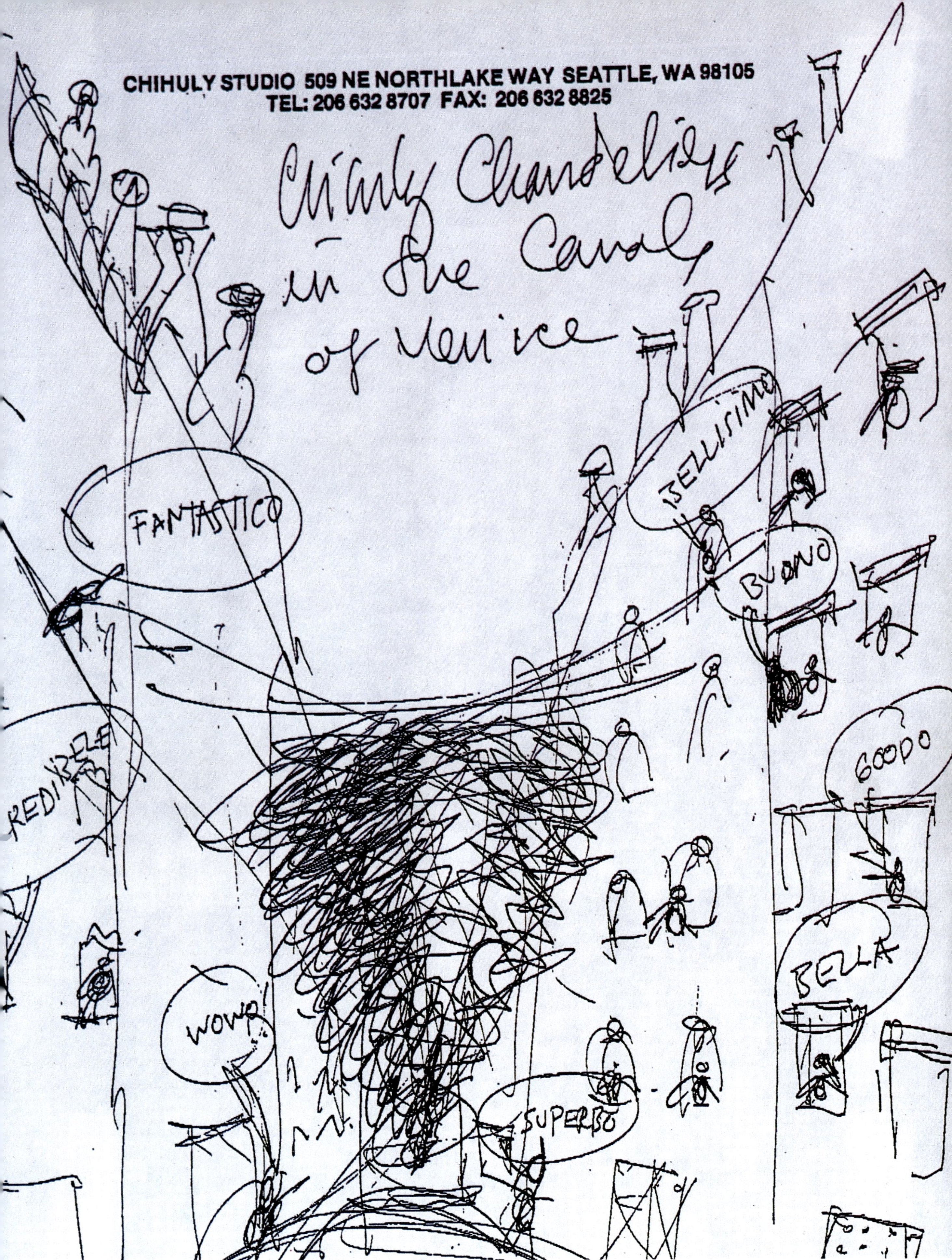

威尼斯吊燈素描
8.5 x 11吋
1994
攝影：C. Garoutte

Venice Chandelier Sketch
8.5 x 11"
1994
photo: C. Garoutte

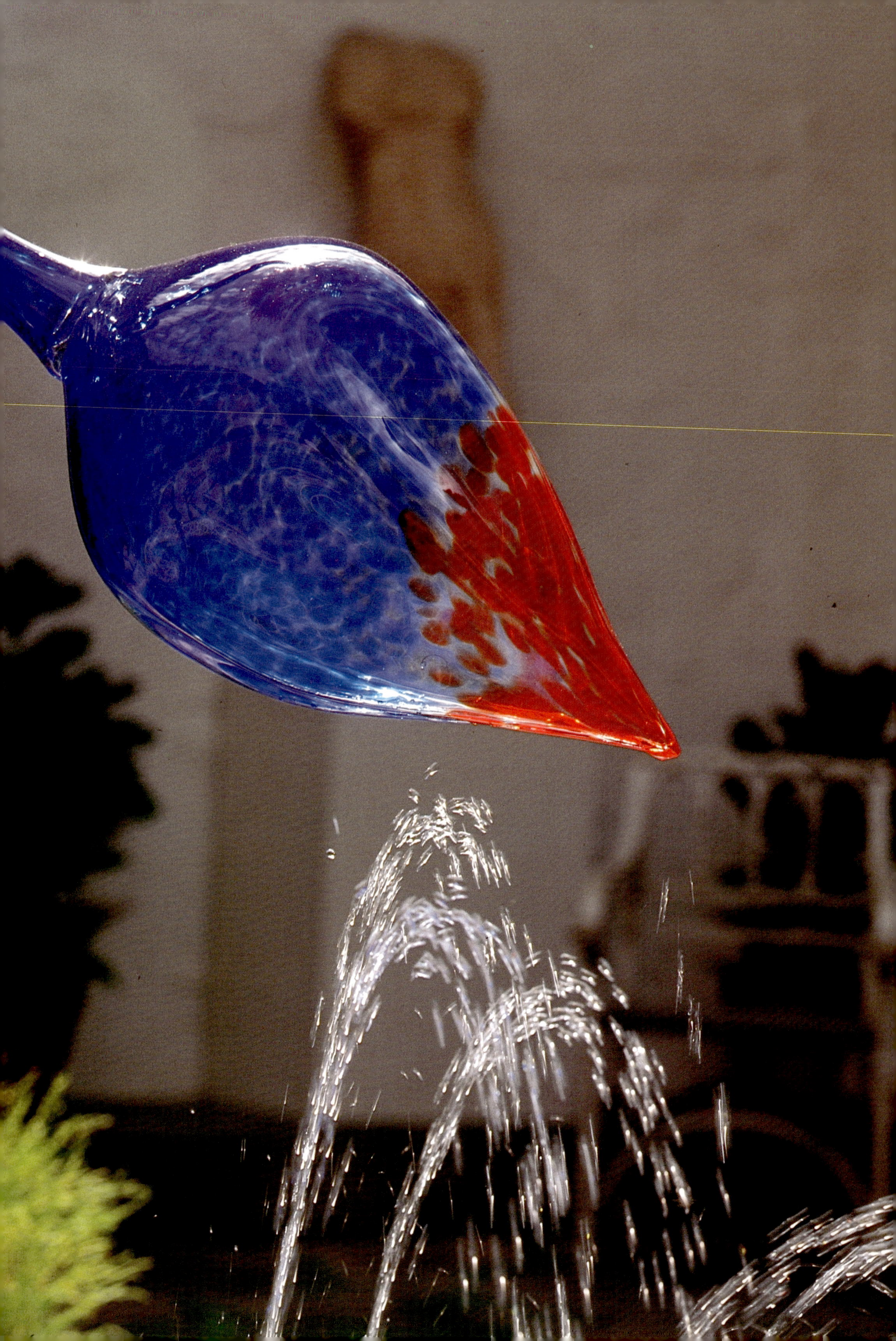

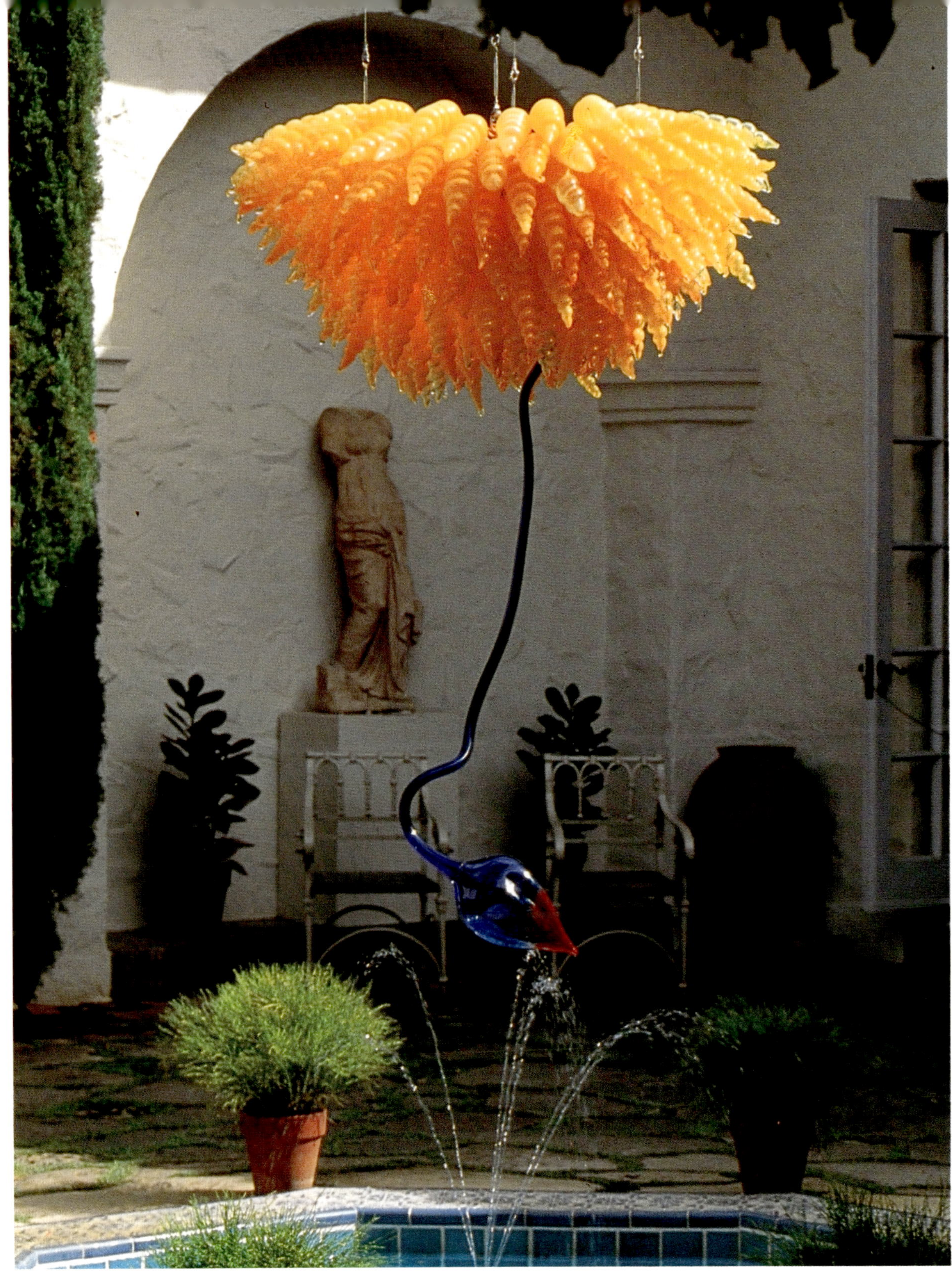

地中海庭院內有鈷藍色花梗的檸檬黃吊燈
84 x 36 x 36吋
"檀香山庭院展"
檀香山藝術學院
檀杳山, 1992
攝影: R. Johnson

Lemon Yellow Chandelier with Cobalt Blue Stem
in the Mediterranean Court
84 x 36 x 36"
"Chihuly Courtyards"
Honolulu Academy of Arts
Honolulu, 1992
photo: R. Johnson

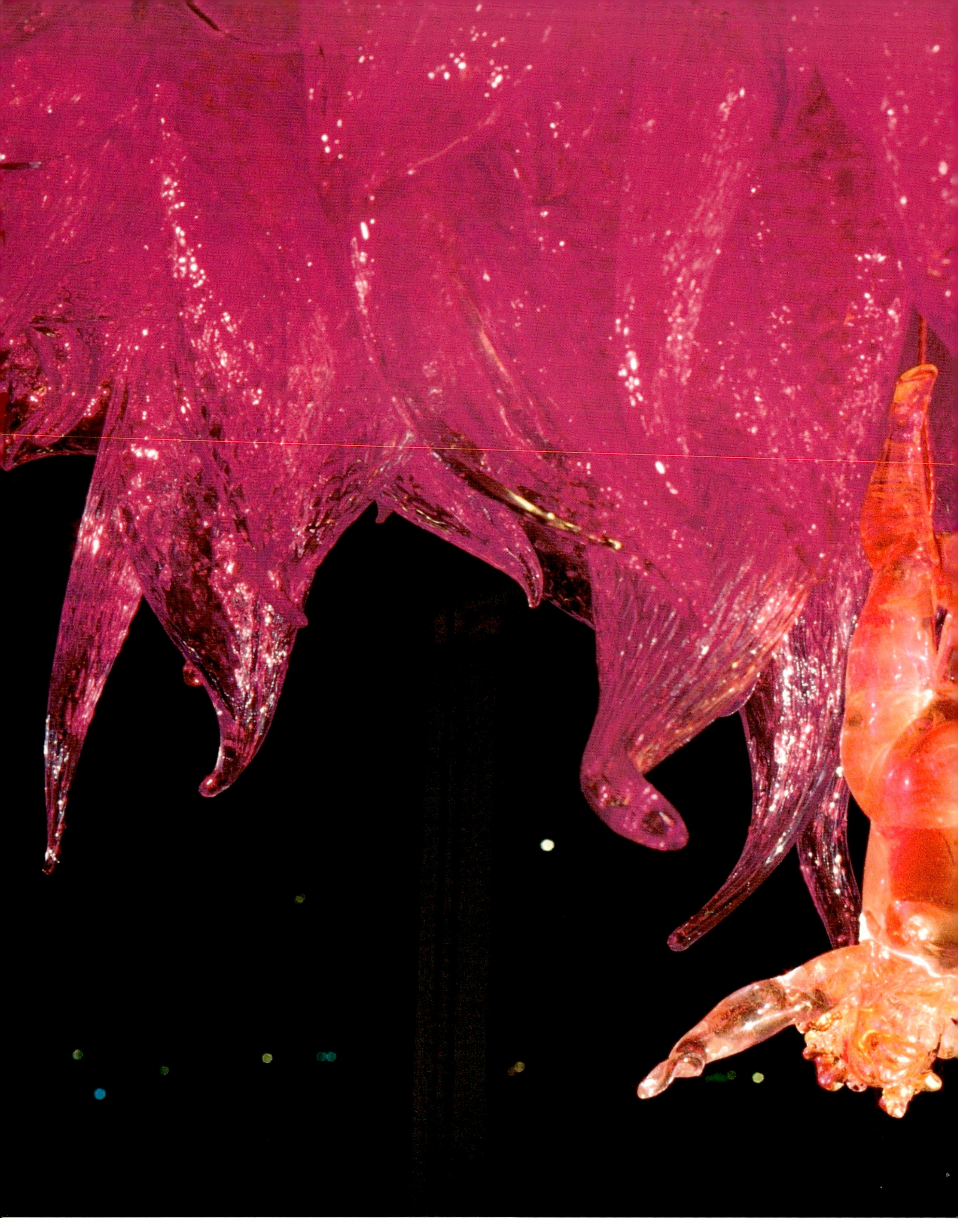

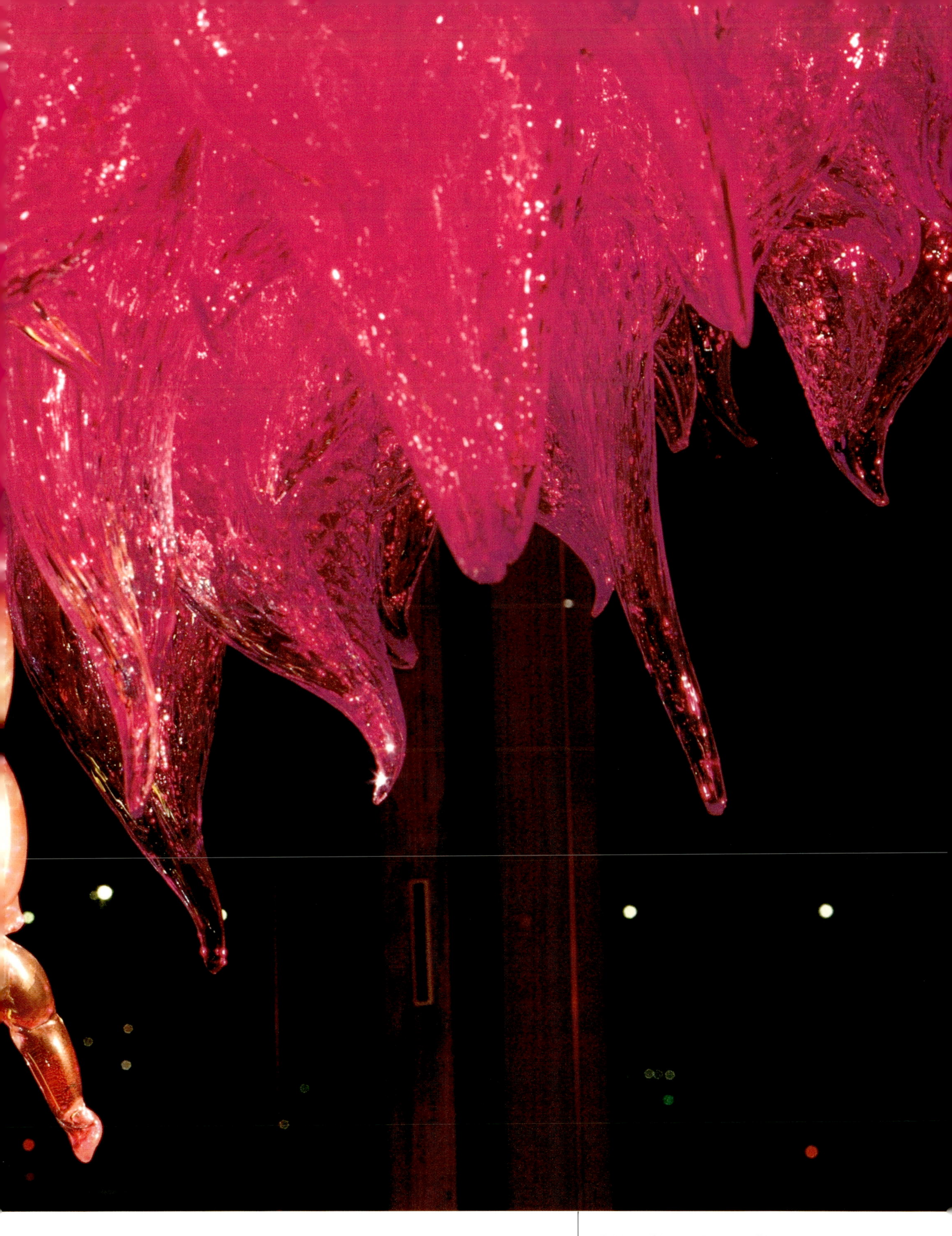

有金色小天使的鉺紅色吊燈(細部)
34 x 54 x 54吋
船屋
西雅圖, 1993
攝影: E. Calderon

Erbium Chandelier with Gilded Putti (detail)
34 x 54 x 54"
The Boathouse
Seattle, 1993
photo: E. Calderon

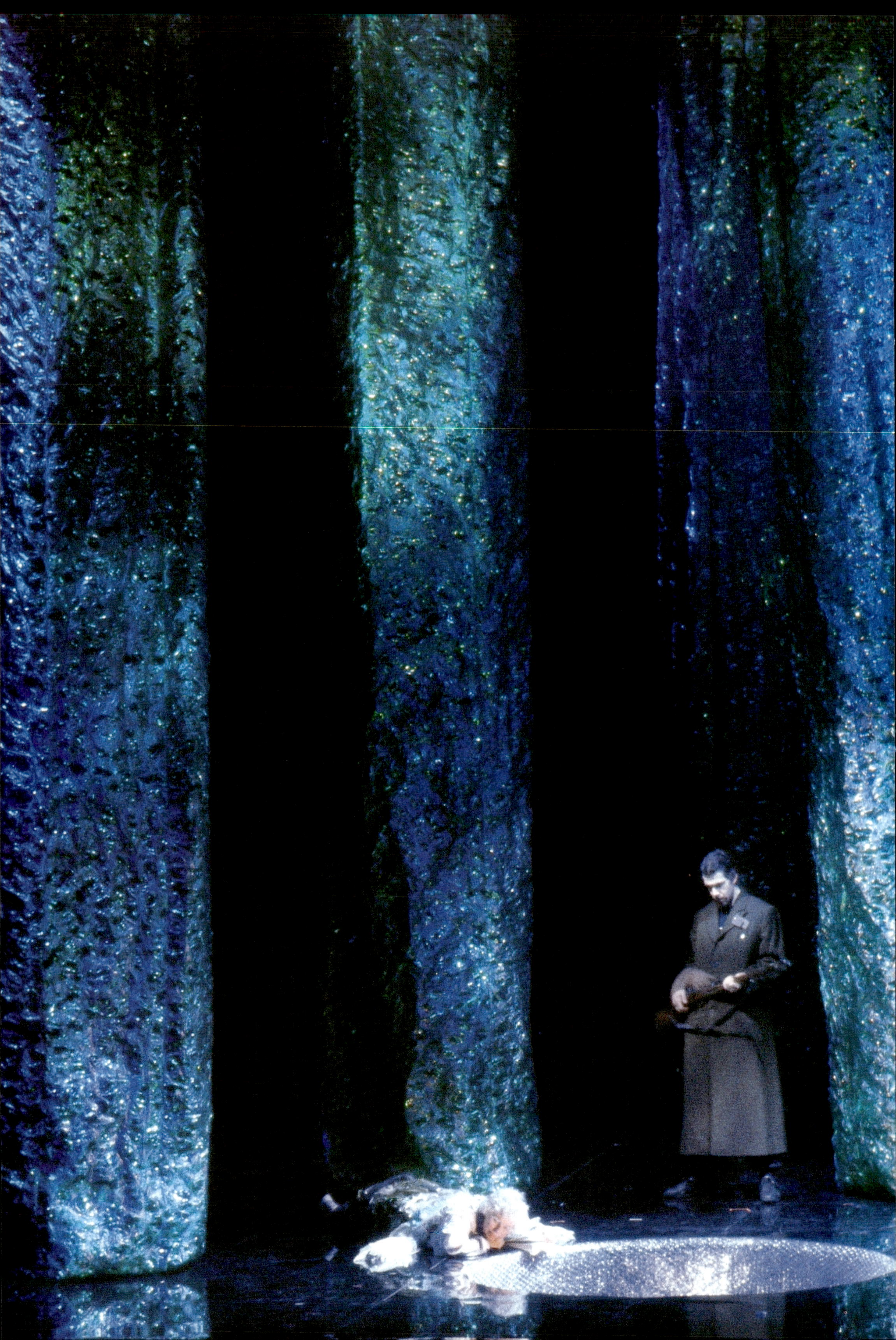

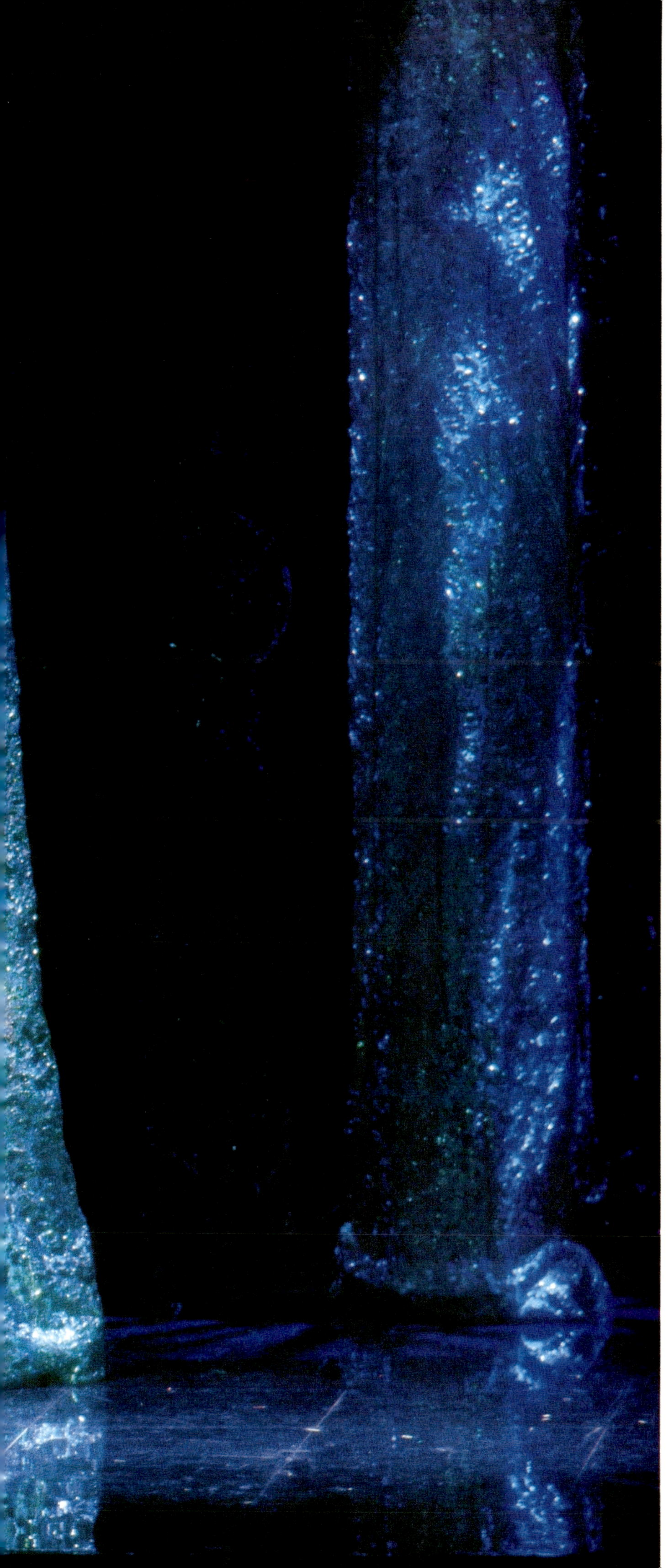

set design

the seattle opera: pelléas et mélisande 1993

西雅圖歌劇院佈景設計：

貝蕾亞絲與梅力松1993年

森林，第一場第一幕
攝影：E. Calderon

Act 1, Scene 1
The Forest
photo: E. Calderon

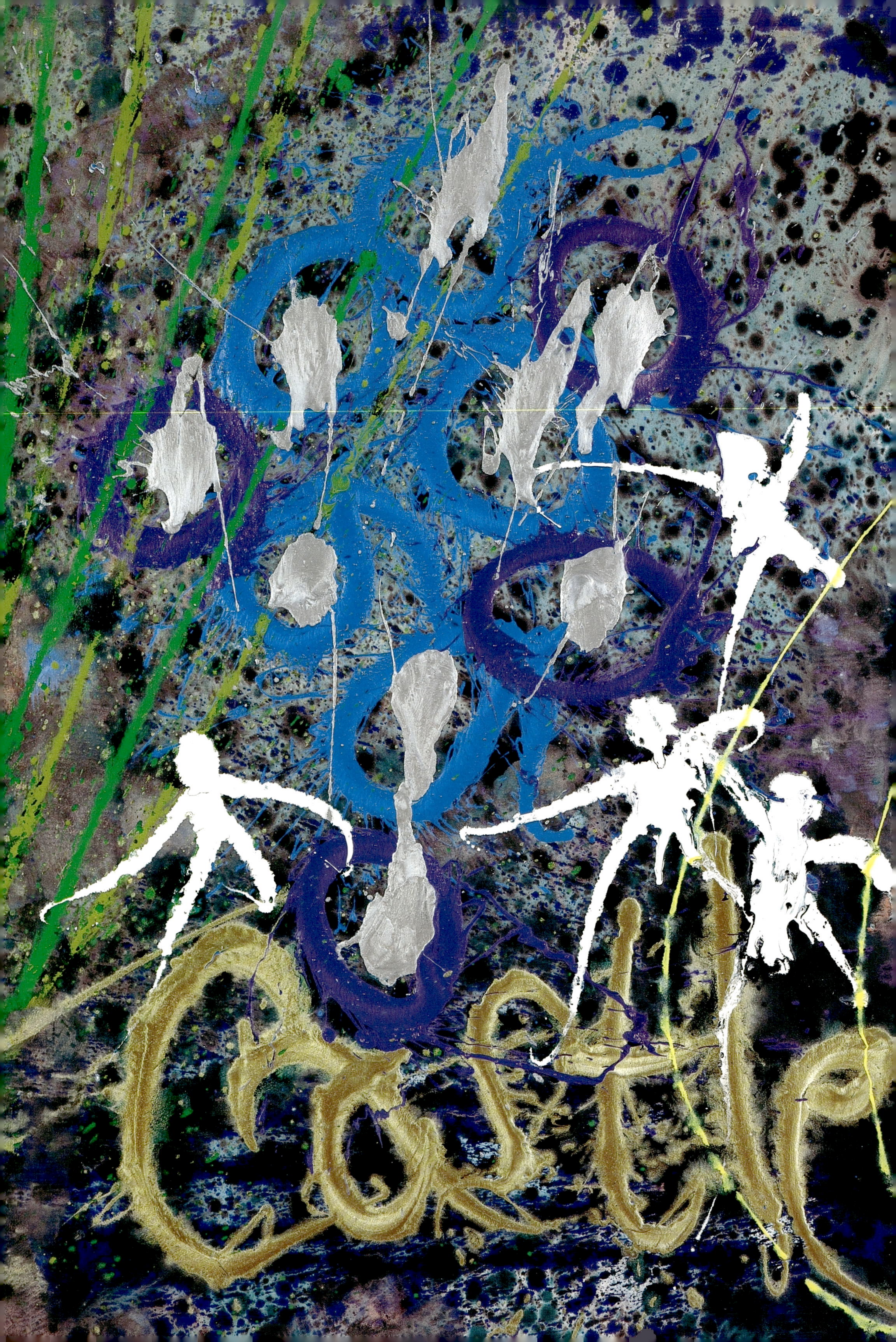
Castle

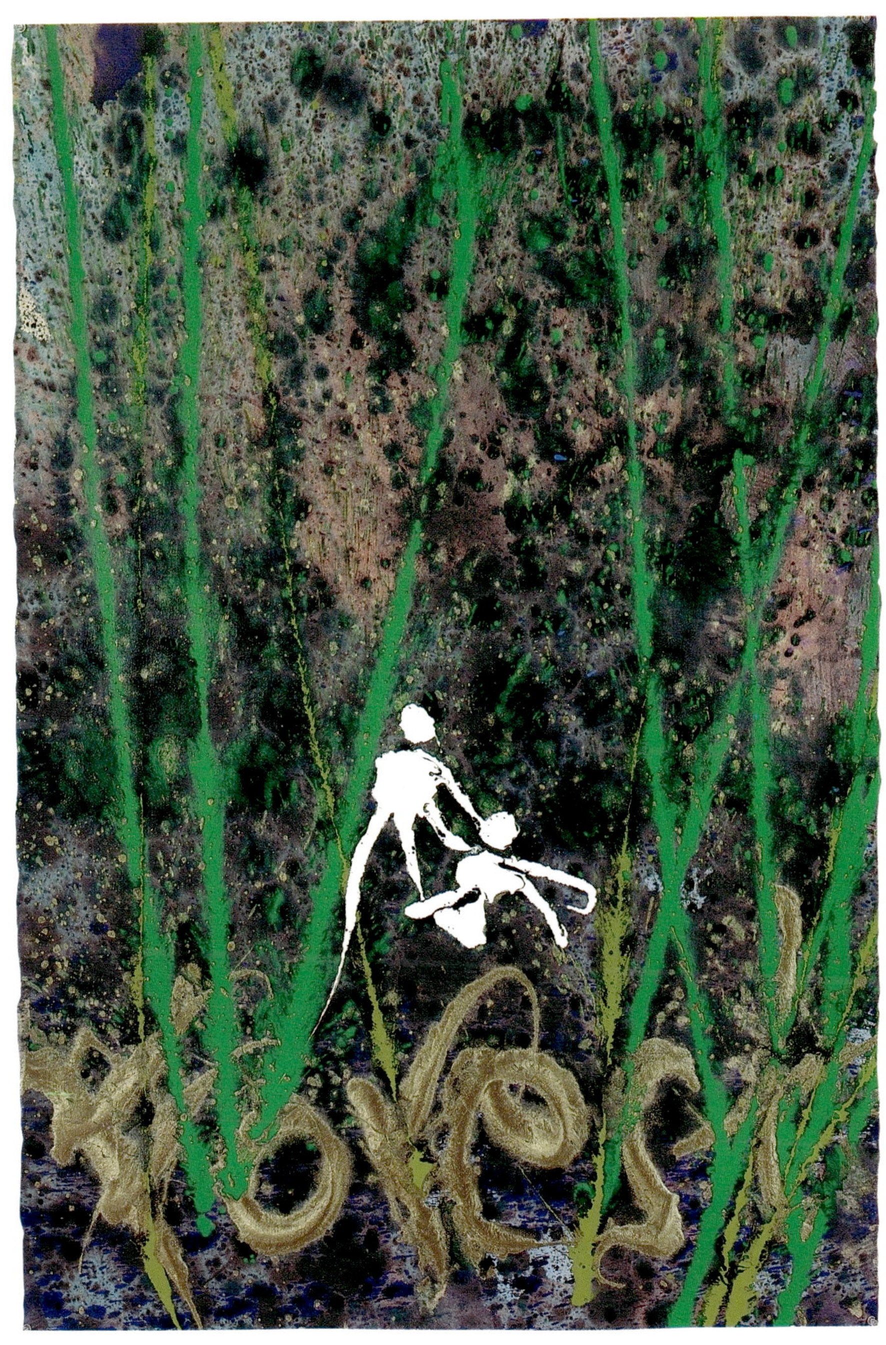

"森林"之素描
60 x 40吋
攝影：M. Seidl

"The Forest" Drawing
acrylic on paper
60 x 40"
photo: M. Seidl

"城堡 "之素描
60 x 40吋
攝影：M. Seidl

"The Castle" Drawing
acrylic on paper
60 x 40"
photo: M. Seidl

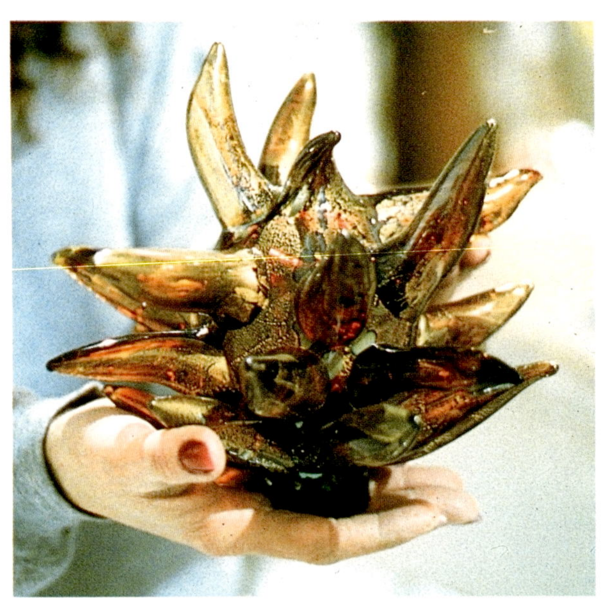

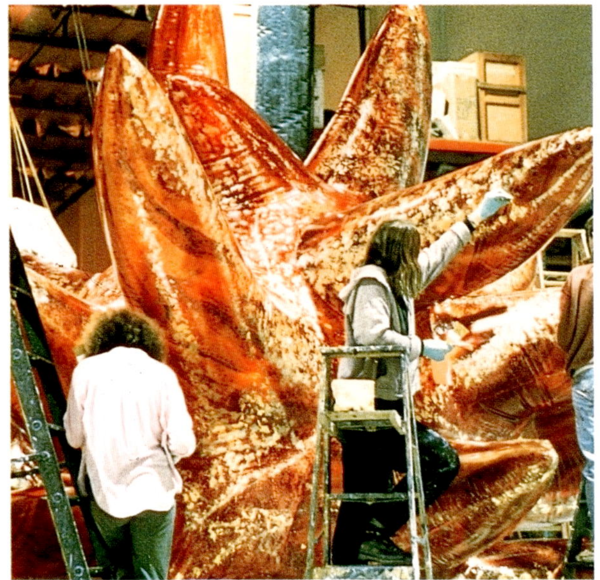

模型與結構
攝影：M. Jervis

Set model and construction
photos: M. Jervis

花園．第三場第一幕
攝影：R. Johnson

Act 4, Scene 1
Golaud's Room
photo: R. Johnson

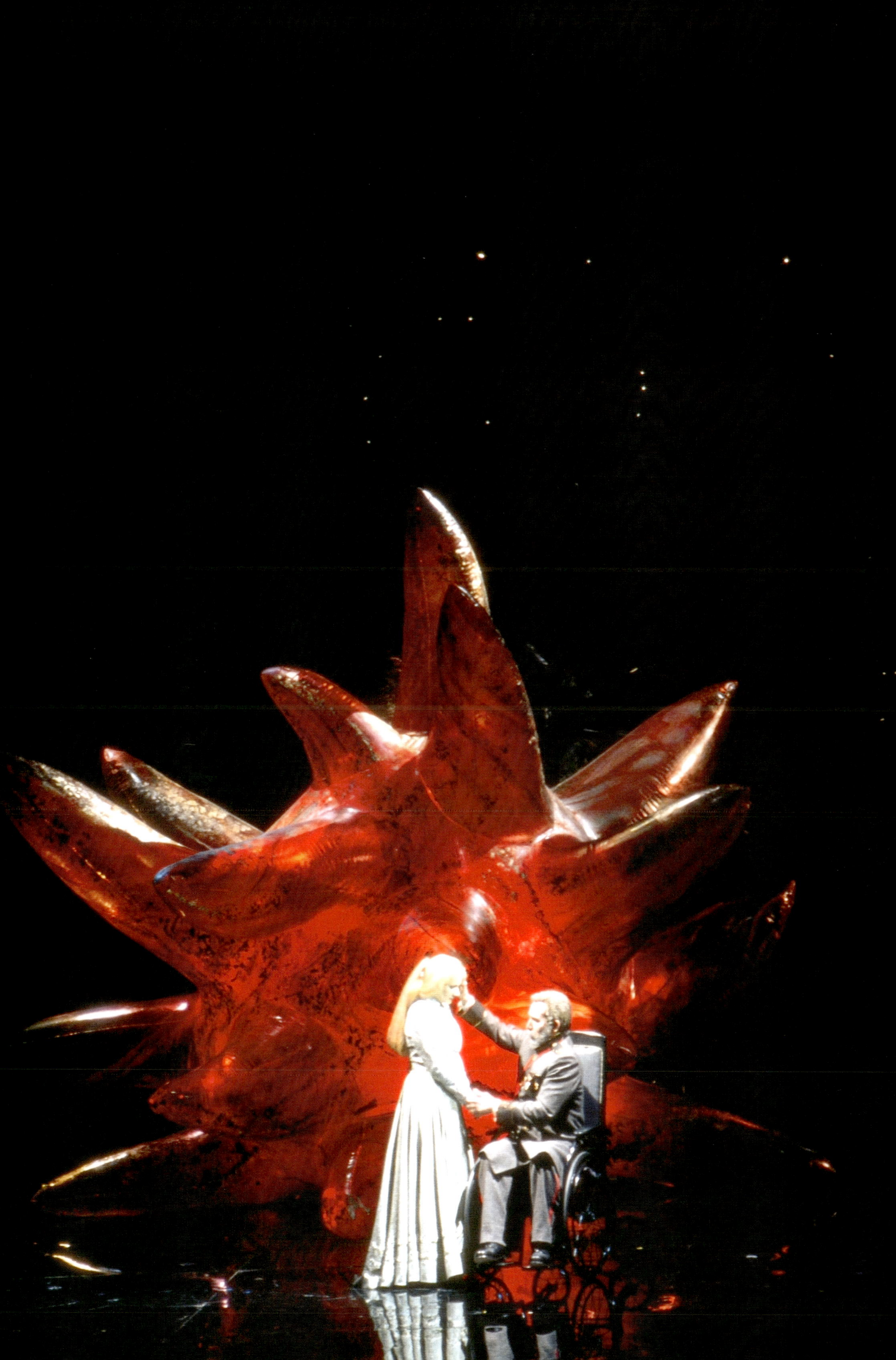

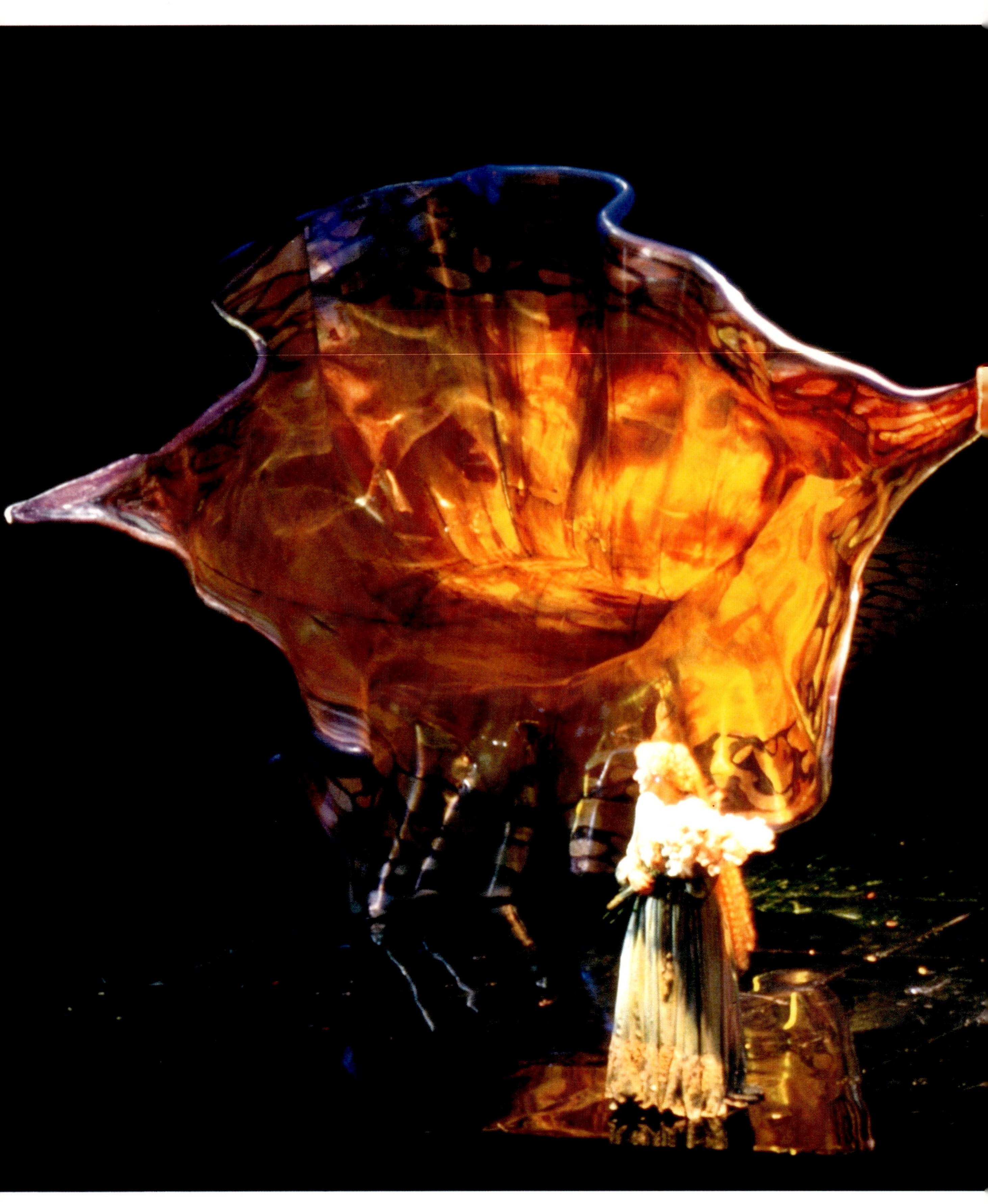

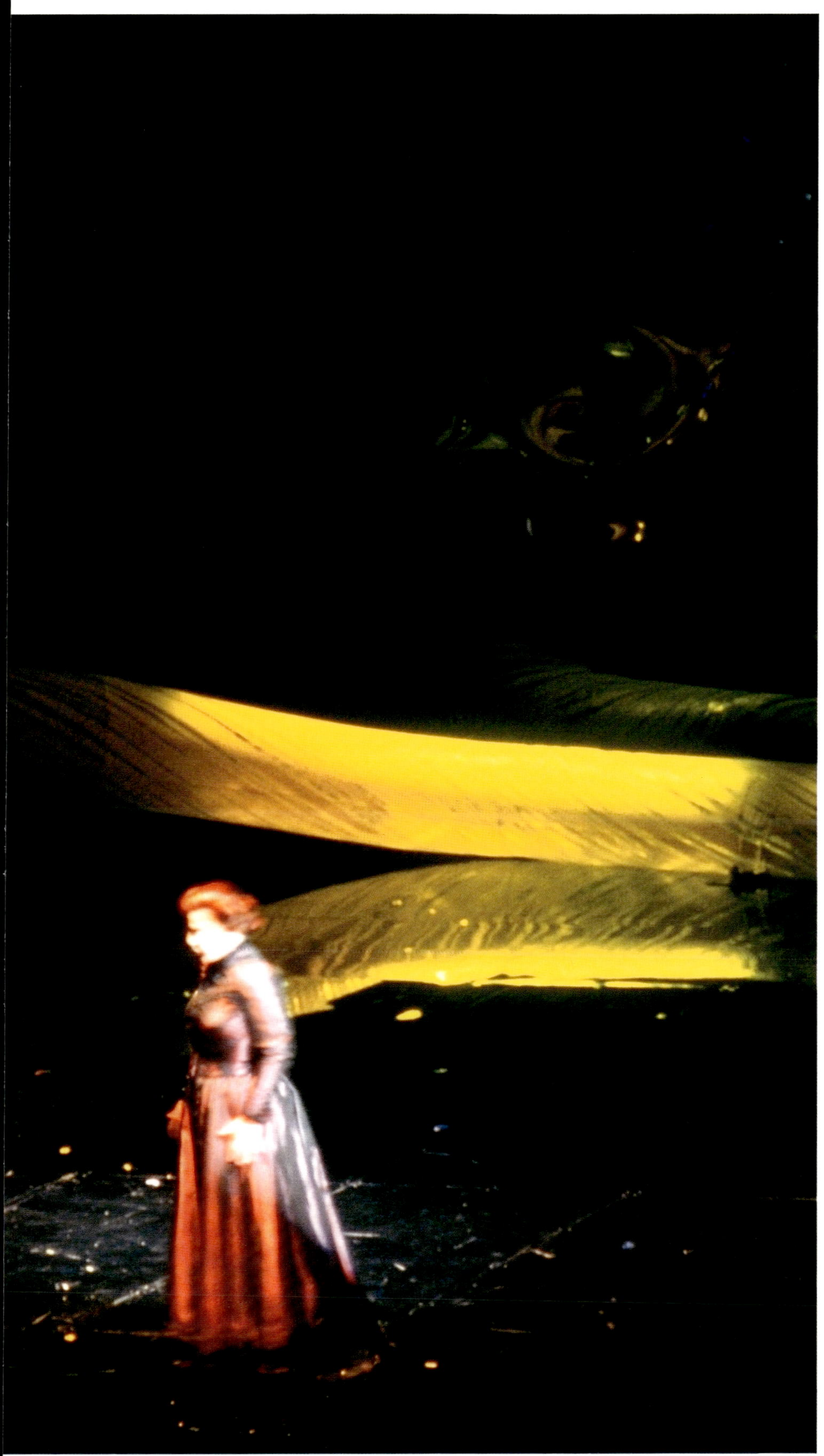

花園，第三場第一幕
攝影：R. Johnson

Act 1, Scene 3
The Garden
photo: R. Johnson

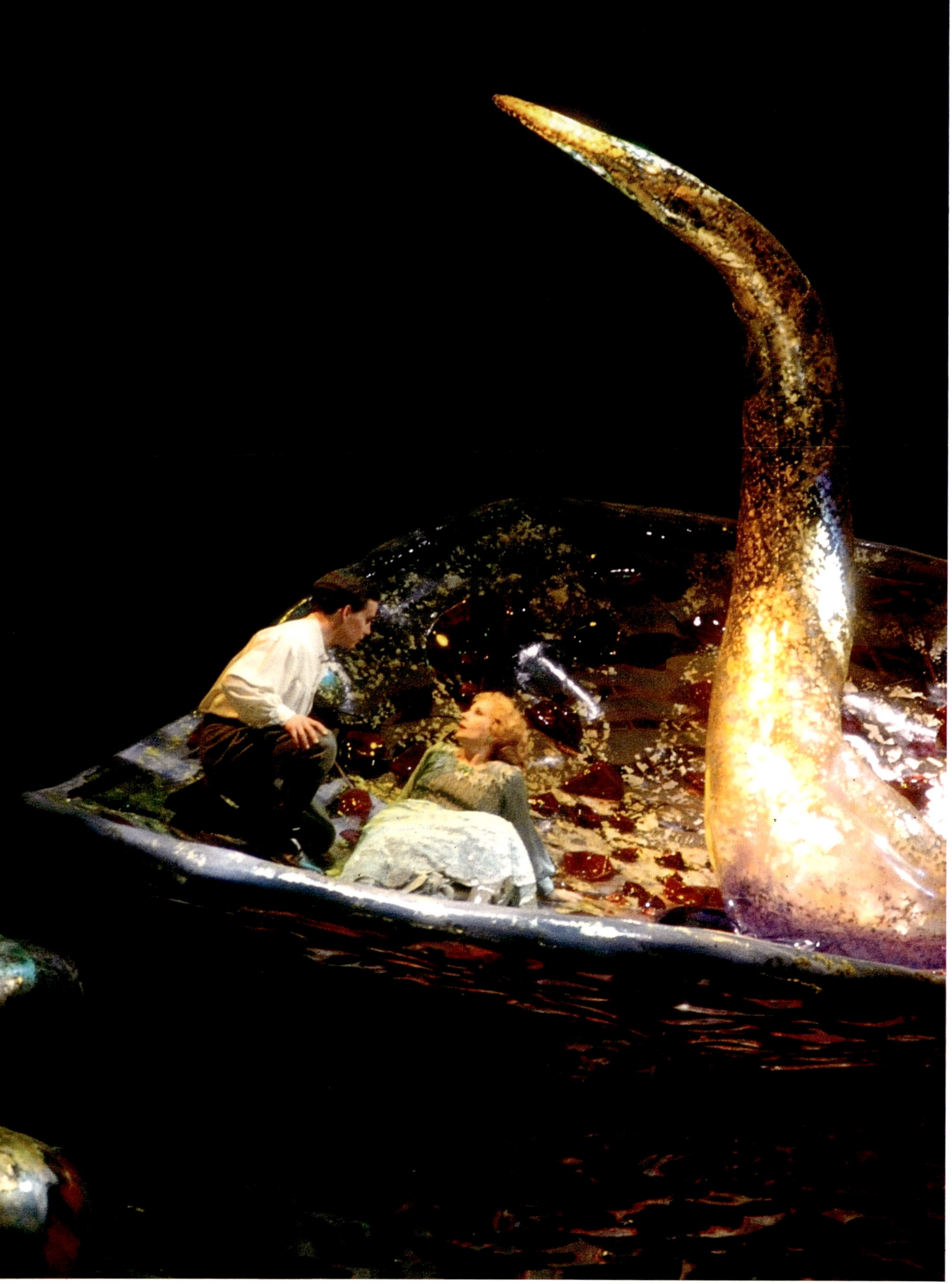

盲人之泉，第二場第二幕
攝影：R. Johnson

Act 2, Scene 2
Blindman's Well
photo: R. Johnson

歌劇素描
船屋
1992
攝影：C. Garoutte

Opera Drawings
The Boathouse
1992
photo: C. Garoutte

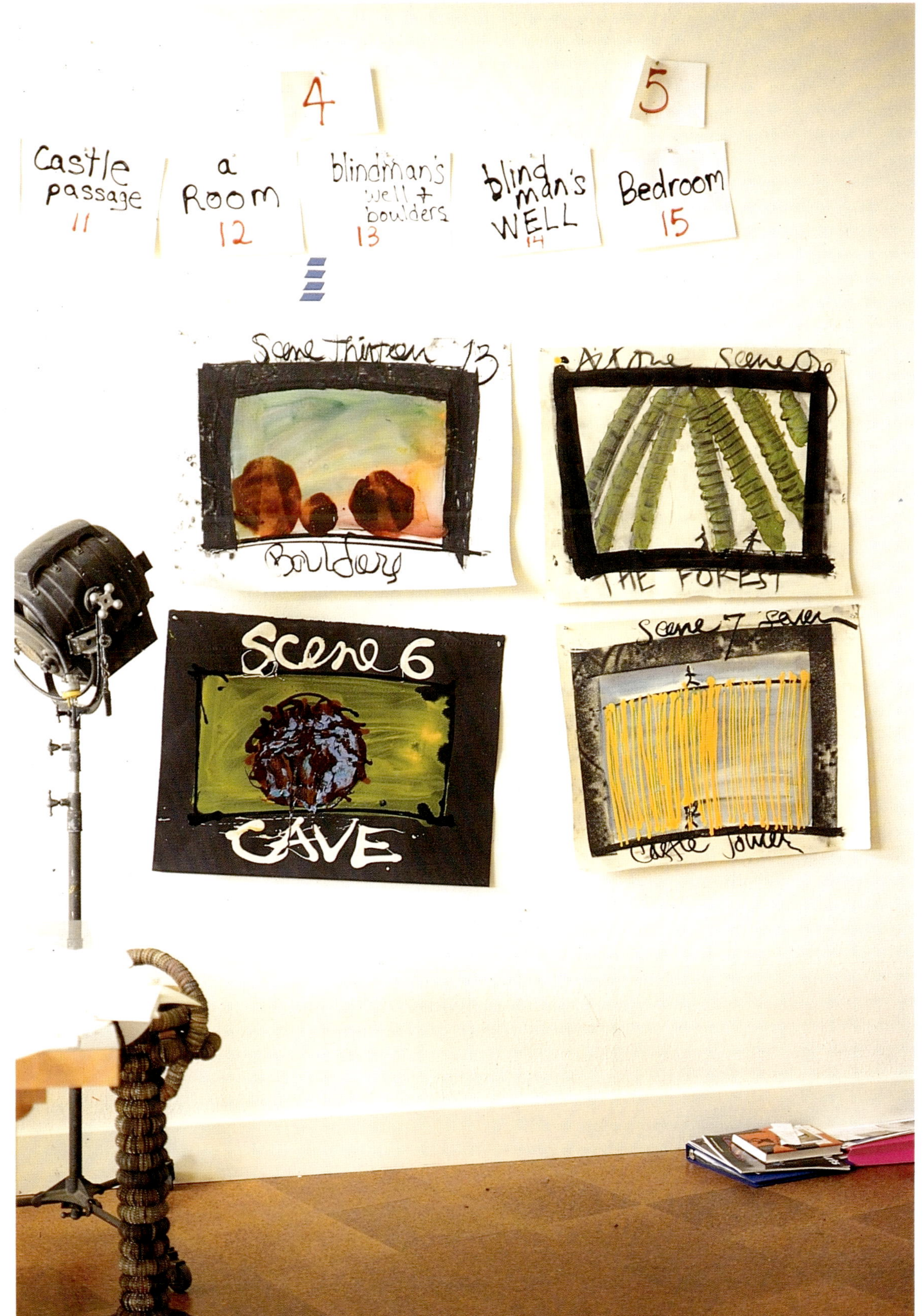

chihuly at union station

tacoma, washington 1994-1999

屈胡利在華盛頓州塔科馬聯合車站

1994 - 1999年

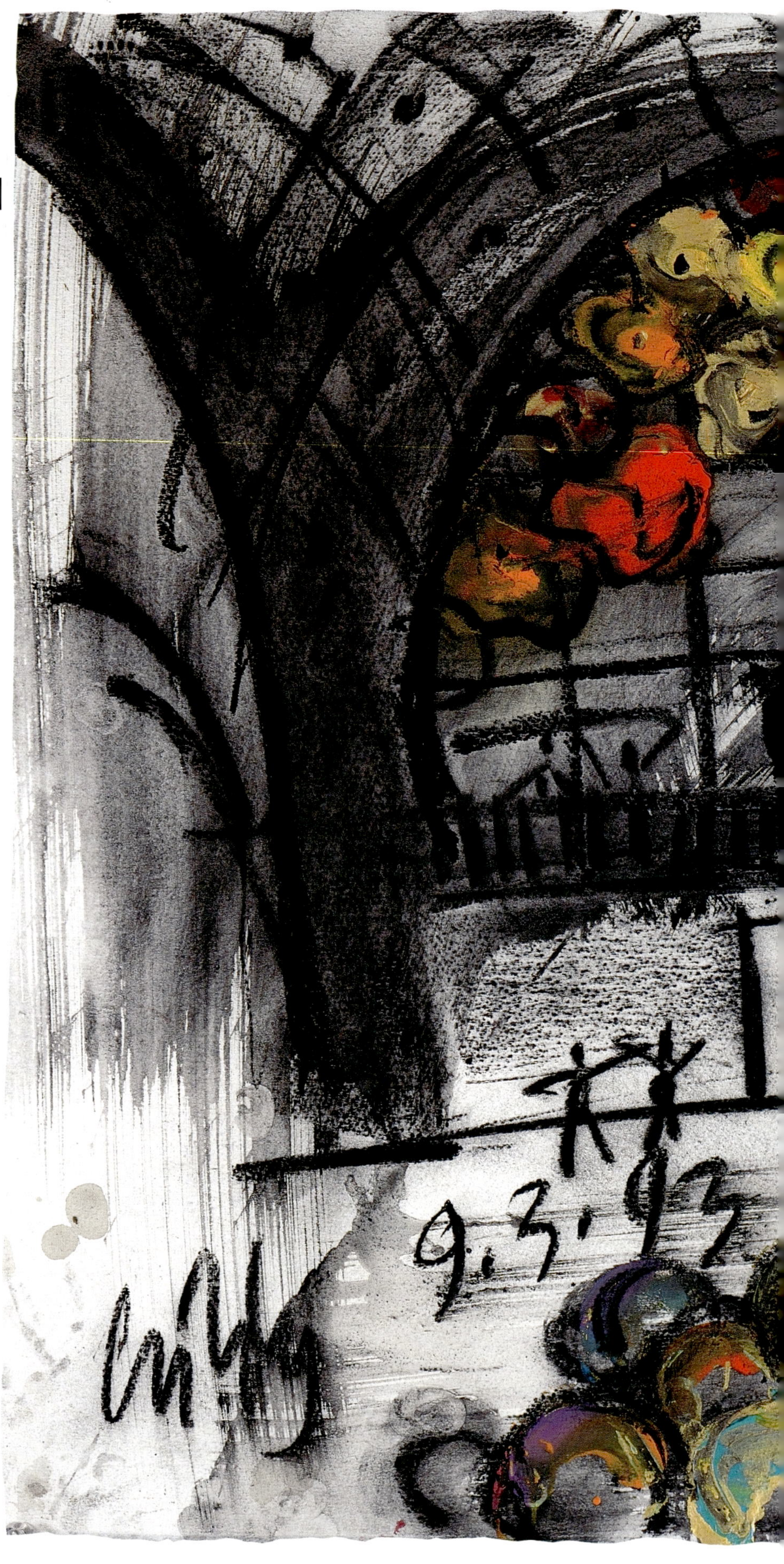

聯合車站素描
22 x 30吋
攝影: C. Garoutte

Union Station Drawing
22 x 30"
photo: C. Garoutte

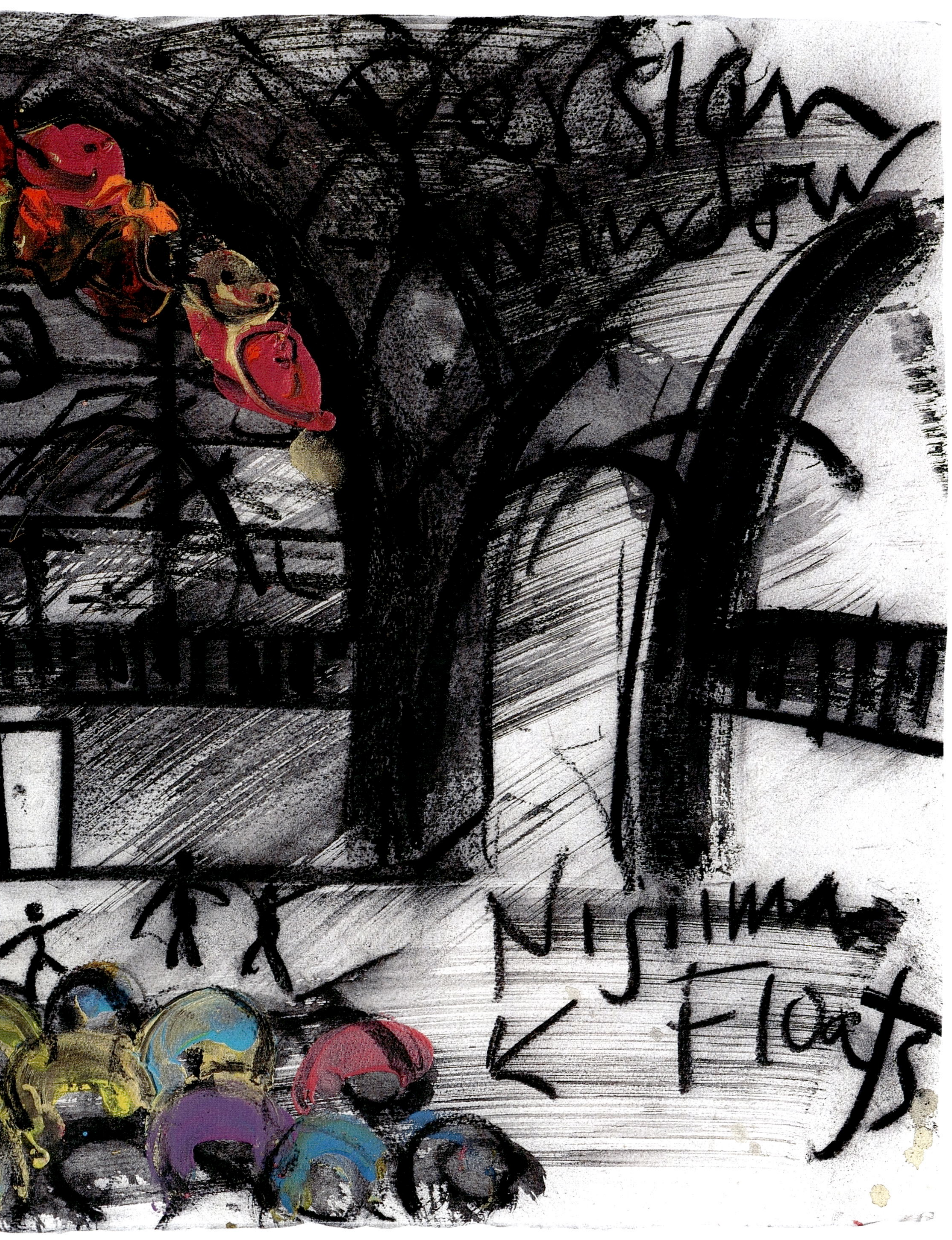
Persian Window
Flats

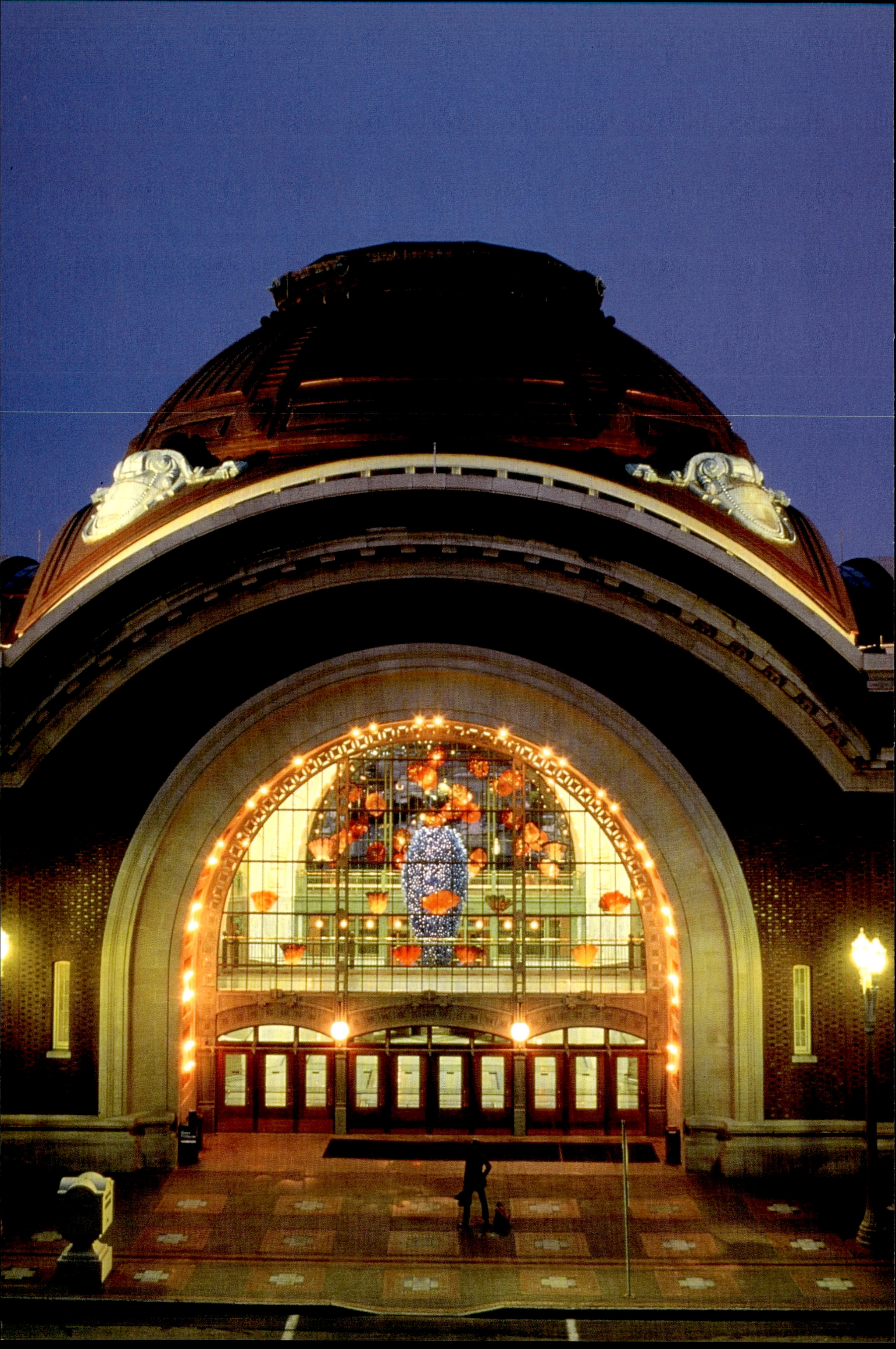

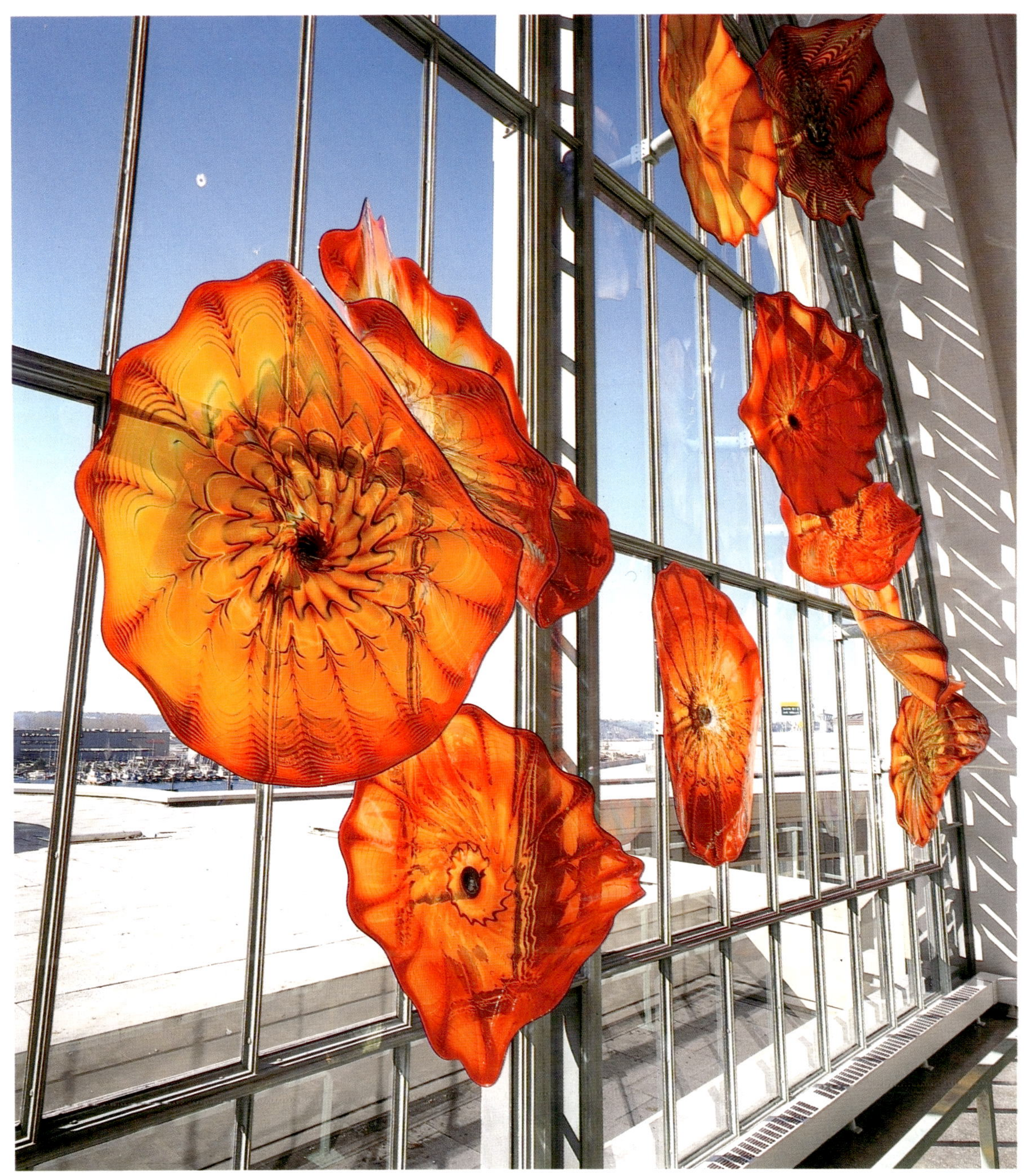

帝王窗
40 x 22 x 3呎
攝影: T. Rishel

Monarch Window
40 x 22 x 3'
photo: T. Rishel

聯合車站
攝影: R. Johnson

Union Station
photo: R. Johnson

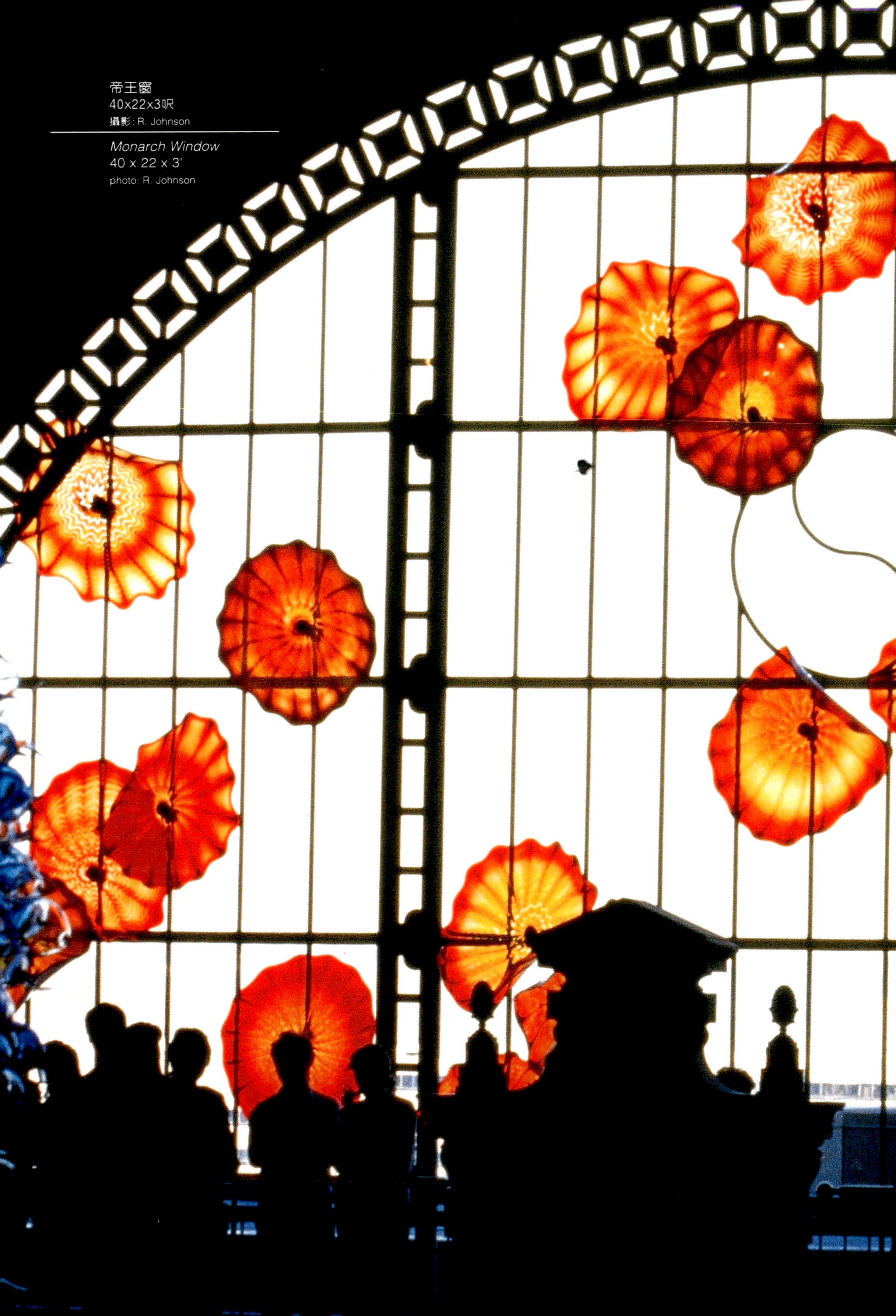

帝王窗
40x22x3呎
攝影: R. Johnson

Monarch Window
40 x 22 x 3'
photo: R. Johnson

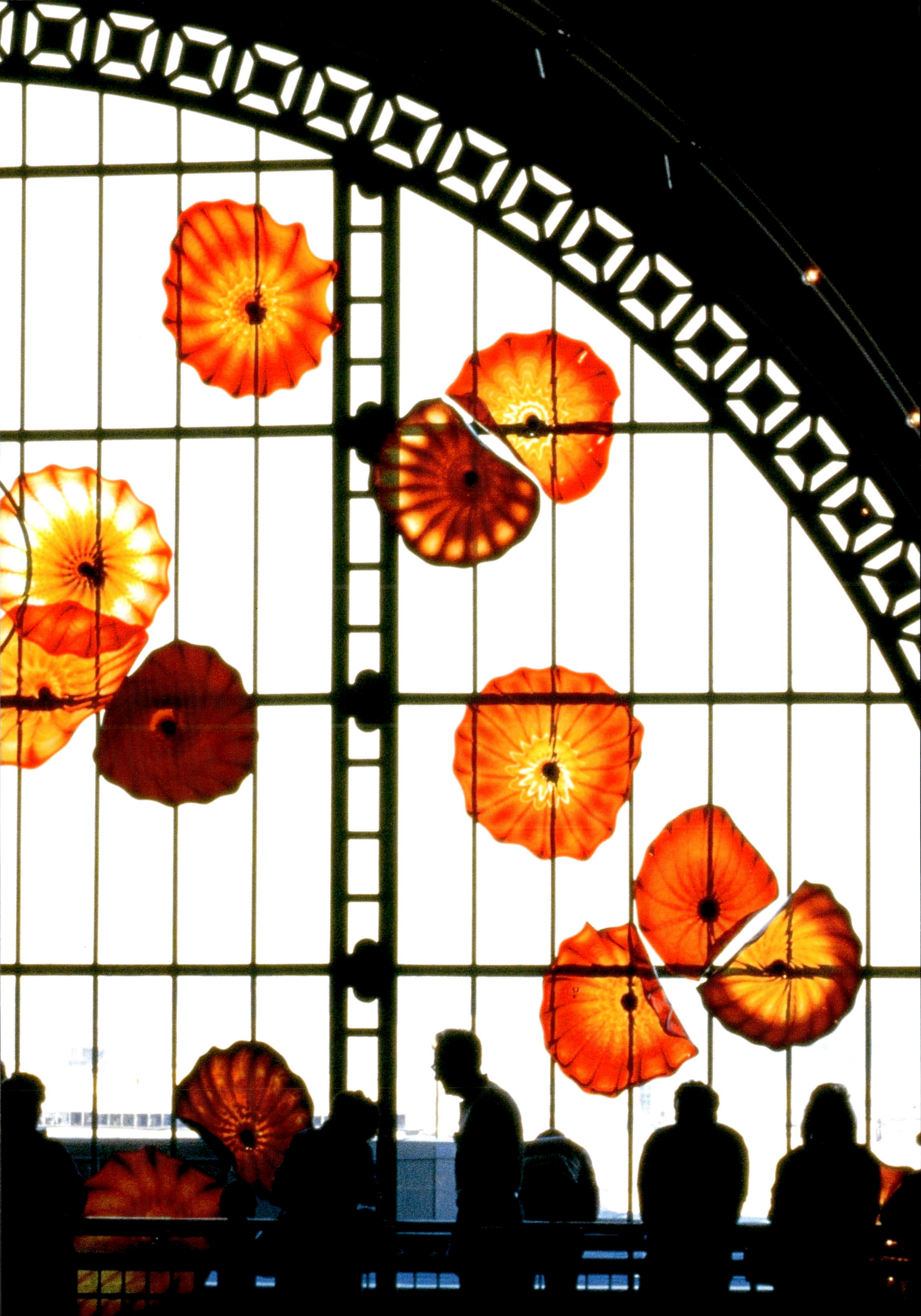

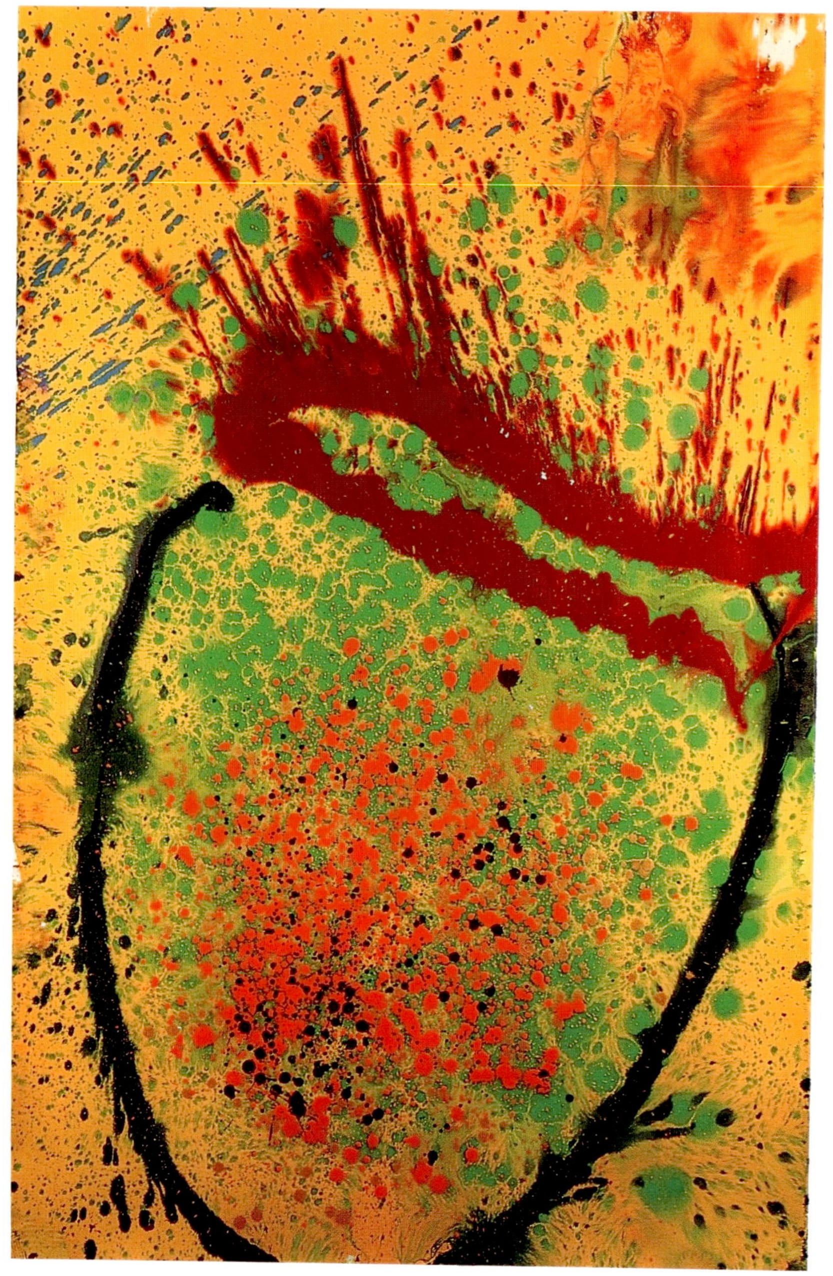

藍之素描
41 x 29吋
攝影 : C. Garoutte

Basket Drawing
acrylic on paper
41 x 29"
photo: C. Garoutte

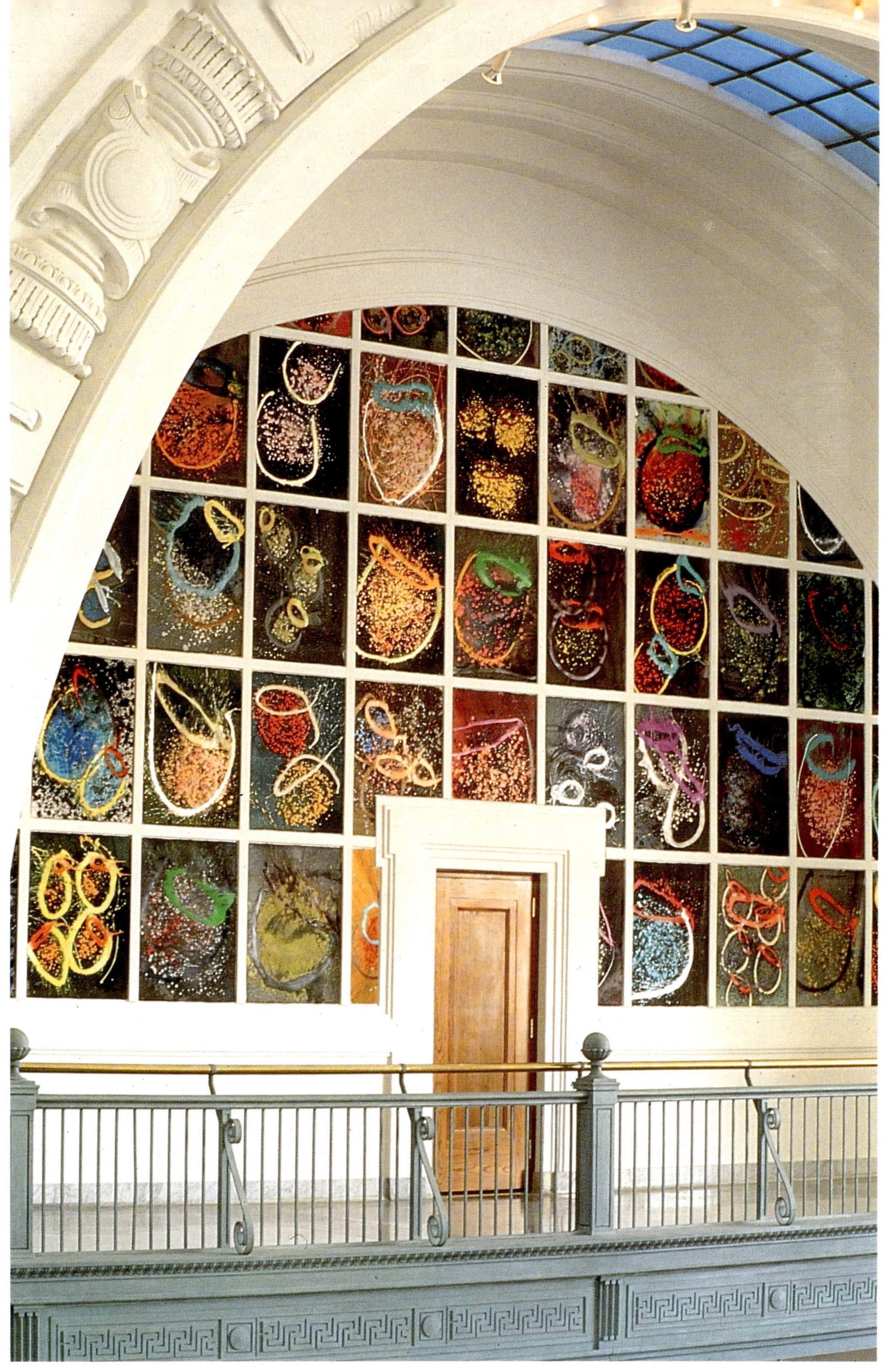

藍壁畫
40 x 22呎
攝影：T. Rishel

Basket Mural
40 x 22'
photo: T. Rishel

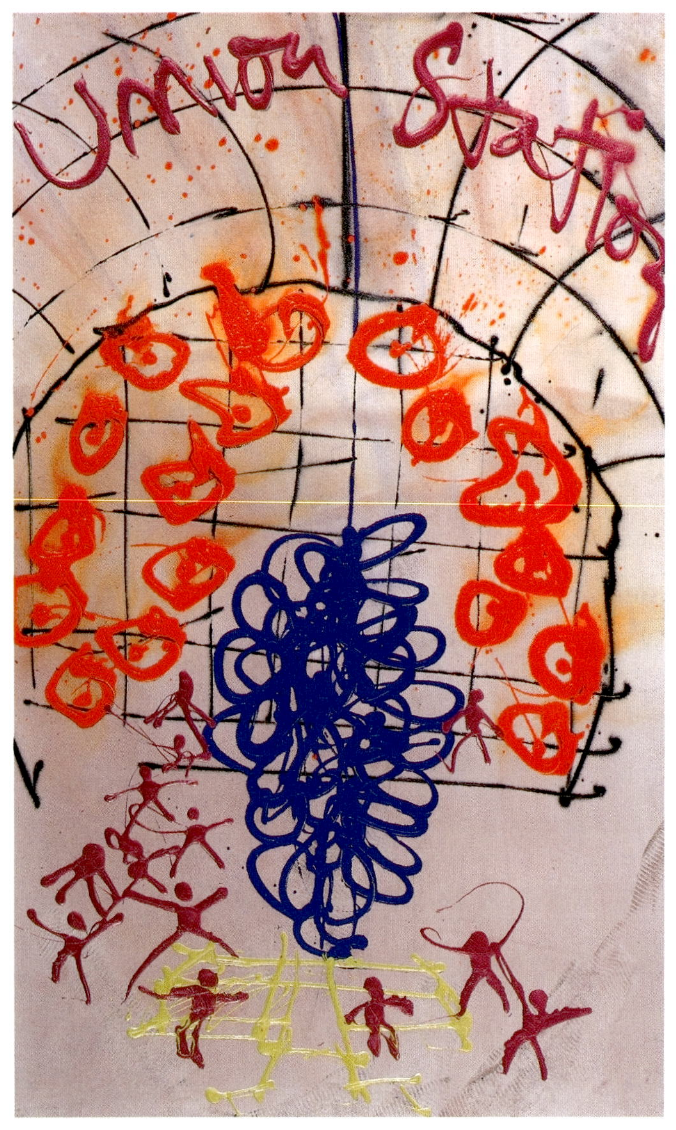

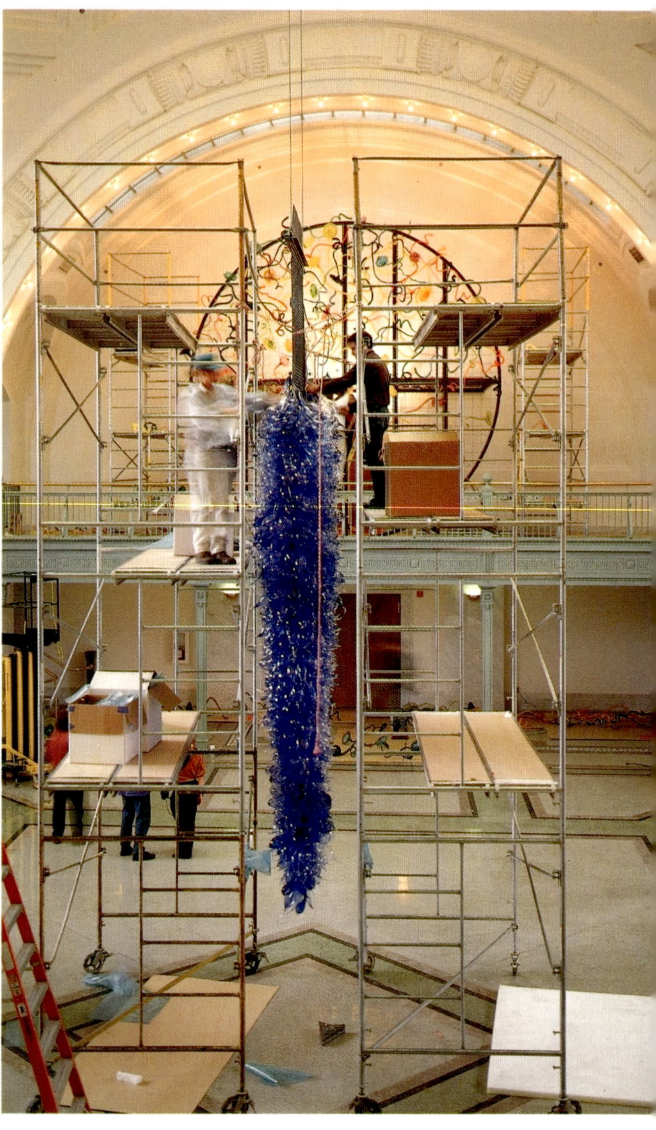

聯合車站之素描
30 x 22吋
攝影：T. Rishel

Union Station Drawing
30 x 22"
photo: T. Rishel

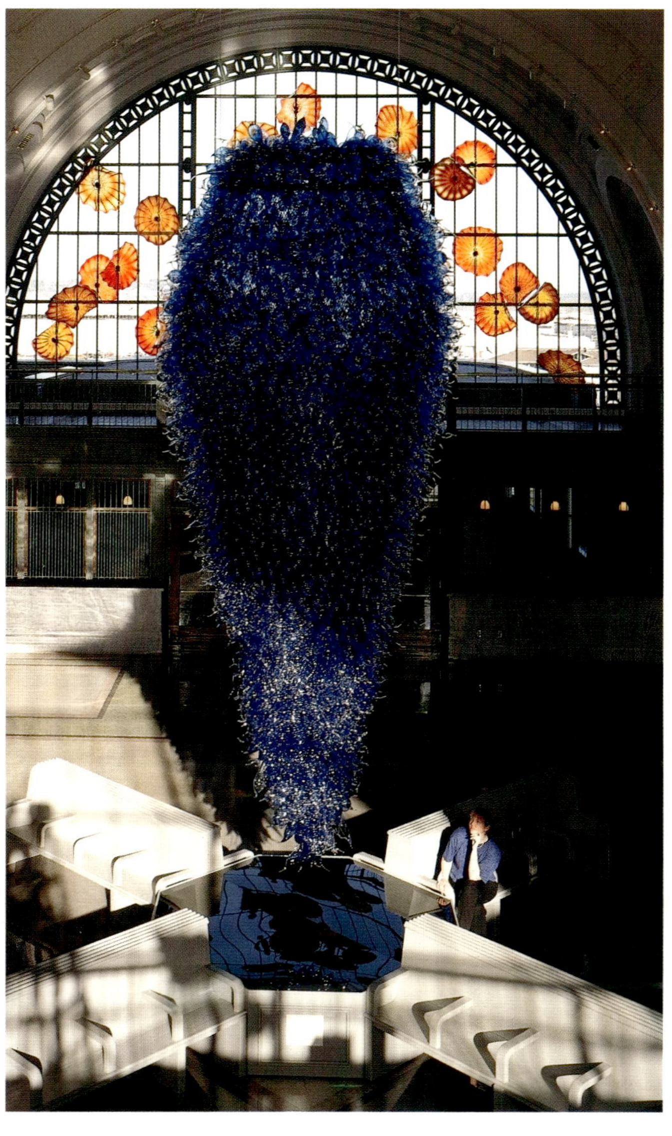

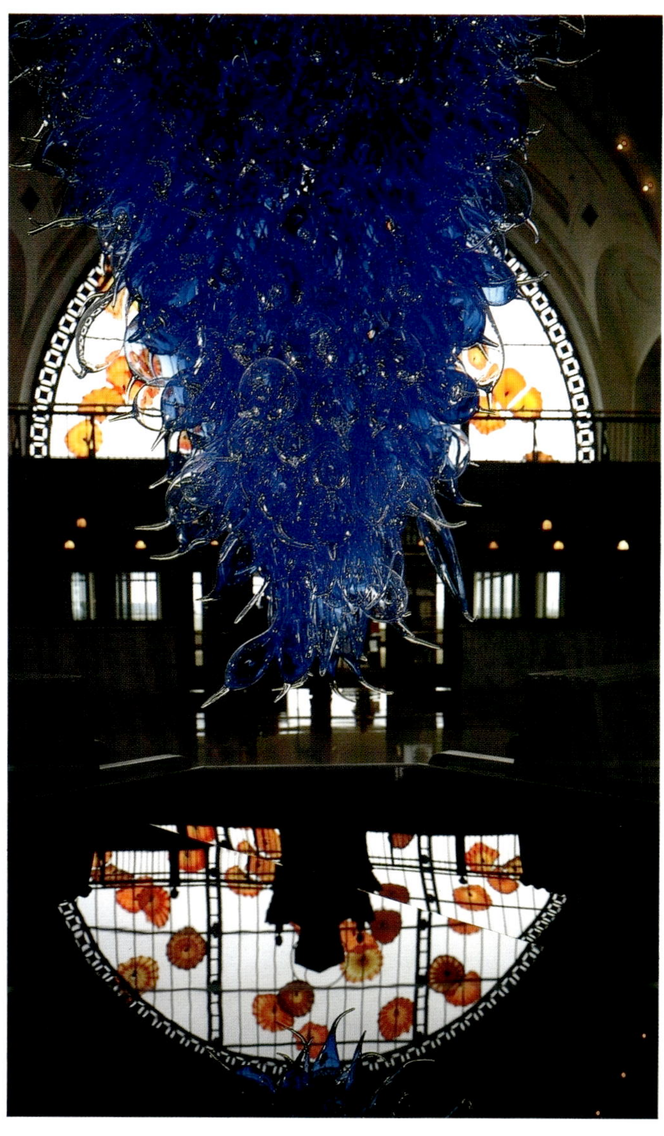

鈷藍色吊燈
20 x 9 x 3呎
攝影：C. Garoutte

Cobalt Blue Chandelier
20 x 9 x 3'
photos: C. Garoutte

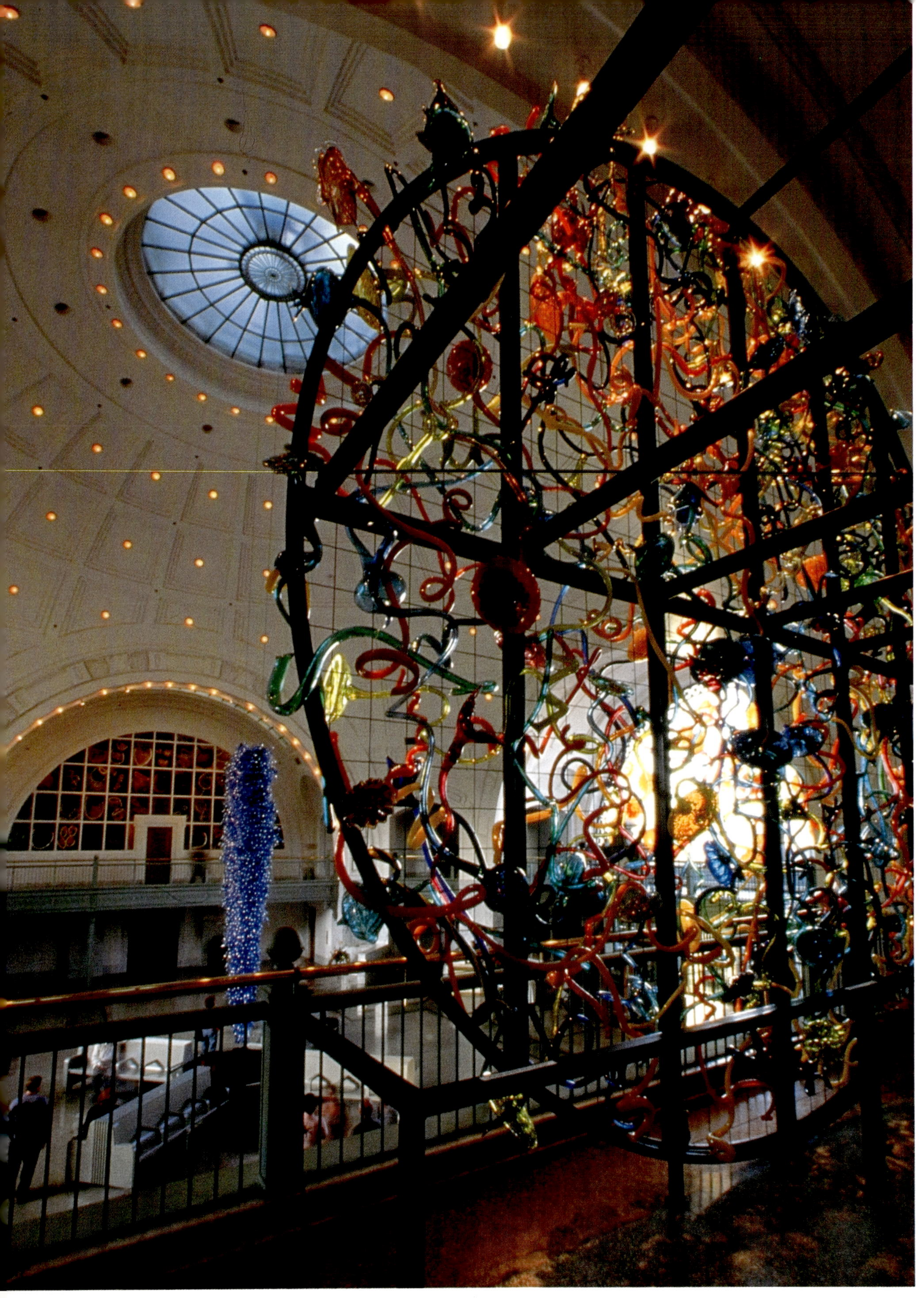

拉卡瓦那花道
直徑：18呎
攝影：R. Johnson

Lakawana Ikebana
18' diameter
photo: R. Johnson

聯合車站裝置
1994年3月
攝影：R. Johnson

Union Station Installation
March, 1994
photo: R. Johnson

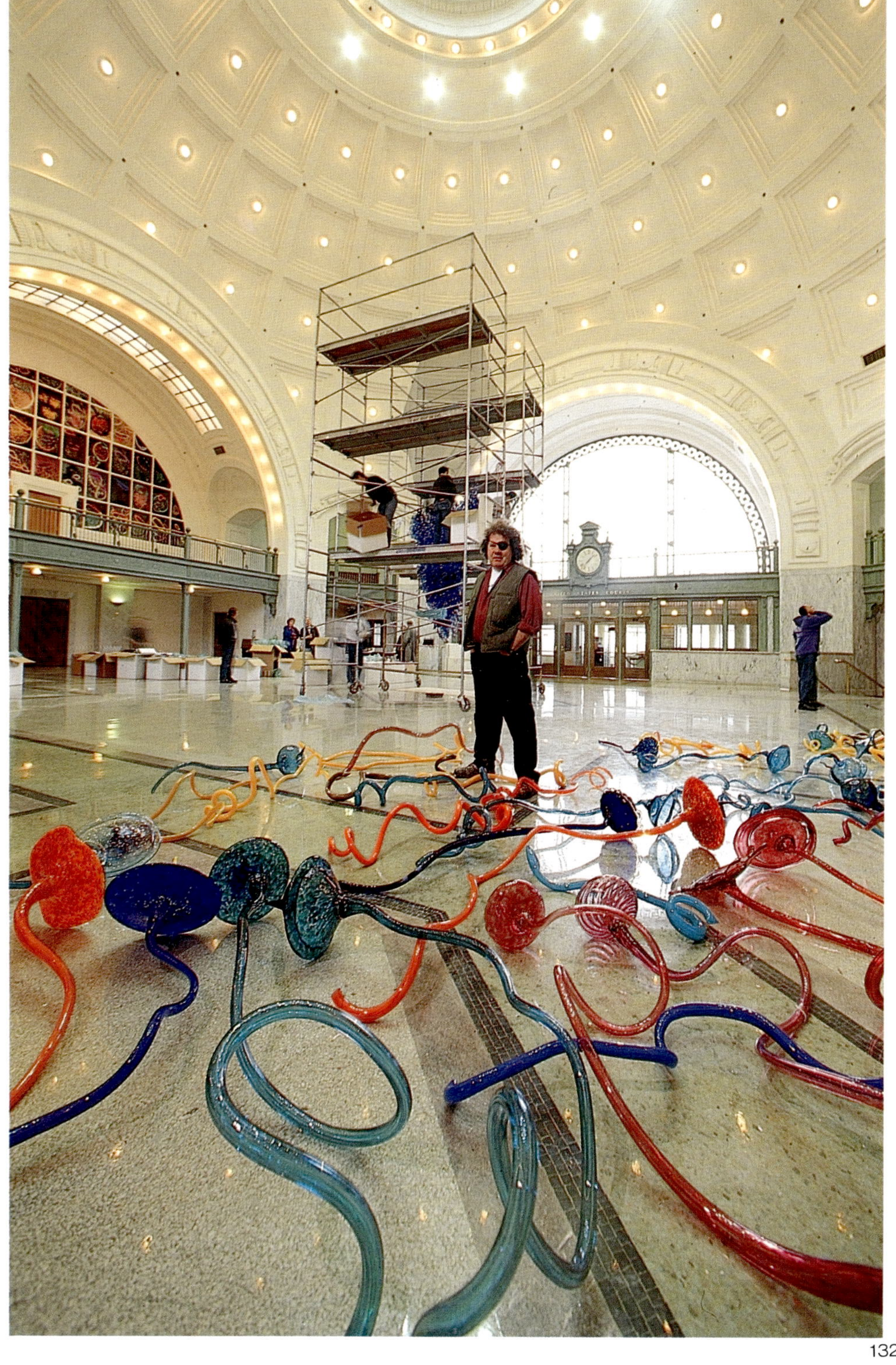

collections
commissions
chronology

收藏
委託製作
年表

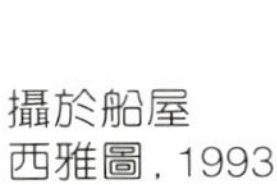

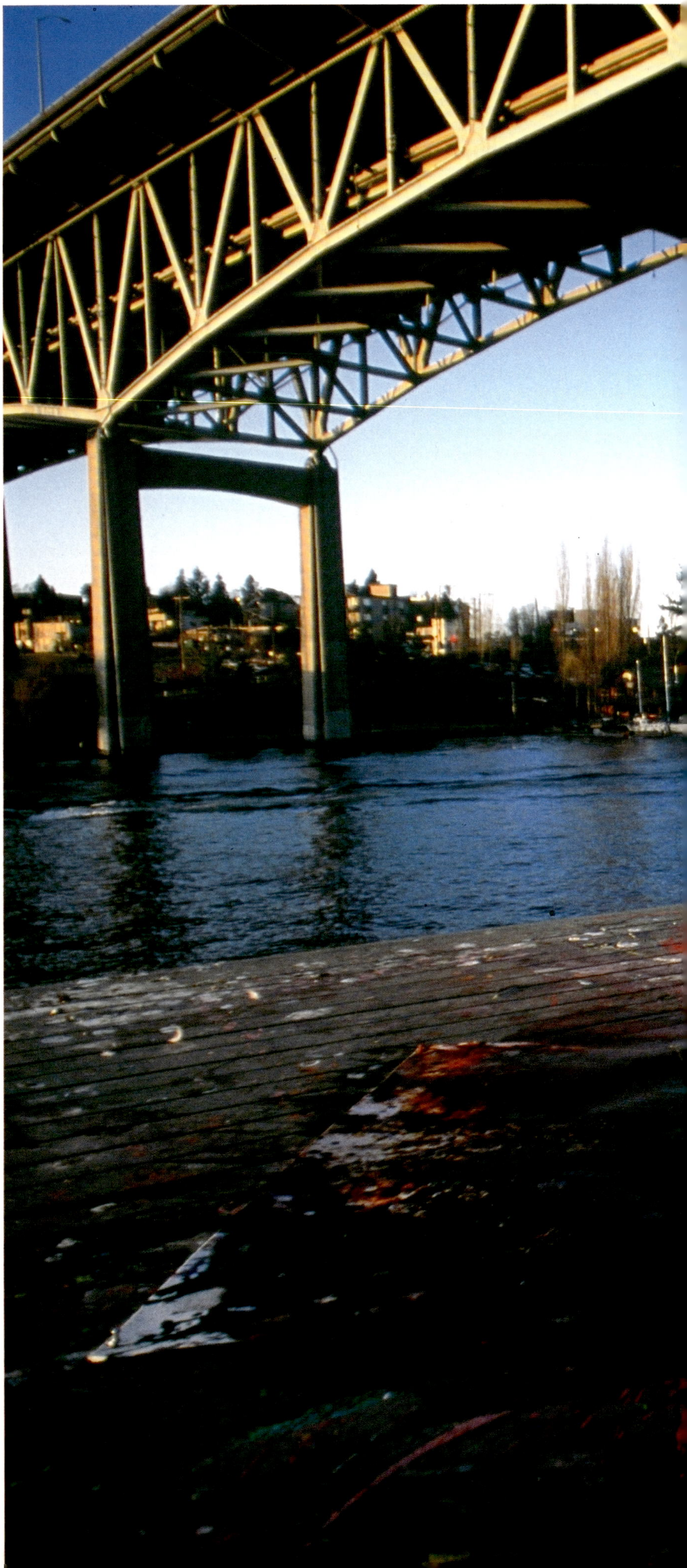

攝於船屋
西雅圖，1993
攝影：R. Johnson

at The Boathouse
Seattle, 1993
photo: R. Johnson

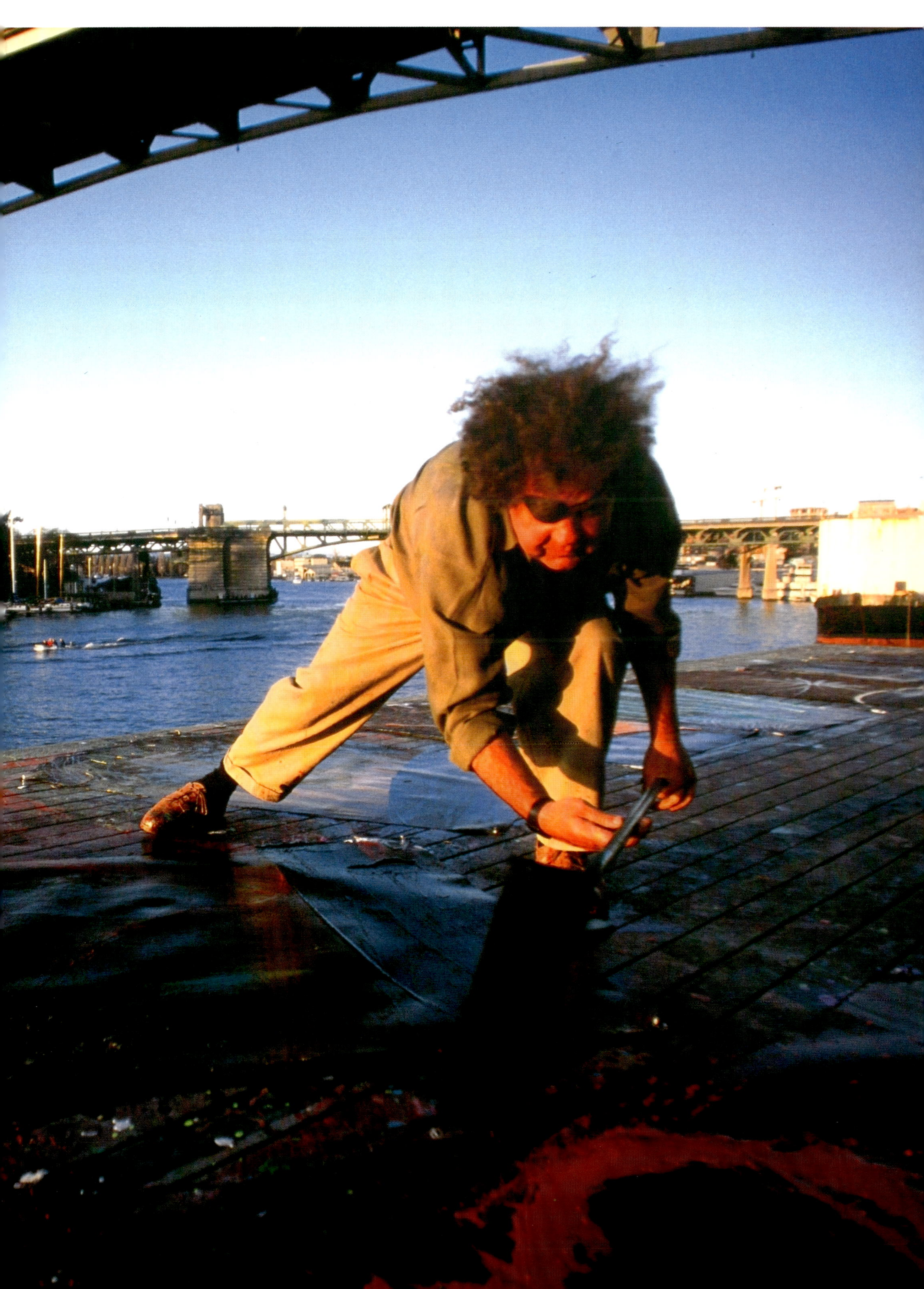

museum collections

Albright-Knox Art Gallery, Buffalo, New York
American Craft Museum, New York, New York
American Glass Museum, Millville, New Jersey
Amon Carter Museum, Fort Worth, Texas
Arkansas Arts Center, Little Rock, Arkansas
Art Gallery of Greater Victoria, Victoria, British Columbia
Art Gallery of Western Australia, Perth, Australia
Art Museum, Arizona State University, Tempe, Arizona
Asheville Art Museum, Asheville, North Carolina
Auckland Museum, Auckland, New Zealand
Australian National Gallery, Canberra, Australia
Azabu Arts and Crafts Museum of Tokyo, Tokyo, Japan
Bellevue Art Museum, Bellevue, Washington
Birmingham Museum of Art, Birmingham, Alabama
Boca Raton Museum of Art, Boca Raton, Florida
Carnegie Museum of Art, Pittsburgh, Pennsylvania
Chrysler Museum at Norfolk, Norfolk, Virginia
The Cleveland Museum of Art, Cleveland, Ohio
Columbus Museum of Art, Columbus, Ohio
The Contemporary Arts Center, Cincinnati, Ohio
Contemporary Arts Center of Hawaii, Honolulu, Hawaii
Cooper-Hewitt Museum, National Museum of Design, Smithsonian Institution, New York, New York
Corning Museum of Glass, Corning, New York
Crocker Art Museum, Sacramento, California
Currier Gallery of Art, Manchester, New Hampshire
Dallas Museum of Art, Dallas, Texas
De Cordova Museum and Sculpture Park, Lincoln, Massachusetts
Denver Art Museum, Denver, Colorado
The Detroit Institute of Arts, Detroit, Michigan
Dowse Art Museum, Aotearoa, New Zealand
Everson Museum of Art, Syracuse, New York
Fine Arts Museum of The South, Mobile, Alabama
Flint Institute of Arts, Flint, Michigan
Glasmuseum Ebeltoft, Ebeltoft, Denmark
Glasmuseum Frauenau, Frauenau, Germany
Glasmuseum Wertheim, Wertheim, Germany
Grand Rapids Museum, Grand Rapids, Michigan
Hawke's Bay Exhibition Centre, Napier, New Zealand
Haaretz Museum, Tel Aviv, Israel
High Museum of Art, Atlanta, Georgia
Hokkaido Museum of Modern Art, Sapporo, Japan
Honolulu Academy of Arts, Honolulu, Hawaii
Hunter Museum of Art, Chattanooga, Tennessee
Indianapolis Museum of Art, Indianapolis, Indiana
Israel Museum, Jerusalem, Israel
J.B. Speed Art Museum, Louisville, Kentucky
Japan Institute of Arts and Crafts, Tokyo, Japan
Jesse Besser Museum, Alpena, Michigan
Kestner Museum, Hannover, Germany
Kobe City Museum, Kobe, Japan
Krannert Art Museum, University of Illinois, Champaign, Illinois
Kunstindustrimuseum Kopenhagen, Copenhagen, Denmark

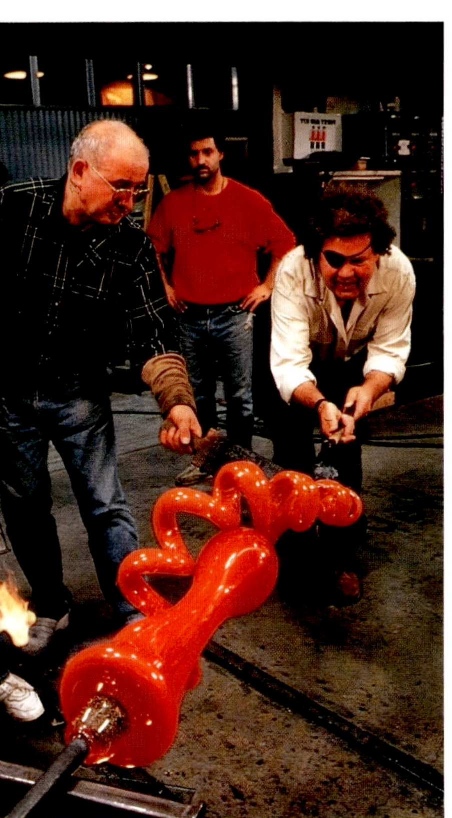

與達里歐派特拉及盧比諾之合影
西雅圖, 1991
攝影: R. Johnson

with Lino Tagliapietra
and Bryan Rubino
Seattle, 1991
photo: R. Johnson

Kunstmuseum, Düsseldorf, Germany
Kunstsammlungen der Veste Coburg, Coburg, Germany
Leigh Yawkey Woodson Art Museum, Wausau, Wisconsin
Lobmeyr Museum, Vienna, Austria
Los Angeles County Museum of Art, Los Angeles, California
Lowe Art Museum, Coral Gables, Florida
Lyman Allyn Art Museum, New London, Connecticut
Madison Art Center, Madison, Wisconsin
Manawatu Museum, Palmerston North, New Zealand
Metropolitan Museum of Art, New York, New York
Milwaukee Art Museum, Milwaukee, Wisconsin
Morris Museum, Morristown, New Jersey
Musée d'art Moderne et d'art Contemporain, Nice, France
Musée des Arts Décoratifs, Paris, France
Musée des Arts Décoratifs, Lausanne, Switzerland
Musée des Beaux Arts et de la Céramique, Rouen, France
Museum of Art and Archaeology, Columbia, Missouri
Museum Bellerive, Zurich, Switzerland
Museum Boymans-van Beuningen, Rotterdam, The Netherlands
Museum für Kunst und Gewerbe, Hamburg, Germany
Museum für Kunsthandwerk, Frankfurt, Germany
Museum of Art, Fort Lauderdale, Florida
Museum of Art, Rhode Island School of Design,
Providence, Rhode Island
Museum of Contemporary Art, Chicago, Illinois
Museum of Contemporary Art San Diego, La Jolla, California
Museum of Fine Arts, Boston, Massachusetts
Muskegon Museum of Art, Muskegon, Michigan
Muzeum Mesta Brna, Brno, Czech Republic
Muzeum Skla A Bizuterie, Jablonec nad Nisou, Czech Republic
National Gallery of Victoria, Melbourne, Australia
National Museum, Stockholm, Sweden
National Museum of American History,
Smithsonian Institution, Washington, D.C.
National Museum of Modern Art, Kyoto, Japan
New Orleans Museum of Art, New Orleans, Louisiana
Newport Harbor Art Museum, Newport Beach, California
North Central Washington Museum, Wenatchee, Washington
Notojima Glass Museum, Ishikawa, Japan
Otago Museum, Dunedin, New Zealand
Palm Beach Community College Art Museum, Lake Worth, Florida
Parrish Museum of Art, Southampton, New York
Philadelphia Museum of Art, Philadelphia, Pennsylvania
Phoenix Art Museum, Phoenix, Arizona
Portland Art Museum, Portland, Oregon
Powerhouse Museum, Sydney, Australia
Princeton University Art Museum, Princeton, New Jersey
Provincial Musée Sterckshof, Antwerpen, Belgium
Queensland Art Gallery, Brisbane, Australia
Renwick Gallery, National Museum of Art,
Smithsonian Institution, Washington, D.C.
Robert McDougall Gallery, Christchurch, New Zealand
Royal Ontario Museum, Toronto, Canada

Saint Louis Art Museum, Saint Louis, Missouri
San Francisco Museum of Modern Art, San Francisco, California
Scitech Discovery Centre, Perth, Australia
Seattle Art Museum, Seattle, Washington
Shimonoseki City Art Museum, Shimonoseki, Japan
Smith College Museum of Art, Northampton, Massachusetts
Spencer Museum of Art, University of Kansas, Lawrence, Kansas
Suntory Museum, Tokyo, Japan
Suomenlasimuseo, Riihimaki, Finland
Tacoma Art Museum, Tacoma, Washington
Taipei Museum of Fine Arts, Taipei, Taiwan
Toledo Museum of Art, Toledo, Ohio
Umeléckoprůmyslové muzeum, Prague, Czech Republic
University Art Museum, University of California, Berkeley, California
University of Michigan, Dearborn, Michigan
Utah Museum of Fine Arts, Salt Lake City, Utah
Victoria and Albert Museum, London, England
Wadsworth Atheneum, Hartford, Connecticut
Waikato Museum, Hamilton, New Zealand
Walker Hill Art Center, Seoul, Korea
Whatcom Museum of History and Art, Bellingham, Washington
Whitney Museum of American Art, New York, New York
Yale University Art Gallery, New Haven, Connecticut
Yokohama Museum, Yokohama, Japan

corporate and public collections

American Embassy, Bratislava, Slovakia
American Embassy, Geneva, Switzerland
American Embassy, London, England
American Embassy, Paris, France
Australian Arts Council, Sydney, Australia
Bader Martin Ross and Smith, P.S., Seattle, Washington
Bass Brothers Enterprises, Fort Worth, Texas
California College of Arts and Crafts, Oakland, California
The City and County of Honolulu, Oahu, Hawaii
Chase Manhattan Bank, New York, New York
Columbia Tower Club, Seattle, Washington
Davis, Wright, Tremaine, Seattle, Washington
Dreyfus Corporation, New York, New York
The Embassy of the Republic of Indonesia, Washington, D.C.
Foster & Marshall, Inc., Spokane, Washington
Genesee Partners, Bellevue, Washington
Dr. Eugene W. Goertzen, Seattle, Washington
The Hearn Company, Chicago, Illinois
Harold Hess Company, Inc., Philadelphia, Pennsylvania
IBM Corporation, New York, New York
Johnson Wax Collection, Racine, Wisconsin
Frances and Sydney Lewis Foundation, Richmond, Virginia
Mercer International, Inc., Vancouver, Canada.
Microsoft Corporation, Redmond, Washington
National Geographic Society, Washington, D.C.
Niijima Glass Art Center, Niijima, Japan
Owens-Corning Fiberglas, Toledo, Ohio

Paccar, Inc, Bellevue, Washington
Pilchuck Glass School, Stanwood, Washington
The Prudential Insurance Company of America, Newark, New Jersey
Safeco Insurance Companies, Seattle, Washington
Seaman's Bank, New York, New York
Seattle First National Bank, Seattle, Washington
Simpson Investment Company, Seattle, Washington
Simpson Paper Company, Seattle, Washington
Stone Container Corporation, Chicago, Illinois
Swedish Hospital, Seattle, Washington
University Hospital, Seattle, Washington
University of Puget Sound, Tacoma, Washington
U.S. News & World Report, Washington, D.C.
Vitro Vidrio Plano, Monterrey, Mexico
Washington University Medical School, Saint Louis, Missouri
Weyerhaeuser Company, Tacoma, Washington

architectural commissions

Joan and Stanford Alexander, Houston, Texas
Paul Allen, Mercer Island, Washington
Mr. and Mrs. E. C. Alvord III, Seattle, Washington
Mr. and Mrs. Leon Berlin, Westmount, Canada
Irvin J. Borowsky and Laurie Wagman, Philadelphia, Pennsylvania
Mr. and Mrs. Jules Brassner, Palm Beach, Florida
Jeff and Susan Brotman, Bellevue, Washington
Mr. Gerard L. Cafesjian, Paradise Valley, Arizona
Joe and Diana Carter, Leawood, Kansas
Mr. and Mrs. Stuart Cauff, Miami, Florida
Chancellor Park, San Diego, California
Mr. and Mrs. Norman Cohn, Radnor, Pennsylvania
Corning World Headquarters, Corning, New York
Crafts Council of Australia, Sydney
Mr. Leonard Dobbs, Long Island, New York
Eric and Barbara Dobkin, Pound Ridge, New York
Mr. and Mrs. Lowell Fine, Atlanta, Georgia
Fleet National Bank, Providence, Rhode Island
Jerome and Mimi Frankel, Delray Beach, Florida
GTE Telephone Operations Headquarters, Irving, Texas
Kathryn and Norman Gerlich, Seattle, Washington
Dr. Rahn Hall, Houston, Texas
Hillhaven Corporation, Tacoma, Washington
Mr. and Mrs. Jerry Holt, Tacoma, Washington
Hyatt Hotel, Adelaide, Australia
Japan-America Society, UNICO Properties, Inc., Seattle, Washington
King and Spalding, Washington, D.C.
Little Caesars World Headquarters, Detroit, Michigan
MCI Communications World Headquarters, Washington, D.C.
Cargill and Donna MacMillan, Indian Wells, California
Madison Stouffer Hotel, Seattle, Washington
Dr. Alan Markowitz and Cathy Pollard, Pepper Pike, Ohio
Dr. and Mrs. Robert Mendelsohn, Betheseda, Maryland
Mr. and Mrs. Paul Milstein, New York, New York

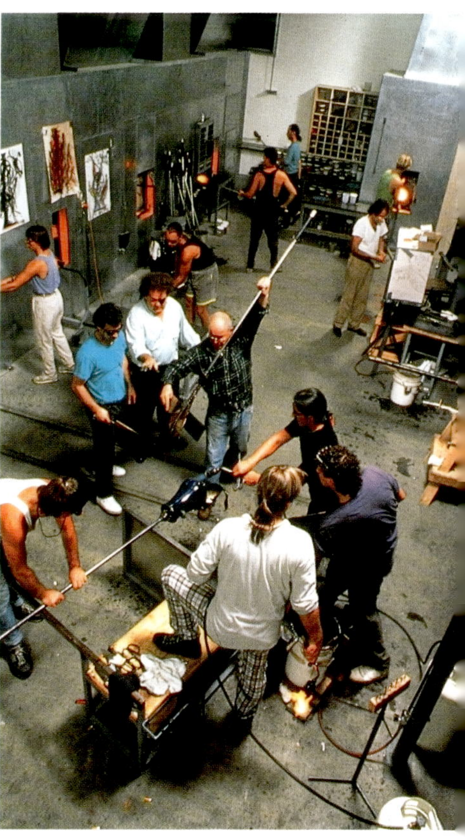

與達里歐派特拉及熱坊工作人員之合影
西雅圖, 1991
攝影: R. Johnson

with Lino Tagliapietra and
the hot shop team
Seattle, 1991
photo: R. Johnson

Richard and Michelle Moodie, Moreland Hills, Ohio
Ohio Arts Council, Library of Science and Engineering,
The Ohio State University, Columbus, Ohio
Pacific Lutheran University, Tacoma, Washington
Mr. and Mrs. Benson Pilloff, Beachwood, Ohio
Rainbow Pavilion, Rockefeller Center, New York, New York
Duane Rath, Key West, Florida
Robins, Kaplan, Miller & Ciresi, Minneapolis, Minnesota
Chapman Root, Ormond Beach, Florida
Frank Russell Building, Tacoma, Washington
S.S. Oceanic Grace, Tokyo, Japan
Seattle Aquarium, Seattle, Washington
Shaare Emeth Synagogue, Saint Louis, Missouri
Mr. and Mrs. Lawrence Schulman, Kenilworth, Illinois
Mr. and Mrs. Jeremy Shamos, Denver, Colorado
Sheraton Seattle Hotel and Towers, Seattle, Washington
Sheraton Hotel, Tacoma, Washington
Mr. and Mrs. Jon Shirley, Bellevue, Washington
Stuart Sloan, Seattle, Washington
Barbaralee Diamonstein-Spielvogel and Carl Spielvogel,
Southampton, New York
George Stroemple, Lake Oswego, Oregon
Tacoma Art Museum, Tacoma, Washington
Tacoma Financial Center, Tacoma, Washington
Tropicana Products, Inc., Bradenton, Florida
United States Border Station, Blaine, Washington
U.S. Bank Centre, Seattle, Washington
David and Nancy Wolf, Cincinnati, Ohio
Yasui Konpira-gu Shinto Shrine, Kyoto, Japan

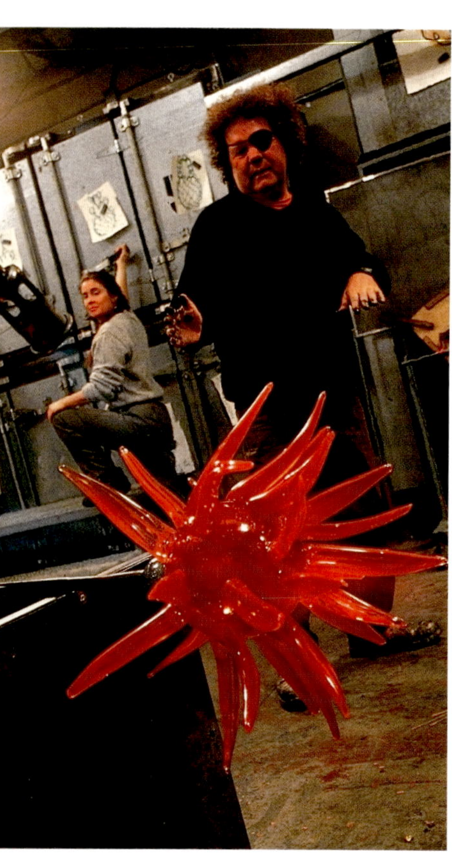

攝於熱坊
西雅圖, 1993
攝影: R. Johnson

in the hot shop
Seattle, 1993
photo: R. Johnson

博物館收藏

美國紐約州布法羅市　艾爾布萊特諾克斯美術陳列館
美國紐約州紐約市　美國工藝博物館
美國紐澤西州密耳維爾市　美國玻璃博物館
美國德州沃茲堡　亞蒙卡特博物館
美國阿肯色州小岩城　阿肯色藝術中心
加拿大英屬哥倫比亞省維多利亞市　大維多利亞美術陳列館
澳大利亞伯斯市　西澳大利亞美術陳列館
美國亞歷桑那州潭碧市　亞歷桑那州立大學藝術館
美國北卡羅萊納州阿士維爾市　阿士維爾美術陳列館
紐西蘭奧克蘭市　奧克蘭博物館
澳大利亞坎培拉市　澳大利亞國家美術陳列館
日本東京市　東京麻布美術工藝博物館
美國華盛頓州貝勒弗市　貝勒弗藝術館
美國阿拉巴馬州伯明罕市　伯明罕藝術館
美國佛羅里達州波卡雷頓市　波卡雷頓藝術館
美國賓夕凡尼亞州匹茲堡市　卡內基藝術館
美國維吉尼亞州諾福克市　諾福克克萊斯勒博物館
美國俄亥俄州克利夫蘭市　克利夫蘭藝術館
美國俄亥俄州哥倫巴士市　哥倫巴士藝術館
美國俄亥俄州辛辛那堤市　當代藝術中心
美國夏威夷州檀香山　夏威夷當代藝術中心
美國紐約州紐約市　庫柏海威特博物館
　　　　　　　　　國家設計博物館
　　　　　　　　　史密斯桑尼亞學會
美國紐約州康寧市　康寧玻璃博物館
美國加州薩克萊曼多市　柯拉克藝術館
美國新罕布夏州曼徹斯特市　庫里美術陳列館
美國德州達拉斯市　達拉斯藝術館
美國麻州林肯市　迪柯多瓦博物館暨雕塑公園
美國科羅拉多州丹佛市　丹佛藝術館
美國密西根州底特律市　底特律藝術協會
紐西蘭奧提羅艾市　道斯藝術館
美國紐約州席拉克斯市　艾佛森藝術館
美國阿拉巴馬州莫比爾市　南方美術博物館
美國密西根州弗苓特市　弗苓特藝術協會
丹麥艾伯托夫特市　玻璃博物館
德國弗勞諾　弗勞諾玻璃博物館
德國威爾辛姆市　威爾辛姆玻璃博物館
美國密西根州大瑞匹茲市　大瑞匹茲博物館
紐西蘭奈皮耶市　霍克灣展覽中心
以色列臺拉維夫市　海瑞蚩博物館
美國喬治亞州亞特蘭大市　高等藝術館
日本札幌　北海道現代藝術博物館
美國夏威夷州檀香山　檀香山藝術學院
美國田納西州契坦諾加市　杭特藝術館

美國印第安那州印第安那玻里斯市　印第安那玻里斯藝術館
以色列耶路撒冷　以色列博物館
美國肯塔基州路易斯維爾市　傑比斯畢藝術館
日本東京市　日本美術工藝學會
美國密西根州艾爾比那市　傑斯貝塞博物館
德國漢諾瓦市　凱斯納博物館
日本神戶市　神戶市立博物館
美國伊利諾州香本市　伊利諾大學克瓦尼特藝術館
丹麥哥本哈根市　哥本哈根工藝博物館
德國杜塞道夫市　美術館
德國科堡　科堡美術館
美國威斯康新州瓦郡市　利約基伍德森藝術館
奧地利維也納市　勞伯梅爾博物館
美國加州洛杉磯市　洛杉磯郡藝術館
美國佛羅里達州柯拉蓋博市　羅威藝術館
美國康乃狄克州新倫敦市　黎曼艾霖藝術館
美國威斯康新州麥迪遜市　麥迪遜藝術中心
紐西蘭北帕莫斯東市　瑪那瓦吐博物館
美國紐約州紐約市　大都會藝術館
美國威斯康新州密耳瓦基市　密耳瓦基藝術館
美國紐澤西州莫里斯鎮　莫里斯博物館
法國尼斯市　現代暨當代藝術館
法國巴黎市　裝飾藝術博物館
瑞士洛桑市　裝飾藝術博物館
法國胡恩市　陶藝美術博物館
美國密蘇里州哥倫比亞市　藝術暨考古博物館
瑞士蘇黎士市　貝勒雷夫博物館
荷蘭鹿特丹市　褒曼司市伯尼根博物館
德國漢堡市　手工藝博物館
德國法蘭克福市　手工業博物館
美國佛羅里達州　羅德岱堡藝術館
美國羅德島普洛維登斯市　羅德島設計學院藝術館
美國伊利諾州芝加哥市　當代藝術館
美國加州優拉市　當代藝術館
美國麻州波士頓市　美術博物館
美國密西根州馬斯柯貢市　馬斯柯貢藝術館
捷克伯諾市　梅司塔伯納博物館
捷克賈勃洛內克尼梭市　思卡娜博物館
澳大利亞墨爾本市　維多利亞國家陳列館
瑞典斯德哥爾摩市　國家博物館
美國華盛頓哥倫比亞特區　史密斯尋尼亞協會美國歷史博物館
日本京都　國家現代藝術館
美國路易斯安那州新奧爾良市　新奧爾良藝術館
美國加州紐波特海濱　紐波特港藝術館
美國華盛頓州威拿奇市　北中央華盛頓博物館

日本石川　能登島玻璃博物館
紐西蘭丹尼丁市　奧大果博物館
美國佛羅里達州湖渥茲市　棕欖灘社區大學藝術館
美國紐約州南安普頓市　帕瑞須藝術館
美國賓夕凡尼亞州費城　費城藝術館
美國亞歷桑那州鳳凰城　鳳凰城藝術館
美國奧勒岡州波特蘭市　波特蘭藝術館
澳大利亞雪梨市　力屋博物館
美國紐澤西州普林司頓市　普林司頓大學藝術館
比利時安特衛普市　省立史特克秀夫博物館
澳大利亞布利斯班市　昆士蘭美術陳列館
美國華盛頓哥倫比亞特區　史密斯桑尼亞學會
國立藝術館
藍維奇陳列館
紐西蘭基督城　羅拔麥道哥陳列館
加拿大多倫多市　皇家安大略博物館
美國密蘇里州聖路易斯市　聖路易斯藝術館
美國加州三藩市　三藩現代藝術館
澳大利亞伯斯市　科技發現中心
美國華盛頓州西雅圖市　西雅圖藝術館
日本下關　下關市立藝術館
美國麻州北安普敦市　史密斯大學藝術館
美國堪薩斯州勞倫斯市　堪薩斯大學史賓塞藝術館
日本東京市　桑多利博物館
芬蘭瑞西梅基市　索曼拉席博物館
美國華盛頓州塔科馬市　塔科馬藝術館
台灣台北市　台北市立美術館
美國俄亥俄州托雷多市　托雷多藝術館
捷克布拉格市　厄梅雷柯普西洛夫博物館
美國柏克萊市　加利福尼亞大學　大學藝術館
美國密西根州迪波恩市　密西根大學
美國猶他州鹽湖城　猶他美術博物館
英國倫敦市　維多利亞暨亞伯博物館
美國康乃狄克州哈特福市　偉沃司圖書館
紐西蘭漢彌爾頓市　威卡多博物館
韓國漢城　渥克丘藝術中心
美國華盛頓州貝林市　華克歷史藝術博物館
美國紐約州紐約市　惠特尼美國藝術館
美國康乃狄克州紐海芬市　耶魯大學藝術陳列館
日本橫濱市　橫濱博物館

公司暨公衆收藏

斯洛伐克亞布拉提斯拉伐　美國大使館
瑞士日內瓦市　美國大使館
英國倫敦市　美國大使館
法國巴黎市　美國大使館

澳大利亞雪梨市　澳大利亞藝術委員會
美國華盛頓州西雅圖市　巴德馬汀羅斯暨史密司
美國德州沃茲堡　貝氏兄弟企業
美國加州奧克蘭市　加州美術工藝學院
美國夏威夷州歐胡市　檀香山城市暨郡
美國紐約州紐約市　鵲司曼哈頓銀行
美國華盛頓州西雅圖市　哥倫比亞塔俱樂部
美國華盛頓州西雅圖市　戴維斯　萊特　崔曼
美國紐約州紐約市　德瑞弗司公司
美國華盛頓哥倫比亞特區　印尼共和國大使館
美國美國華盛頓州司坡坎市　佛斯特馬歇爾有限公司
美國華盛頓州貝勒弗市　堅尼希合作社
美國華盛頓州西雅圖市　尤金哥雅琛博士
美國伊利諾州芝加哥市　席恩公司
美國賓州費城　赫羅哈斯有限公司
美國紐約州紐約市　IBM公司
美國威斯康新州哈辛市　強生衛克司收藏中心
美國維吉尼亞州瑞奇曼市　法蘭西與西尼路易斯基金會
加拿大溫哥華市　梅爾塞國際有限公司
美國華盛頓州瑞德蒙市　微軟公司
美國華盛頓哥倫比亞特區　國家地理協會
日本三島市　三島玻璃藝術中心
美國俄亥俄州托雷多市　歐文康寧纖維玻璃館
美國華盛頓州貝勒弗市　帕卡有限公司
美國華盛頓州史坦伍德市　彼恰克玻璃學校
美國紐澤西州紐瓦克市　美國普羅登席保險公司
美國華盛頓州西雅圖市　賽飛可保險公司
美國紐約州紐約市　席曼司銀行
美國華盛頓州西雅圖市　西雅圖第一國家銀行
美國華盛頓州西雅圖市　辛普森投資公司
美國華盛頓州西雅圖市　辛普森紙業公司
美國伊利諾州芝加哥市　史東貨櫃公司
美國華盛頓州西雅圖市　瑞典醫院
美國華盛頓州西雅圖市　大學醫院
美國華盛頓州塔科馬市　普桑大學
美國華盛頓哥倫比亞特區　美國新聞與世界報導
墨西哥蒙特芮　維羅威迪歐帕拉諾
美國密蘇里州聖路易斯市　華盛頓大學醫學院
美國華盛頓州塔科馬市　威耶赫塞公司

建築裝飾

美國德州休士頓市　瓊與史丹福亞歷山大
美國華盛頓州梅爾塞島　保羅艾倫
美國華盛頓州西雅圖市　艾爾福德三世夫婦
加拿大西茂德　里昂伯林夫婦
美國賓州費城　歐文包羅斯基與勞瑞衛格曼

美國佛羅里達州棕櫚灘　朱兒伯斯納夫婦
美國華盛頓州貝勒弗市　傑夫與蘇珊伯特曼
美國亞歷桑那州天堂谷　傑洛卡夫斯吉恩先生
美國堪薩斯州利木市　喬與戴安娜卡特
美國佛羅里達州邁阿密市　斯圖亞特寇夫夫婦
美國加州聖地牙哥市　法官公園
美國賓州拉德諾市　諾曼柯恩夫婦
美國紐約州康寧市　康寧世界總部
澳大利亞雪梨市　澳大利亞工藝委員會
美國紐約州長島　里歐納達伯先生
美國紐約州磅橋　艾力克與芭芭拉達伯金
美國喬治亞州亞特蘭大市　勞威爾汎夫婦
美國羅德島普羅維登斯市　旗艦國家銀行
美國佛羅里達州岱爾瑞海濱　傑洛米與咪咪法蘭克
美國德州歐文市　吉悌電話作業總部
美國華盛頓州西雅圖市　凱薩琳與諾曼喬利茲
美國德州休士頓市　洛恩霍爾博士
美國華盛頓州塔科馬市　希爾海溫公司
澳大利亞阿德雷德市　席雅大飯店
美國華盛頓州西雅圖市　美日協會UNICO財產有限公司
美國華盛頓哥倫比亞特區　金恩與斯帕汀
美國密西根州底特律市　小凱撒世界總部
美國華盛頓哥倫比亞特區　MCI傳播世界總部
美國加州印第安威爾士市　卡吉兒與多娜麥克米倫
美國華盛頓州西雅圖市　麥迪遜史脫佛飯店
美國俄亥俄州匹伯帕克　艾倫馬克威茲與凱茜波樂博士
美國馬里蘭州貝茲西達市　羅拔曼德莎女士博士
美國紐約州紐約市　保羅密斯坦夫婦
美國俄亥俄州摩蘭希爾市　理查與密雪兒慕迪
美國俄亥俄州哥倫巴士市　俄亥俄州立大學
科學工程圖書館
俄亥俄藝術委員會
美國華盛頓州塔科馬市　太平洋路塞朗大學
美國俄亥俄州濱林市　班森庇洛夫夫婦
美國紐約州紐約市　洛克斐勒中心彩虹廳
美國佛羅里達州奇威斯特市　杜安那芮斯
美國明尼蘇達州明尼亞玻利斯市　羅賓士　加布朗　米勒與西瑞西
美國佛羅里達州歐蒙海濱　恰普曼魯特
美國華盛頓州塔科馬市　法蘭克魯塞爾大廈
日本東京市　海洋藝術館
美國華盛頓州西雅圖市　西雅圖水族館
美國密蘇里州聖路易斯市　沙赫艾米斯西那貢格
美國伊利諾州凱尼渥茲市　勞倫斯舒曼夫婦
美國科羅拉多州丹佛市　傑洛米沙摩夫婦
美國華盛頓州西雅圖市　夏樂頓西雅圖飯店與大廈

美國華盛頓州塔科馬市　夏樂頓飯店
美國華盛頓州貝勒弗市　強雪萊夫婦
美國華盛頓州西雅圖市　斯圖亞特史洛恩
美國紐約州南安普敦市　芭芭拉岱夢斯坦史賓弗吉與卡爾史賓弗吉
美國奧勒岡州湖歐斯維哥　喬治斯楚安布
美國華盛頓州塔科馬市　塔科馬藝術館
美國華盛頓州塔科馬市　塔科馬金融中心
美國佛羅里達州布來登頓市　熱帶產品有限公司
美國華盛頓州泊蘭市　美國勃登車站
美國華盛頓州西雅圖市　美國銀行中心
美國俄亥俄州辛辛那提市　大衛與南茜沃爾夫
日本京都　安井金比羅神道神社

chronology

1941 Born September 20, Tacoma, Washington, to Viola and George Chihuly, a union organizer

1956 Older brother, George, killed in Naval aviation practice flight

1957 Father dies

1959 Enrolls in University of Puget Sound, Tacoma

1960 Transfers to University of Washington, Seattle, in interior design

1961-62 Melts and fuses glass in his basement studio in south Seattle • Becomes rush chairman of Delta Kappa Epsilon fraternity

1962-63 Travels to Europe and Near East • In Israel works on a kibbutz.

1963 Re-enters University of Washington, studying interior design and architecture under Hope Foote and Warren Hill • In weaving classes with Doris Brockway begins incorporating glass into tapestries

1964 Returns to Europe, visiting Leningrad and making first of many trips to Ireland • Receives Seattle Weavers Guild Award

1965 Meets textile designer Jack Lenor Larsen • Awarded highest honors from the American Institute of Interior Designers (now the American Society of Interior Designers) • Receives Bachelor of Arts degree in interior design, University of Washington • Works as designer for John Graham Architects, Seattle • Experimenting on his own, blows glass for the first time • Encouraged by Russell Day

1966 Works as commercial fisherman in Alaska to earn money for graduate studies in glass • On a full scholarship, enters University of Wisconsin, Madison, to study glass blowing with Harvey Littleton

1967 Receives Master of Science degree from University of Wisconsin • Enrolls in Master of Fine Arts program at Rhode Island School of Design (RISD), Providence • Teaches glass courses and works on large-scale environmental sculptures incorporating neon, plastic and other materials • Meets Italo Scanga

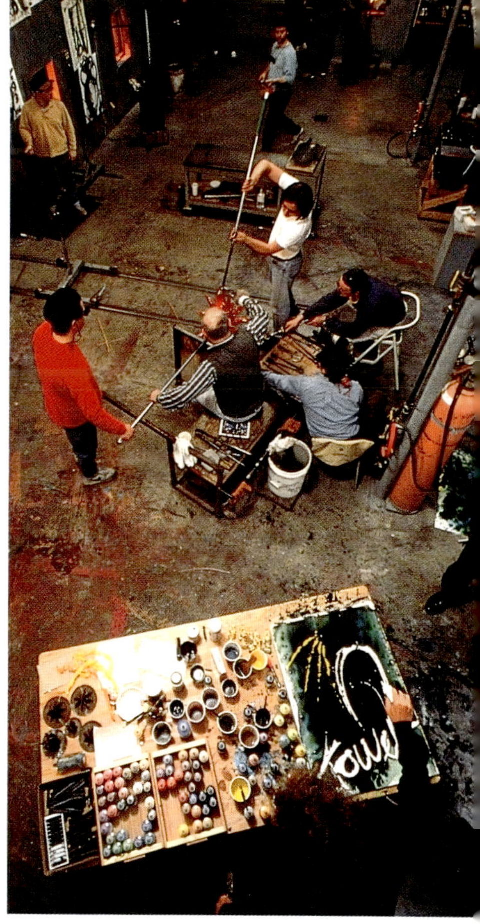

熱坊
西雅圖，1993
攝影：R. Johnson

the hot shop
Seattle, 1993
photo: R. Johnson

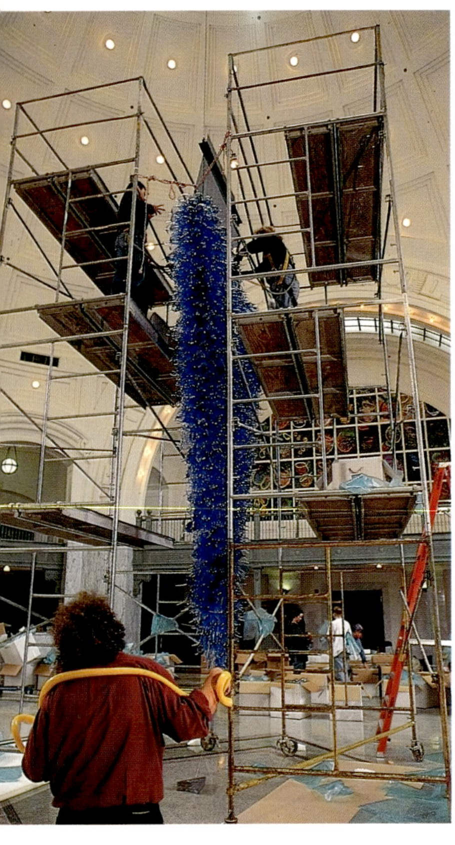

"屈胡利在聯合車站"展覽中之
鈷藍色吊燈裝置
塔科馬, 1994
攝影: R. Johnson

installation of
Cobalt Blue Chandelier for
"Chihuly at Union Station"
Tacoma, 1994
photo: R. Johnson

1968 Receives Master of Fine Arts degree from RISD • Teaches at Haystack Mountain School of Crafts in Maine for the first of four summers • Awarded Tiffany Foundation grant for work in glass and Fulbright Fellowship to study glass in Venice • The first American glass blower to work on the island of Murano, begins at Venini factory

1969 Continues at Venini • Makes pilgrimage to visit Erwin Eisch in Germany as well as Jaroslava Brychtova and Stanislav Libensky in Czechoslovakia • Returns to RISD to establish glass department • Included in "Objects USA," a collection compiled by Paul J. Smith and Lee Nordness for Johnson Wax Company that toured the U.S. and Europe, premiering at the National Collection of Fine Arts, Smithsonian Institution, Washington, D.C.

1970 Meets James Carpenter at RISD and begins four-year collaboration • Included in "Toledo Glass National III," a circulating exhibition organized by the Toledo Museum of Art, Ohio

1971 Has solo exhibition with James Carpenter at the Museum of Contemporary Crafts (now the American Craft Museum), New York • With a grant from the Union of Independent Colleges of Art, starts the Pilchuck Glass School north of Seattle on property donated by arts patrons John Hauberg and Anne Gould Hauberg

1972-73 Returns to Venice and blows glass with James Carpenter at Venini to prepare for "Glas Heute" exhibition at the Museum Bellerive, Zurich • Works on architectural glass projects with Carpenter, including *Leaded Glass Door* for the Toledo Museum of Art • Included in traveling show, "American Glass Now," organized by the Toledo Museum of Art and the Museum of Contemporary Crafts

1974 Tours European glass centers with Thomas Buechner, director, Corning Museum of Glass • Experiments on new "glass drawing pick-up techniques" at Pilchuck • Builds glass studio at Institute of American Indian Art, Santa Fe

1975 Receives National Endowment for the Arts grant • Develops *Navajo Blanket Cylinder* series • Helps start glass program at University of Utah's Snowbird Art School outside Salt Lake City • Solo exhibition of *Blanket Cylinders* at Utah Museum of Fine Arts, Salt Lake City, and Institute of American Indian Art, Santa Fe

1976 Collaborates with Seaver Leslie on *Irish* and *Ulysses Cylinders*, with Flora Mace fabricating glass drawings • Travels with Leslie to Great Britain on lecture tour; loses sight in left eye in automobile accident • Henry Geldzahler, curator of contemporary art at the Metropolitan Museum of Art, New York, purchases three *Navajo Blanket Cylinders* for the permanent collection • Western Association of Art Museums circulates solo exhibition • Receives an Individual Artist's Grant and, with Kate Elliott, a Master Craftsman Apprenticeship Grant from the National Endowment for the Arts

1977 Becomes head of RISD sculpture department • Begins *Pilchuck Basket* series at Pilchuck, inspired by seeing Northwest Coast Indian baskets at Washington State Historical Society, Tacoma • Exhibits at Seattle Art Museum with Italo Scanga and James Carpenter in show curated by Charles Cowles

1978 Exhibition "Baskets and Cylinders: Recent Work by Dale Chihuly" shown at the Renwick Gallery, Smithsonian Institution, Washington, D.C. • Meets William Morris, beginning an eight-year working relationship

1979 Works in Baden, Austria, with Benjamin Moore, William Morris and Michael Scheiner • Has one-man shows at Lobmeyr, Vienna, and Museu de Arte, São Paulo, Brazil • Relinquishes gaffer position when shoulder becomes dislocated in body surfing accident • Included in major traveling exhibition, "New Glass," organized by the Corning Museum of Glass

1980 Becomes artist-in-residence at RISD after resigning as head of glass department • Begins *Sea Form* series • Individual exhibition mounted at Haaretz Museum, Tel Aviv, Israel • Executes large-scale, acid-etched, hand-blown stained glass windows for Shaare Emeth Synagogue in Saint Louis, with the assistance of Eric Hopkins and Eve Kaplan

1981 Begins *Macchia* series • Works in Austria with Benjamin Moore, Richard Royal, and Jeff Held • Has solo exhibitions at Lobmeyr, Vienna, and Rosenthal, Berlin • Returns to work at RISD •Travels to Scotland with William Morris and continues on to Orkney Islands • Spends summer and fall at Pilchuck, preparing for solo show at the Tacoma Art Museum

1982 "Chihuly Glass" exhibition focusing on *Sea Forms* opens at Tacoma Art Museum and travels through 1984 to five American museums • Works at various glass blowing facilities throughout the country

1983 Sells "Boathouse" studio in Rhode Island • Moves to Seattle to live and work

1984 Honored by RISD as President's Fellow • Receives Visual Artist's Award from American Council for the Arts and first of three Washington State Governor's Art Awards • Traveling exhibition, "Chihuly: A Decade of Glass," opens at the Bellevue Art Museum, Washington, and travels to 13 museums throughout the United States and Canada through 1987

1985 Commissioned to make large-scale architectural installations, including one at the Seattle Aquarium as King County Arts Commission's Honors Awards Artist • Experiments with *Flower Forms* • Renovates Buffalo Shoe Building as studio in Seattle

1986 Named Fellow of the American Craft Council • Receives honorary doctorates from the University of Puget Sound and RISD as well as Governor's Art Award from Rhode Island • Returns to cylinder format with *Soft Cylinder* series • Begins *Persian* series working with gaffer Martin Blank • Builds his first glass blowing studio at the Van de Kamp Building in Seattle • Survey exhibition, "Dale Chihuly: Objets de Verre," organized by the Musée des Arts Décoratifs, Palais du Louvre, Paris, opens and travels in Europe and the Middle East through 1991

1987 Completes *Rainbow Frieze* installation at Rockefeller Center, New York • Honored as University of Washington Alumni Legend • Retrospective "Chihuly Collection" installed permanently at the Tacoma Art Museum

1988 In Seattle begins *Venetian* series with maestro Lino Tagliapietra, inspired by seeing a private collection of Venetian Art Deco vases • Receives honorary doctorate from California College of Arts and Crafts, Oakland

1989 Continues to work with Lino Tagliapietra, Richard Royal and Benjamin Moore as gaffers on Venetian series • Blows glass in Niijima, Japan, and at RISD and California College of Arts and Crafts • Special individual exhibition at Bienal de São Paulo travels to Santiago, Chile • At Pilchuck works with Italian maestro Pino Signoretto, experimenting with additions of *putti* to *Venetians* • Begins to experiment with Tagliapietra adding flower forms to *Venetians* for the *Ikebana* series

1990 Survey exhibition, "Dale Chihuly: Japan 1990," presented by Azabu Museum of Arts and Crafts, Tokyo • Renovates Seattle Pocock racing shell factory on Lake Union into new "Boathouse," incorporating glass blowing shop, studio and residence • Develops *Venetians* further with Lino Tagliapietra and Pino Signoretto in Seattle

1991 Exhibition "Chihuly: Venetians," originating at the Umeléckoprůmyslové muzeum, Prague, travels in Europe • Completes major private and public architectural installations, including a tea room at the Yasui Konpira-gu Shinto Shrine in Kyoto, Japan, and a wall piece at GTE Telephone Operations Headquarters in Irving, Texas • Participates in "Masterpieces" workshop at Pilchuck with Lino Tagliapietra, Richard Marquis and William Warmus • Begins to experiment with *Niijima Float* series, working with gaffer Richard Royal

1992 Exhibits temporary installation of *Niijima Floats* at the American Craft Museum • Traveling exhibition of *Venetians* shown at major museums in Sweden, Germany, The Netherlands and Belgium

1992 Creates major new architectural installations for traveling exhibition organized by the Seattle Art Museum, "Dale Chihuly: Installations 1964-1992"; recreates *20,000 pounds of Ice and Neon* (1971) temporary installation • Development of chandeliers begins with the *SAM Chandelier* • Solo exhibitions featuring large-scale installations held at the Contemporary Arts Center, Cincinnati; the Honolulu Academy of Arts, Hawaii; and the Taipei Fine Arts Museum, Taiwan • Executes temporary installation of *Niijima Floats* at the Marco Museum, Monterrey, Mexico • Commissioned for large-scale architectural installations by Little Caesars World Headquarters, in Detroit and Corning Glass in Corning, New York • Designs stage sets for 1993 Seattle Opera production of Claude Debussy's *Pelléas et Mélisande* • New glass series, *Pilchuck Stumps*, grows out of these designs • Receives first National Living Treasure Award given in the United States

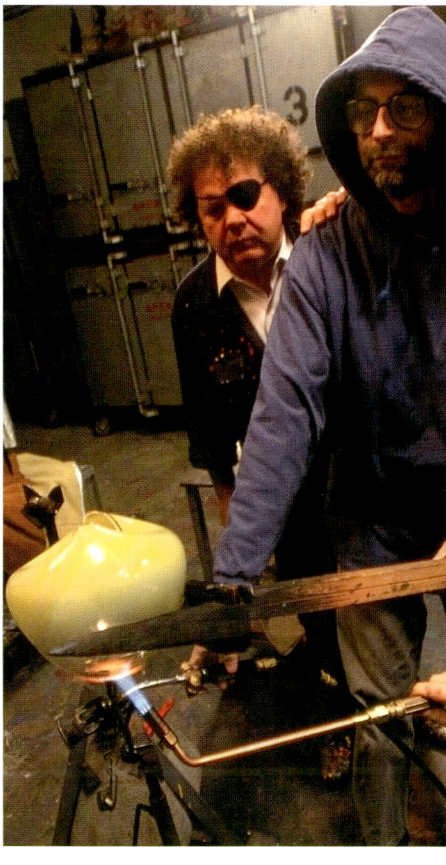

與倍里歐特一同製作籃系列
西雅圖, 1993
攝影: R. Johnson

with Charles Parriott,
working on the *Basket* series
Seattle, 1993
photo: R. Johnson

1993 "Chihuly: Form from Fire" begins tour in U.S. at the Lowe Art Museum, Miami • "Chihuly in Australia: Glass and Works on Paper," opens at the Powerhouse Museum, Sydney, Australia, and travels to the National Gallery of Victoria, Melbourne • "Chihuly Installations: 1964-1992" tours the U.S. • Seattle Opera premiers stage sets for *Pelléas et Mélisande* • Mayor Norm Rice declares March 13 "Dale Chihuly Day" in Seattle • Creates his first suite of etchings, inspired by *Pelléas et Mélisande* • *"alla Macchia"* opens at the Art Museum of Southeast Texas, Beaumont, and tours U.S • Named the 1993 Alumnus Summa Laude Dignatus by the Alumni Association, University of Washington, Seattle • Chihuly Glass used as a backdrop for President Bill Clinton's Speech at the Asian Pacific Economic Conference in Seattle, Washington

1994 *"alla Macchia"* travels to Laguna Gloria Art Museum, Austin, Texas • "Chihuly in Australia: Glass and Works on Paper" continues to tour, traveling to Scitech Discovery Centre, Perth, Australia • "Chihuly in New Zealand"opens at the Dowse Art Museum, Aotearoa, New Zealand. • "Chihuly Baskets," opens at the North Central Washington Museum, Wenatchee, Washington • "Dale Chihuly Center for Glass" opens in Tacoma Washington's Union Station • "Chihuly: Form from Fire" travels to Samuel P. Harn Museum of Art, University of Florida, Gainsville, Florida • "Chihuly and the Opera Sets" featured in Gala Celebration at the Renwick Gallery, Smithsonian Institution, Washington, D.C. • Receives American Academy Achievement Golden Plate Award

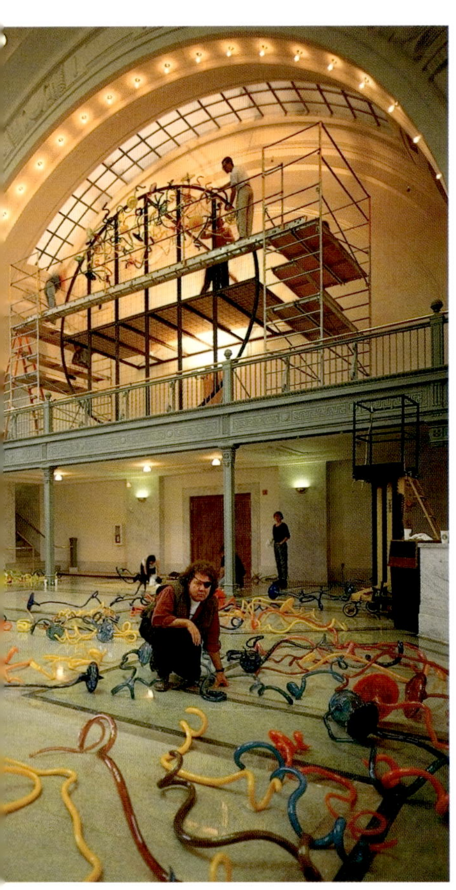

"屈胡利在聯合車站"展覽中之
拉卡瓦那花道裝置
塔科馬，1994
攝影：R. Johnson

installation of
Lakawana Ikebana for
"Chihuly at Union Station",
Tacoma, 1994
photo: R. Johnson

德爾·屈胡利年表

1941	●九月二十日生於美國華盛頓州塔科馬市，母親為葳歐拉屈胡利；父親是喬治屈胡利，為一聯合會發起人。
1956	●哥哥喬治於海軍航空飛行演習中罹難。
1957	●喪父。
1959	●進入塔科馬市普桑大學就讀。
1960	●轉學西雅圖的華盛頓大學；主修室內設計。
1961－62	●在南西雅圖的地下工作室鑽研玻璃的融化及接合
	●成為DKE兄弟會的主席。
1962－63	●遊歷歐洲與近東
	●在以色列研習kibbutz。
1963	●返回華盛頓大學，受教於荷柏福特及渥仁希爾，修習室內設計與建築
	●在紡織課與多莉絲布勞威首先將玻璃結合到掛毯繡帷中。
1964	●回到歐洲訪遊列寧格勒，首次前往愛爾蘭
	●獲頒西雅圖紡織公會獎。
1965	●結識織品設計師傑克里諾賴桑，獲頒美國室內設計師協會最高榮譽獎(現為美國室內設計師學會)
	●取得華盛頓大學室內設計學士學位
	●於西雅圖的約翰克亨建築師事務所擔任設計師
	●首次獨自實驗吹製玻璃
	●受到羅素戴的肯定。
1966	●為賺取玻璃研究課程的學費，在阿拉斯加從事漁夫工作
	●因獲全額獎學金，得於麥迪遜市威斯康新大學與哈維里托頓共同研究玻璃吹製。
1967	●取得威斯康新大學理學碩士學位
	●進入普羅維登斯的羅德島設計學校修習美術碩士課程
	●教授玻璃課程並參與大型的景觀雕塑，在材質中加入氖、塑膠及其他材料
	●結識義塔洛史坎加。
1968	●取得羅德島設計學校美術碩士學位
	●於緬因州的海斯達克山工藝學校任教四年
	●獲提芬妮基金會贊助與富爾布來特獎助金，得至威尼斯從事玻璃研究
	●為首位至慕拉諾島之美籍玻璃吹製工作者，並開始於凡尼尼廠工作。
1969	●繼續工作於凡尼尼
	●完成一趟朝聖之旅，到德國的艾爾文　依斯克及捷克的捷洛斯拉瓦　布瑞克托瓦和史丹尼斯拉夫　林本斯基
	●返回羅德島設計學校設立玻璃學系
	●參加「美國作品巡迴展」
	●由強生渥克斯公司之保羅史密斯和李諾得尼司策劃，巡迴至全美與歐洲首站為華盛頓哥倫比亞特區史密司桑尼亞協會之國

立美術展覽館。

1970 ●在羅德島設計學校結織詹姆士卡本特，展開爲期四年的合作
●參加美國俄亥俄州托雷多美術館舉辦之「托雷多第三屆全國玻璃展之巡迴展。

1971 ●於紐約當代工藝博物館(現爲美國工藝博物館)與卡本特舉行個展
●獲獨立藝術學院協會獎助金，並以贊助人約翰荷柏和安柯得荷柏所捐贈之財產，在西雅圖北方著手創立比恰克玻璃學校。

1972－73 ●返回威尼斯，與卡本特合力吹製玻璃，籌劃於蘇黎士貝勒瑞夫博物館舉辦「今日玻璃」展覽，並與卡本特從事建築玻璃設計案，其中包括托雷多藝術館之「鉛玻璃門」
●參加由托雷多藝術館與當代工藝博物館主辦之「今日美國玻璃」展。

1974 ●與康寧玻璃博物館館長湯姆士布歇爾同訪歐洲各玻璃中心
●於彼恰克實驗創作新式「玻璃繪製技巧」
●於聖大非美國印第安藝術協會設立玻璃工作室。

1975 ●獲得國家藝術贊助金
●創作那瓦荷毛氈圓筒系列作品
●協助塩湖市郊區之猶他大學雪鳥藝術學院玻璃課程的開設
●於塩湖市猶他美術館及聖大非藝術協會舉辦毛氈圓筒個展。

1976 ●與西佛李斯利合力完成「愛爾蘭」以及「尤利西斯圓桶」作品，並且與佛羅拉麥思共同完成玻璃畫的製作
●與李斯利一同前往英國作巡迴演講；因車禍而導致左眼失明
●紐約大都會博物館之當代藝術主任亨利傑澤勒蒐購三件「那瓦荷毛氈圓筒」作品作爲永久收藏
●西方藝術館協會爲他舉行巡迴個展，獲頒「個人藝術家獎」並另與凱特艾略特共同獲得國家頒贈的「工藝大師獎」。

1977 ●成爲羅德島設計學校雕刻系系主任
●在塔科馬市的華盛頓州立歷史社區中無意地看到美國西北岸印第安部落的籃子，靈感大受激發，開始著手〝比恰克籃〞系列作品的創作
●與義塔洛史坎加和詹姆士卡本特於西雅圖藝術館共同展出，由查理士寇利斯負責策劃。

1978 ●於華盛頓特區史密斯索尼恩中心的瑞威克藝廊舉辦「籃與圓筒：德爾屈胡利近作」展覽
●結識威廉莫里斯，兩人展開長達八年的工作搭擋關係。

1979 ●與班傑明摩爾威廉莫里斯以及麥可史金尼爾，於奧地利巴登共同創作，於維也納洛伯梅爾及巴西聖保羅兩地舉行個展
●由於衝浪發生意外，肩膀脫臼，因而辭去系主任聯務，參加康寧玻璃博物館籌辦之「新玻璃」巡迴展。

1980 ●辭去玻璃系系主任的職務後，成爲羅德島設計學校的專屬特駐藝術家

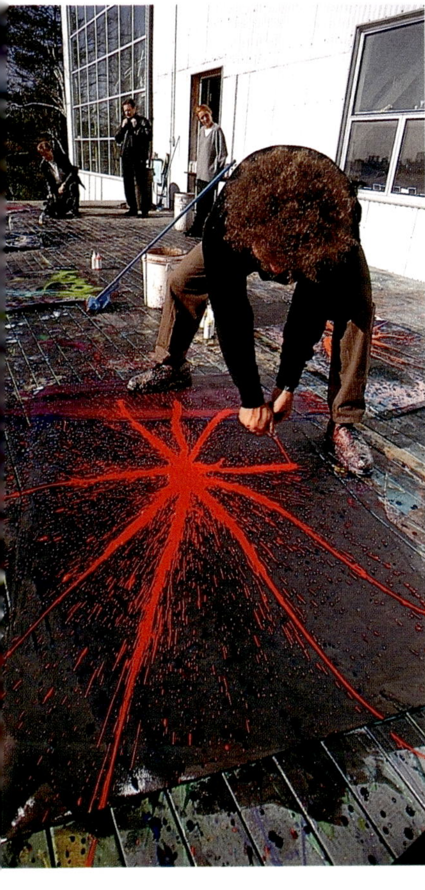

攝於船屋
西雅圖, 1993
攝影: R. Johnson

at the Boathouse
Seattle, 1993
photo: R. Johnson

- 著手〝海之形〞系列作品的創作
- 於以色列臺拉維夫的哈瑞茲博物館舉行個展
- 在艾瑞克霍布金斯及依芙卡帕蘭的協助下，爲聖路易的猶太教會堂製作大型手吹的酸蝕彩色玻璃。

1981
- 開始創作「馬其亞」系列作品
- 與班傑明摩爾、瑞奇羅伊爾及傑夫荷德於奧地利共同創作
- 於維也納的洛伯梅爾及柏林的羅森索舉行個展
- 回到羅德島設計學校工作
- 與威廉莫里斯同遊蘇格蘭，並繼續前往歐克尼島
- 夏、秋兩季留在比恰克，籌備將於塔科馬藝術館舉辦之個展。

1982
- 於塔科馬藝術館舉辦「屈胡利玻璃展」，展出主題爲「海之形」，該展並在其他五所美國博物館繼續展出，至1984年結束
- 在全國各地的玻璃吹製機構工作。

1983
- 出售羅德島的「船屋」工作室，遷至西雅圖居住及工作。

1984
- 被尊爲羅德島設計學校校長榮譽會員
- 獲美國藝術協會頒發的「視覺藝術家獎」及三名「華盛頓州州長藝術獎」中之第一名
- 舉辦「屈胡利：十年玻璃」巡迴展，首站於華盛頓州的貝勒串美術館，並繼續於美國及加拿大的十三個博物館展出，爲期至1987年。

1985
- 受委託製造大型建築裝置，包括在西雅圖水族館擔任皇家群藝術委員會的榮譽獎藝術家
- 開始「花形」之實驗創作
- 改建水牛鞋大樓爲西雅圖的工作室。

1986
- 爲美國工藝協會會員
- 普桑大學及羅德島設計學校授予榮譽博士學位，並獲頒羅德島州長藝術獎
- 再度創作「軟圓桶」系列作品
- 與馬可布蘭克開始合力創作「波斯」系列作品
- 在西雅圖的坎培大樓建立個人首間專屬玻璃吹製工作室
- 由巴黎羅浮宮裝置藝術博物館籌辦「德爾·屈胡利：玻璃展」，並歐洲及近東巡迴展出，爲期至1991年。

1987
- 在紐約的洛克斐勒中心完成「彩虹飾帶」裝置
- 榮尊爲華盛頓大學校友傳奇
- 塔科馬藝術館設立永久屈胡利作品回顧。

1988
- 因觀察私人收藏的威尼斯裝飾藝術瓶而受到啓發
- 在西雅圖與玻璃師傅里諾，達里歐派特拉共同開始創作威尼斯系列
- 獲奧克蘭的加州美術工藝學院頒授榮譽博士學位。

1989
- 繼續與里諾·達里歐派特拉、理查羅伊爾及班傑明摩爾合力創作「威尼斯」系列
- 分別於日本三島、羅德島設計學校及加州美術工藝學院吹製玻璃

- 於聖保羅雙年展舉行個人特展，並至智利聖地牙哥巡迴展出
- 於此恰克與義大利籍大師皮諾，席格諾雷多合作，試驗將「小愛神」添加於「威尼斯」系列作品上
- 與達里歐派特拉開始嚐試將「花形」加於「威尼斯」而成爲「花道」系列。

1990
- 於日本東京的麻布藝術工藝博物館舉辦「德爾·屈胡利—日本1990」展
- 將位於聯合湖上的西雅圖賽船船體工廠改建爲新的「船屋」，其中兼置玻璃吹製室、工作坊及居住房舍
- 在西雅圖與里諾，達里歐派特拉及皮諾，席格諾雷多展開進一步的「威尼斯」創作。

1991
- 「屈胡利：威尼斯」展於布拉格的烏梅列克魯密斯洛夫博物館開展，並至歐洲各地巡迴展出
- 完成數件重要的私人及公共建築物裝置，包括日本京都的安井金比羅神道神社的茶室及德州艾文市的電話作業總部的牆面裝置
- 與里諾，達里歐派特拉、李察·馬奇斯及威廉·渥慕斯一同加入比恰克的「鉅作」工作坊
- 與李察·羅伊爾著手「三島浮球」系列作品的實驗創作。

1992
- 於美國工藝博物館展出暫時性裝置「三島浮球」
- 「威尼斯」展繼續於瑞典、德國、荷蘭、比利時之各大博物館巡迴展出
- 爲西雅圖藝術館所籌劃的巡迴展「德爾·屈胡利：裝置藝術1964－1992」，創作新的建築裝置作品，並重新製作他1971年的作品「2萬的霓虹與冰」暫時性裝置
- 進行「吊灯」系列創作，首件作品爲「山姆吊灯」
- 於辛辛那提當代藝術中心，夏威夷的檀香山藝術學院及台灣的台北市立美術館舉辦大型裝置個展
- 於墨西哥蒙特瑞市的馬爾可博物館展出「三島浮球」暫時性裝置作品
- 爲底特律的小凱撒企業世界總部及紐約的康寧玻璃器皿公司製作大型的建築裝置
- 爲1993年西雅圖歌劇院的德布希歌劇「貝蕾亞絲與梅力松」設計舞台佈景
- 自舞台佈景設計所得的靈感而創作新作「比恰克樹椿」
- 獲頒美國首座「當代國寶」獎。

1993
- 於邁阿密勞伊藝術館展開美國巡迴展「屈胡利：火之形」
- 於澳大利亞雪梨力屋博物館展開「屈胡利澳大利亞：玻璃與紙上創作」展覽並且巡迴至墨爾本之國立維多利亞藝廊
- 「屈胡利裝置藝術：1969－1992」於美國巡迴展出
- 爲德布西劇作「貝蕾亞絲與梅力松」在西雅圖的演出製作舞台佈景
- 西雅圖市長諾曼雷斯定三月十三日爲「德爾·屈胡利日」

- 從「貝蕾亞絲與梅力松」一劇獲得靈感，創作其首件蝕刻系列創作
- 「阿拉馬其亞於比蒙特的東南德克薩斯藝術館展出並巡迴全美
- 獲頒西雅圖華盛頓大學校友會1993年榮譽校友頭銜
- 於華盛頓州西雅圖市舉行的亞太經濟會議中柯林頓演講現場採用屈胡利的玻璃作品爲背景。

1994
- 「阿拉馬其亞」作品於德州奧斯汀市的葛羅莉亞湖藝術館巡迴展出
- 「屈胡利在澳大利亞：玻璃與紙上創作」展覽繼續巡迴展出，展至澳大利亞伯斯市科技發現中心
- 「屈胡利在紐西蘭」於紐西蘭奧狄洛亞的道斯藝術館展出
- 「屈胡利籃」於華盛頓州威那奇中北部華盛頓博物館展出
- 「德爾屈胡利玻璃中心」於塔科馬市聯合車站內展出
- 「屈胡利：火之形」巡迴至佛羅里達州佛羅里達大學山姆哈恩藝術館中展出
- 「屈胡利與歌劇佈景」於華盛頓特區史密司桑尼亞協會雷威克藝廊中展出以歡欣慶祝爲主題
- 獲頒美國學術成就金牌獎。

屈胡利：建築中的玻璃

發 行 人：黃才郎
發 行 者：高雄市立美術館
策劃編輯：張艾茹、曾媚珍、陳宏基、陳雪妮
執行編輯：屈胡利工作室、陳美智
承　　印：秋雨印刷股份有限公司
設　　計：北川梅根、吳國華
版　　面：Helvetica Light, Helvetica Black
翻　　譯：曾子容，羅雯霞，陳美智

Chihuly：Glass in Architecture

Director: Tsai－Lang Huang
Published by: Kaohsiung Museum of Fine Arts
Organized by: Ai-Ru Chang, Mei-Chen Tseng.
Hung-Chi Chen, Hsieh-Ni Chen.
Edited by: Chihuly Studio, Mei-Chih Chen.
Printed by: Chiu Yu Printing Co., Ltd.
Designed by: Megan Kitagawa、Kao-Hua Wu
Typeface：Helvetica Light，Helvetica Black
Translated by: Tzu－Jung Tseng，Wen－Hsia Lo，Mei－Chih Chen

From Dale Chihuly's studio,
special thanks to：

Parks Anderson
Karen Chambers
Mark Englehardt
Diana Johnson
Karin Johnson
John Landon
Rob Millis
Heidi Myer
Bryan Ohno
Barry Rosen
Joanna Sikes

for their efforts in making this exhibition
and catalog a reality.